STUDIES IN THE BÁBÍ AND BAHÁ'Í RELIGIONS
(formerly *Studies in Bábí and Bahá'í History*)

Anthony A. Lee, General Editor

'ABDU'L-BAHÁ WITH THE BAHÁ'Í COMMUNITY OF CHICAGO
in Lincoln Park, Chicago, May 5, 1912.

STUDIES IN THE
BÁBÍ AND BAHÁ'Í RELIGIONS

VOLUME SIX

General Editor
ANTHONY A. LEE

COMMUNITY HISTORIES

Edited by
RICHARD HOLLINGER

KALIMÁT PRESS
LOS ANGELES

First Edition.

Manufactured in the United States of America.

Library of Congress Cataloging in Publication Data
(Revised for vol. 6)

Studes in Bábí and Bahá'í history.

Vols. 5- have title: Studies in the Bábí and Bahá'í religions.
(Studies in the Bábí and Bahá'í religions)
Includes bibliographies and indexes.
Contents: v. 1 [no title]–v. 2. From Iran east and west /
edited by Juan R. Cole and Moojan Momen–[etc.]–v. 5. Studies
in honor of the late Hasan M. Balyuzi / edited by Moojan Momen.
v. 6. Community histories / edited by Richard Hollinger.
1. Baha'i Faith–History. 2. Babism–History.
I. Momen, Moojan. II. Series.
BP330.S78   1982   297'.9'09   83-227

ISBN 0-933770-16-2 (v. 1)
ISBN 0-933770-76-6 (v. 6)

CONTENTS

INTRODUCTION:
BAHÁ'Í COMMUNITIES IN THE WEST, 1897-1992

by Richard Hollinger

In his ground-breaking work on slavery in South Carolina, Charles Joyner notes: "All history is local history, somewhere. And yet how little this obvious fact is reflected in the scholarship . . ."[1] A similar observation could be made about the scholarship on Bahá'í history. There is a significant body of literature on the history of the Bahá'í Faith in the West, for example, but very little has been published on the history of local Bahá'í communities.[2] Historians describe *the* Bahá'í community without having examined in depth any particular Bahá'í community.

This volume is intended as a first effort to fill this gap in the literature. The essays by Duane Herrmann and Phillip Smith document the history of the Bahá'í Faith in Kansas and Great Britain, respectively. The articles by Deborah Clark, Roger Dahl, Peggy Caton, and Will C. van den Hoonaard focus on specific local communities in the United States and Canada: Baltimore, Maryland; Kenosha, Wisconsin; Sacramento, California; and St. John, New Brunswick.

vii

These local communities were, of course, affected by national and international trends in the Bahá'í Movement and their histories should be viewed in that wider context. Three of the Bahá'í communities discussed in this volume—Baltimore, Kenosha, and Enterprise (Kansas)—date back to 1897-1898. During this period the Bahá'í Faith was being spread in the West almost exclusively by means of a course of lectures developed by Ibrahim Kheiralla (a Lebanese convert) which began with metaphysical teachings and ended with instruction on the Bahá'í religion.[3] When students had completed the lessons, they were asked to write a letter to 'Abdu'l-Bahá, the head of the Faith in Palestine, declaring their belief. If they did so, they were invited to join the Bahá'í community. Beyond this, there appear to have been meetings, in the Chicago Bahá'í community at least, that were intended for Bahá'ís only.[4]

The communities that developed during this period, as a result, seem to have had a fairly clear definition of membership, which probably contributed to the development of Bahá'í identities among the members. Kheiralla's message, which interpreted biblical prophecies as having been fulfilled by the Báb, Bahá'u'lláh, and 'Abdu'l-Bahá, also provided a powerful basis of a new identity for at least some members of the new Bahá'í communities. Nevertheless, it is not clear that all the Bahá'ís of this period viewed the Bahá'í Faith as an independent religion. The presentation Kheiralla offered was centered on interpretation of the Bible and could have given the impression that the Faith was a movement within Christianity.

Many of Kheiralla's students were highly individualistic in their approach to religion and had already been involved in other alternative religious groups.[5] The Bahá'í teachings (however they were understood) were on the fringes of American religious belief, and most active church members would not have been willing to attend Bahá'í classes. Kheiralla himself observed that most of his students were persons who had left their churches and were "true seekers . . . always looking about for some new religion."[6] These individuals were not subject to the same social constraints as active churchgoers. Such persons may have been attracted by some aspects of the Bahá'í teachings without accepting the Bahá'í scriptures as a primary source of their religious beliefs.

Even for those who accepted the Bahá'í teachings with fewer reservations, it took some time to develop personal identities in which the Bahá'í Faith was a central element. During the years 1900 to 1904, this process was facilitated in the larger Western communities by visits from several Iranian Bahá'í teachers, including Mírzá Abu'l-Faḍl Gulpaygání and Mírzá Asadu'lláh Iṣfahání. These teachers, especially the former, taught that the Bahá'í Faith was an independent religion and emphasized its unique laws and rituals.[7] The publication and distribution of Bahá'í scriptures and of some introductory literature also contributed to an independent conception of the Faith. Some Bahá'ís who found this difficult to accept left the community during this time.[8] However, an active core of believers seems to have adopted this understanding.

While this process of consolidation was taking place in some of the oldest Western communities, the Bahá'í Faith was also spreading fairly rapidly in new localities elsewhere in North America and Europe. Consequently, while a small group of active believers with strong Bahá'í identities emerged within a few years of the founding of the first Bahá'í communities, a significant number of Bahá'ís at any given time were new to the community and probably had weak Bahá'í identities.

In 1899, according to a list compiled about the end of that year, approximately 84% of the Bahá'ís in the West resided in four cities: New York City; Chicago; Kenosha; and Cincinnati, Ohio. These ranged in size from 69 in Cincinnati to 712 members in Chicago. Another 7% resided in seven communities in the midwestern and eastern regions of the United States (including Baltimore and Enterprise) ranging in size from 6 to 23 persons; and a roughly equal number of Bahá'ís were isolated or lived in localities with only one or two Bahá'ís. There was only one Bahá'í group on the West Coast: San Francisco, with 14 members (1%).[9] While most of the Bahá'í communities were relatively small (the median size was 19), the larger communities may be regarded as more representative of the Bahá'í experience in 1899. (The average community size was 113.)

The Bahá'í population at the turn of the century was centered in the midwestern and northeastern regions of the United States, almost exclusively in urban areas. There were Bahá'ís from various social classes, but there were few blacks, Jews, or Catholics in the Bahá'í population then.[10] Few Bahá'ís lived in rural areas. The movement had not spread significantly outside of the networks of Protestants, in urban industrial centers of the United States, where it had first taken hold. It was some time before it transcended these networks and penetrated the social barriers imposed by religion, ethnicity, and geography.

On the other hand, the geographic dispersion of the Bahá'í population to other urban centers in the West began rather quickly. According to figures collected by the United States Census in 1906, there were 24 Bahá'í communities in the United States at that time.[11] The average community had a membership of 53, but the average attendance at Bahá'í community meetings was probably less than 20.[12] Most of the new communities were in the Midwest and Northeast. However, between 1906 and 1908 several new communities were established in the Pacific Northwest.[13] Between 1900 and

1907, Bahá'í groups were also formed in Honolulu, Hawaii; Stuttgart, Germany; London and Manchester, England; Paris, France; and Montreal, Canada.[14] Hence, there was a trend toward geographic diffusion as well as a trend toward the development of smaller communities.

This pattern of geographic diffusion without a substantial growth in the Bahá'í population appears to have continued until the 1930s. According to the 1916 census of religions, there were 2,884 Bahá'ís in 57 communities in the United States; thus the average community had 50 members.[15] The number of persons who signed a petition to 'Abdu'l-Bahá circulated in 1918 suggests that the average attendance at Bahá'í meetings was about 29 and that as many as 30% of the active Bahá'ís in North America may have then resided on the West Coast.[16] By 1921, there were at least six times as many Bahá'í communities as there were in 1899.[17] However, a careful analysis by Robert Stockman suggests that the number of active Bahá'ís in the United States had not increased significantly.[18] We can deduce from this that there was great deal of flux in the membership of the Bahá'í community; a significant number of persons must have drifted in and out of local communities during this period.

This pattern was particularly distinct in newly formed Bahá'í communities, which tended to exhibit the characteristics of "voluntary associations" popular with the urban middle class. This essay follows Bahá'í usage in referring to these groups as "communities," but such social configurations fit this description only in the broadest sense of the term; they might more accurately be likened to social clubs or religious study classes. New communities were usually begun when one person (or a family) in a locality opened a home for Bahá'í meetings; often these would begin as study classes conducted by outside teachers. Eventually, one or more local Bahá'ís might take responsibility for conducting the meetings. Often when such key individuals left a community, the other members did not identify strongly enough with the Bahá'í Faith to take on a leadership role. In such instances, Bahá'í communities might become temporarily inactive or disappear altogether. An example of the latter is provided in Will C. van den Hoonaard's essay on the St. John community in this volume.

The rapid fluctuation in Bahá'í membership necessarily retarded the development of Bahá'í community life. This was exacerbated, for a time, by the lack of a generally accepted body of Bahá'í beliefs and the absence of clear boundaries to Bahá'í community membership. During the 1890s, individuals had been obliged to write letters declaring their faith in Bahá'u'lláh and 'Abdu'l-Bahá before they could become members of Bahá'í communities. However after 1900, there was no such requirement in most places. Bahá'í meetings, therefore, were generally open to anyone.

The major gatherings in most Bahá'í communities were weekly meetings that were usually held on Sundays. In many communities these were the only Bahá'í gatherings. These meetings typically included prayers, readings from the Bahá'í sacred writings and from the Bible, a prepared talk on some aspect of Bahá'í history or the Bahá'í teachings, the reading of letters from Bahá'ís in other localities, a discussion of community business, and sometimes the singing of hymns.[19] If someone unfamiliar with the Bahá'í teachings attended, an introductory talk would be given. The Nineteen-Day Feasts, social and devotional meetings called for in Bahá'í scriptures, were held in many communities beginning about 1906. But these, too, were often open meetings. In 1909 (by which time Feasts were held in most of the larger communities), Charles Mason Remey, a widely traveled Bahá'í, complained that there were almost no meetings being held just for believers.[20]

In many communities, anyone who attended Bahá'í meetings was regarded as a member of the Bahá'í community, and would have been counted in the census statistics cited above. However, many of those who attended Bahá'í meetings had not accepted Bahá'u'lláh as a prophet, had little commitment to the community, and held beliefs that were in conflict with the Bahá'í teachings. For example, between 1904 and 1912 Anna Monroe, who is not known to have ever expressed a belief in the Bahá'u'lláh, attended Bahá'í meetings in the San Francisco Bay Area and in Washington, D.C.— and even held Bahá'í meetings in her home in Berkeley.[21] Her correspondence shows that she held 'Abdu'l-Bahá in high esteem, but that there were other spiritual teachers, such as Emmanuel Swedenborg, from whose writings she also drew inspiration and whom she may have regarded as equals of 'Abdu'l-Bahá. Near the end of her life, for reasons that are not clear, she stopped attending Bahá'í meetings. Marion Yazdi, reflecting the standards of membership that developed later, recalled that Monroe "never became a Bahá'í."[22] But Monroe was considered a member of the Bahá'í community while she was attending Bahá'í meetings. [23]

The lack of clear community boundaries impeded the development of Bahá'í identities, especially in the smaller, newly established communities. However, in the cities with the greatest number of Bahá'ís, such as Chicago and New York, communities appear to have evolved into social configurations that were significantly different from those of smaller communities. These large communities were characterized by a wide variety of meetings and activities that drew families and individuals into interlocking social networks similar to those of a small town (or parish) church.[24] In some specific ways, such as the organization of choirs and the development of philanthropic endeavors, they emulated church activities. As in many of the small communities, large communities held Sunday meetings to which non-Bahá'ís were allowed (or even encouraged) to attend. But their presence probably did not have the same impact on the proceedings that it would have had in a small community. On the other hand, if some persons regularly attended a number of different Bahá'í functions, they might develop Bahá'í identities, and be assimilated into the Bahá'í community.

In Chicago, at least, there are indications that the development of social networks within the community led to strong bonds of reciprocal obligation between the members. One example of this sense of mutual obligation is related by Roger Dahl in his essay on Kenosha in this volume. He notes that the Bahá'ís of Chicago arranged for the housing of a destitute and elderly Bahá'í from Kenosha. Their sense of obligation does not seem to have stemmed from a personal relationship with this woman; rather, they felt obliged to care for her because she was part of the community.

These large communities became centers of Bahá'í activity upon which many smaller communities depended for intellectual, moral, and material support. Even before 1900, members of the New York and Chicago communities had begun to support smaller communities in a number of ways. They conducted classes and meetings in small communities; corresponded with Bahá'ís in these places; published Bahá'í literature; and circulated copies of unpublished materials that illuminated various aspects of the Bahá'í teachings. In 1908, New York Bahá'ís launched the first English-language Bahá'í newsletter, *The Bahai Bulletin*, noting in the first issue its importance to small Bahá'í communities: "We in the large cities have no idea what this would mean to more isolated believers in small towns and villages . . . To them a paper coming regularly with news of the Cause would mean life itself."[25] The function of *The Bahai Bulletin* was later assumed by *Star of the West*, which was published by the Chicago Bahá'ís. In 1909, the Bahá'ís of Chicago organized the first annual Bahai Temple Unity convention, attended by delegates from various Bahá'í communities, to facilitate the construction of a Bahá'í House of Worship in North America. All of these activities tied the Bahá'ís of small communities to a larger movement and, in the process, strengthened the Bahá'í identities of the members.

These activities, because they provided forums for discussing the Bahá'í teachings, also contributed to the emergence of a normative body of belief among the most active North American Bahá'ís. Even before 'Abdu'l-Bahá's visit in 1912, most of the leading Bahá'ís, though possibly a minority of those who attended local Bahá'í meetings, appear to have accepted the Bahá'í scriptures as their primary source of spiritual truth. Other religious teachings might be studied, but they would be interpreted and judged in the light of the Bahá'í teachings. Dreams, visions, and other forms of inspiration were also important in the culture of the community and were sometimes understood to validate certain forms of artistic expressions. For example, the design for the Bahá'í House of Worship in Wilmette, Illinois, was legitimized, in part, by the architect's assertion that it was "an inspiration of the creator . . . a copy of a Temple that exist[s] in the spirit world."[26] Personal inspiration could also provide proof of the truth of Bahá'í teachings, evidence for beliefs that were not known to have been addressed in Bahá'í scriptures and, to a more limited extent, esoteric meanings of the Bahá'í teachings. However, it was not acceptable for such inspiration to replace Bahá'í scripture as the primary source of doctrine for the community.[27]

Although there was a degree of agreement among leading Bahá'ís concerning these matters, and this consensus was reflected in most of the published literature and much of the public discourse of the community, individualism remained at the heart of the American Bahá'í ethos. Because of this, some Bahá'ís could defy the norms of the accepted Bahá'í epistemology by, for example, circulating documents that they claimed were letters received from 'Abdu'l-Bahá through "spiritual telepathy."[28] Views that were at variance with the general understanding of the Bahá'í teachings continued to be presented in Bahá'í meetings, and such opinions were occasionally found in Bahá'í publications. While Bahá'ís might express their personal disagreement with such ideas, they were reluctant to impose their views on others, even when there was a widespread consensus on a particular subject. Thus Marie Watson prefaced her criticism of a Bahá'í publication with the following disclaimer: "No one can dictate to another . . . but I must insist *for myself*, to sanction only the Principles of the Revelation as set forth by Baha'o'llah and Abdul Baha." (Emphasis added.)[29]

One Bahá'í, Charles Mason Remey, for years conducted a campaign to purge Bahá'í literature, and presentations at Bahá'í meetings, of ideas that could not be supported by Bahá'í scriptures. These efforts did achieve results, but they are significant primarily because they were so unusual. Although other Bahá'ís may have sympathized with Remey, few were willing to take such initiatives.

However, attitudes began to change in 1917 and 1918 as a result of a watershed event that has become known as the Chicago Reading Room Affair.[30] This controversy centered around the activities held at a Bahá'í Reading Room that had been established in Chicago, apparently as a way of reaching non-Bahá'ís with the Bahá'í message. This was supported by a number of the leading Bahá'ís of Chicago, and for a short time it seems to have been the center of Bahá'í activity in the city. However by 1917, there was a serious division in the community between those who supported the Reading Room and those who opposed the activities there. Separate meetings were held by the two rival factions, each of which claimed to be the "Chicago Bahai Assembly" (i.e., community). Under normal circumstances, the matter would have been referred to 'Abdu'l-Bahá for resolution, but World War I had cut off communication with Palestine, making this impossible. Therefore, a committee was appointed, by persons who had gathered in Chicago to commemorate the one-hundredth anniversary of Bahá'u'lláh's birth, to investigate this division in the Chicago community. The Committee of Investigation concluded that the activities at the Reading Room constituted Covenant-breaking and that the participants, therefore, should be expelled from the Bahá'í community and shunned by the believers. This ruling was ratified by the delegates at the Bahai Temple Unity Convention of 1918.

Although there were a variety of accusations made against the Reading Room group and a number of unusual circumstances that led to this radical action, the primary argument for this decision was that the Reading Room group had split off from the Chicago Bahá'í community to form a separate and rival community, an act expressly forbidden by 'Abdu'l-Bahá.[31] Behind this legalistic argument, however, lay worlds of meaning.

The dominant view of the relationship of the Bahá'í Faith to other religious teachings, which centered on the concept of "progressive revelation," allowed Bahá'ís at once to validate and transcend the teachings of the major world religions. Bahá'ís could also embrace the teachings of new religious movements, with some reservations, on the basis that they were (unknowingly) inspired by the spirit of the new age. However, the teachings of a few groups, such as Theosophists and Freemasons, were difficult for Bahá'ís to encompass. Theosophists asserted that their teachings were the distillation of truths found in all religions, and therefore the true essence of all religion—a claim that was difficult to fit into the Bahá'í paradigm without ceding the primacy of Bahá'í scripture as the basis for spiritual truth. Beyond this, Theosophy, because it claimed to have captured the esoteric truth found in every religion, presented a paradigm into which the Bahá'í Faith could potentially be incorporated.

This potential was realized in the writings of W. W. Harmon, a Theosophist from the Boston area. He published books and circulated lessons within the Bahá'í community that offered esoteric interpretations of Bahá'í scriptures and explanations of the stations of Bahá'u'lláh and 'Abdu'l-Bahá that were influenced by the teachings of Theosophy. He was careful to note in his writing that the "Bahai Movement" was not responsible for his conclusions and that he was not "entering into the field of interpretation of the teachings of Baha'o'llah." This itself is evidence that explanations that contradicted or significantly exceeded the obvious meaning of the scriptures were regarded with some suspicion in certain Bahá'í circles.[32] Harmon's teachings had been a source of controversy as early as 1912, and they faced increasing criticism as they became more influential.[33] The crux of the dispute in Chicago was that the Harmon lessons and other Theosophical teachings were being used in classes given at the Reading Room.

Many of the other accusations levelled against the Reading Room group—that they spread negative rumors about prominent Bahá'ís and sought to take over the leadership of the Bahai Temple Unity, for example—could have been directed at other contemporary Bahá'ís, including some of their most outspoken opponents. It was the theological challenge to the dominant Bahá'í paradigm that imbued these accusations with special meaning. If there was the possibility that Theosophy could absorb the Bahá'í Faith theologically, there was a fear that the Bahá'í community could be dominated by persons sympathetic to Theosophy. In this context, the "Harmonites" came to be seen as conspirators who sought to usurp or infiltrate the legitimate leadership of the Bahá'í community so that they could contaminate the Bahá'í movement with Theosophical doctrines.

The Reading Room Affair, which affected a number of local Bahá'í communities in North America, continued to have repercussions throughout the 1920s. The incident marked a significant step towards defining the boundaries of the Bahá'í community. Although they were far from defeated as a force within the Bahá'í community, Bahá'ís who espoused Theosophy or other metaphysical teachings were put on the defensive. After 1918, Bahá'í leaders exhibited a greater willingness to exercise control over Bahá'í publications and presentations.

On the other hand, some prominent Bahá'ís, such as Roy Wilhelm and Agnes Parsons, felt that the conduct of the investigation had been inappropriate and sought to cultivate a more tolerant attitude in the community.[34] While the Reading Room Affair served to discredit metaphysical teachings, it did not challenge the participation of Bahá'ís in churches, other religious groups or movements for social change, which had also contributed to the ambiguity of community boundaries.

In fact, the involvement of Bahá'ís with other groups that promoted teachings similar to those of the Bahá'í Faith, appears to have been increasing at the very time when metaphysical teachings were coming under attack. About the time of 'Abdu'l-Bahá's visit to the West (1911-1913), Bahá'ís began to place increasing emphasis on the Bahá'í social teachings in their public presentations of the Faith. Individuals might be attracted to specific Bahá'í teachings and could on that basis be considered Bahá'ís. This view seemed to be supported by some of 'Abdu'l-Bahá's public statements. For example, he was reported to have said: "To be a Bahá'í simply means to love all the world; to love humanity and try to serve it; to work for universal peace and universal brotherhood."[35] Responding to such exhortations, Bahá'ís became active in movements promoting peace, an international language, racial equality, and feminism.[36] At about this time, a view developed among some Western Bahá'ís that the purpose of the Bahá'í Faith was to spiritualize and broaden the perspective of existing organizations and movements. One such Bahá'í argued: "The Bahai Revelation is not to be organized. It remains an ideal, a force, a principle. Since organizations must be, let the old organizations remain, as many of them as prove useful. Infused with the Bahai Spirit, they can no longer conflict, duplicate or contend."[37] Some asserted that the Bahá'í Faith was the "esperanto of religions," whose purpose was to "coordinate the existing sects and religions but not attempt to replace them."[38] A number of prominent Bahá'ís felt that Bahá'ís could (and should) be active members of non-Bahá'í religious organizations. In 1911, for example, Tudor Pole encouraged the Bahá'ís of London not to leave their churches to form another sect.[39]

During the 1910s and 1920s, many Bahá'ís, especially in the New York and Boston areas, affiliated with churches that had adopted progressive social programs, and they hired liberal clergymen to make public presentations on the Bahá'í Faith.[40] As early as 1908, Dr. Oliver M. Fisher, an Episcopalian minister, was active in the New York Bahá'í Community, where he lectured on the *Seven Valleys*; in 1910 he offered lectures on the Bahá'í Faith in London and held Bahá'í meetings his home there.[41] Subsequently, Christian ministers were associated with a number of American Bahá'í communities, and as Phillip Smith observes in his essay on Great Britain, a Unitarian minister was elected to the National Spiritual Assembly there in 1927. The close association of Christian ministers with the Bahá'í community suggests that at least some Bahá'ís attended their churches. Jackson Armstrong-Ingram has argued that the affiliation of leading

American Bahá'ís with churches impeded the development of distinctive community devotional life in the United States.[42] This might also account for the slow development of a distinct Bahá'í identity and practice in Great Britain.

The lack of a clear consensus on the meaning of Bahá'í identity and on the definition of membership in Bahá'í communities was partly rooted in the absence of local and national institutions whose authority was fully accepted by all Bahá'ís.[43] The Executive Board of the Bahai Temple Unity, was the first ongoing Western Bahá'í institution with more than a local scope of responsibility. Initially focusing on the task of establishing a Bahá'í Temple (*mashriqu'l-adhkár*), the body gradually took on broader responsibilities, but it generally functioned as a board of directors answerable to the delegates who elected it. The delegates themselves might achieve a consensus in a crisis such as the Reading Room Affair, but there was no regular forum at which they could consult and vote on the complex web of issues relating to Bahá'í identity.

Boards of Counsel (the precursors to Local Spiritual Assemblies), seem to have exercised more authority at a local level, but they did not always function with clear mandates to make decisions on all matters for the community. Sometimes their decisions were ratified by a general vote of the believers. In any case, most communities did not have elected consultative bodies; instead they had community officers who were elected or chosen in an informal manner by the community. As Mariam Haney, a Bahá'í since 1900, explained: ". . . the affairs of the Cause were administered by individuals who seemed naturally to have the necessary ability to function."[44] Thus, at both a national and local level, Bahá'í organization at this time could be described as a participatory democracy.

However, in the early 1920s this began to change. Shoghi Effendi, the grandson and appointed successor to 'Abdu'l-

Bahá, drawing on the principles outlined in the Will and Testament of 'Abdu'l-Bahá and in other Bahá'í scriptures, began to alter the existing Bahá'í community practices in significant ways. Local Spiritual Assemblies of nine adult members were to be elected in every community that was large enough, and they were to have the authority to govern the affairs of the community. National Spiritual Assemblies were to have authority independent of the delegates who elected them. Only persons who had declared their belief in Bahá'u'lláh were to attend Nineteen-Day Feasts or vote in Bahá'í elections.[45] The dissemination and implementation of these principles in the North American Bahá'í communities took until about the mid-1930s, and these efforts were not without opposition.

Bahá'ís who did not believe that the Bahá'í Faith should be organized, who felt that excluding non-Bahá'ís from some Bahá'í meetings contradicted the spirit of the Bahá'í teachings, or who opposed what they perceived as the dictatorial tendencies of Bahá'í administrators, coalesced around *Reality* magazine (published from 1919-1929) and the New History Society (founded in 1929). These organizations promoted the idea of an inclusive Bahá'í movement rather than an organized Bahá'í religion. However, neither of them appear to have had widespread support among Western Bahá'ís; both were able to continue their activities primarily because of the financial support of wealthy individuals.[46]

After 'Abdu'l-Bahá's Will and Testament began to be circulated in 1923, it became more difficult to advocate an anti-organization position, because this document included an outline for the development of Bahá'í organization. Nevertheless, many Bahá'ís continued to be troubled by what they viewed as intrusive aspects of the new Bahá'í administrative practices. When the Local Spiritual Assembly of Los Angeles sought to control the Bahá'í meetings held by Ed-

ward Getsinger, for example, he questioned their right to
intervene in his personal activities and decried the "drift in
the Cause toward *sectarianization*."[47]

Such tension between older Bahá'ís and the newly established Bahá'í institutions was common, but the broader trend
was toward acceptance of institutional authority. By 1925,
support for the concept of a Bahá'í movement was so weak
that *Reality* magazine sought a rapprochement with the National Spiritual Assembly.[48] Ultimately, however, neither
Reality nor the New History Society was willing to submit to
the authority of Bahá'í administrative institutions. Those who
continued to be involved with these groups either distanced
themselves from the Bahá'í community or were excommuni-
cated, which effectively ended their influence among Bahá'ís.

This outcome, which became evident by the end of the
1920s, illustrates the changes that had occurred in the Bahá'í
community by this time. Fifteen years earlier, the activities
of *Reality* magazine and the New History Society probably
would have continued within the community. As there was
then no mechanism for resolving the differing concepts of
Bahá'í community and Bahá'í identity, it is likely that most
Bahá'ís would have viewed them not as opposition groups,
but as representatives of different schools of thought within
the Bahá'í Faith.

Although they did, in fact, have a profound effect on the
New York Bahá'í community, the activities of the New History Society and *Reality* magazine were intended to influence
the direction of the Bahá'í Faith at a national and international level. But the authority of both the Guardian and of
the National Spiritual Assembly of the Bahá'ís of the United
States and Canada, the legitimacy of which they attempted
to challenge, had been firmly established within the Bahá'í
community by the late 1920s. There were still minor disagreements about the jurisdiction of the National Assembly

in local affairs and its relationship to National Convention delegates until the mid-1930s.[49] But by 1930, the National Spiritual Assembly was able to focus its attention on the implementation of administrative changes in local communities.

In 1931, for example, for the first time the National Assembly directed that local communities should be confined to the legal metropolitan boundaries of the town or city; those who lived outside these boundaries were to form separate communities.[50] The impact of this policy is noted in several of the essays in this volume.[51] The implementation of this new rule obviously had important consequences for persons who were cut off from the communities to which they had belonged, but the loss of members was also sometimes traumatic for the rest of the community. For example, when the Berkeley Bahá'í community broke off from the San Francisco Bahá'í community, which then included all Bahá'ís in the San Francisco Bay Area, it was the San Francisco Bahá'ís who were upset by the change.[52]

The National Spiritual Assembly also began to coordinate teaching activities in various parts of the country. During the late 1920s and early 1930s, many new local communities were established by teachers whose presentations had been approved by the National Assembly. As a result of the activities of these teachers, there was also a substantial change in membership in some of the established communities. Extended Bahá'í study classes were held in many local communities to insure that community members had a thorough understanding of the Bahá'í teachings and the principles of Bahá'í Administration.

As we can see from the articles on Kansas and Baltimore, this process of reeducation may have also functioned as a way of identifying and removing from the membership lists those individuals who were not Bahá'ís according to the new standards. In the 1930s, it became customary in most local communities in North America for persons to be required to attend study classes for as long as a year before being allowed to enroll in the Bahá'í community.[53] This prevented the development of the ambiguous boundaries of membership that had existed during earlier years and resulted in much greater consistency in Bahá'í beliefs.

As the Kansas essay illustrates, some persons left Bahá'í communities when the membership requirements changed, but they were probably outnumbered by new converts. According to the 1936 census of religions, there were then 2,584 Bahá'ís in the United States in 88 Bahá'í communities.[54] Although this estimate may be slightly high, and there is some question about whether the Bahá'í population grew significantly in the previous decade, there can be little doubt that were many new converts during this time and that their presence and involvement in Bahá'í activities changed the nature of Bahá'í communities.[55]

A survey of local communities conducted in 1937 illustrates some of the changes that had taken place in Bahá'í community life. The majority of the Bahá'ís in these communities were reported to have been enrolled after the "establishment of the administrative order."[56] Hence the majority of Bahá'ís, and the total membership of some communities, had by then been socialized into a Bahá'í culture that placed great stress on organization. This did not simply entail an acceptance of the authority of Bahá'í institutions. New Bahá'ís understood that when they had accepted the Bahá'í Faith they had also joined a community in which they were obliged to be active workers. In 1937, there was an average of 6.3 committees per community, or one committee for every 4.8 persons.[57] Many tasks that had previously been handled by individuals, such as the planning of the Nineteen-Day Feast or the maintenance of a Bahá'í Library, were now handled by committees. This came to be viewed as the proper way to accomplish most tasks; and, as the example of Edward Getsinger suggests, activities that were not under the control of an institution were seen as improper. Mariam Haney, writing in the mid-1940s, observed that in the period prior to the establishment Local Spiritual Assemblies, "even the committees did not preclude the friends from serving and teaching in accordance with their own guidance. Those were the days when the 'rugged individualism' of Americans was greatly in evidence."[58] We can infer from this statement that such individual activities were no longer the norm when she wrote this. Although, as Deborah Clark observes with regard to Baltimore, some local committees may have been quite small, it seems probable that most active Bahá'ís were on a committee.

This suggests that, in comparison to earlier periods, there was a high level of commitment among the membership. The level of participation in Bahá'í meetings also seems to have grown from earlier decades. Attendance at Feast in 1937, for example, was estimated to be, on average, 56%; in 1918, it was probably about 38%.[59] Further evidence of this commitment can be seen in the high number of Bahá'ís who "pioneered" to new localities to establish new communities in the following decade. Between 1937 and 1944, 241 Bahá'ís—5% to 10% of the North American Bahá'í population—became Bahá'í pioneers.[60]

Of course, this is evidence not just of high levels of commitment, but also of changing priorities in Bahá'í communities. By the end of the 1930s, North American Bahá'í communities had been transformed into an organizational type that one sociologist has termed a "mission," an organization in which a high proportion of resources is directed towards evangelical activities.[61] Beginning in 1937 in North America, and in 1940 in Great Britain, plans were developed to focus the resources of Bahá'ís almost exclusively on the recruitment of new members. After World War II, North American Bahá'ís began systematically to spread the Bahá'í Faith in Western Europe, establishing a number of new communities.[62] After 1937, the Bahá'í population of the United States doubled roughly every thirteen years until the 1960s, when growth became more rapid.[63] The Bahá'í population of Canada seems to have grown at a faster rate—doubling every five or six years—but the membership was not measured in the thousands until the 1960s.[64] Bahá'í evangelical activities in North America, some of which were attempts to attract specific minorities, began to change the demographic composition of the Bahá'í population. By 1937, about 6% of the North American Bahá'ís were former Catholics and about 2% were former Jews.[65] Both groups were underrepresented in the Bahá'í community in comparison with the larger population. This is probably because both groups had developed cohesive social networks that were difficult to penetrate; Catholics and Jews were less like to convert to any other religion than were Protestants.[66] However, several surveys suggest that Catholic and Jewish representation in Bahá'í communities did increase. In 1953, for example, 15.6% of the Bahá'ís of New York City were from a Jewish background, an increase of 10.7% from 1937.[67] In a 1968 survey of new Bahá'í converts in the United States, 15% were former Catholics and 4% were formerly Jewish.[68] Finally, a 1979 study of the membership of the Los Angeles Bahá'í community found that 7.6% of the members were former Catholics and 9.3% had been Jewish.[69]

There were significant numbers of African-Americans in one community—Washington, D.C.—even before 'Abdu'l-Bahá's visit there in 1912. In the later 1910s and 1920s, blacks became members of at least 19 other Bahá'í communities. By 1937, they comprised about 5% of the North American Bahá'í population and were found in 34 communities, with the largest number in Chicago.[70] Their representation within the Bahá'í community was not equal to their percentage of the U.S. population. However, if a comparison is made just of the populations of the states in which there were Bahá'í communities, African-Americans were overrepresented in the community.[71] By 1950, blacks were estimated by one observer to comprise 15% of some local communities.[72] In the 1968 survey cited above, 13% of the new Bahá'ís were found to be black.[73] These percentages reflect the composition of Bahá'í communities before a surge of black conversions in 1970 and 1971.

This cultural diversity affected the development of communities in a variety of ways. In some localities, there was opposition to interracial meetings from groups such as the Ku Klux Klan,[74] and some communities were investigated by government agencies such as the FBI, presumably because organizations that sponsored integrated meetings were suspected of being influenced by Communism.[75] Such interference, when it was overt, may have contributed to a sense of community solidarity. On the other hand, cultural differences may have contributed to a diminished intimacy in the social relationships within communities. In several instances, individual members of Bahá'í communities openly opposed the integration of Bahá'í meetings. Although such positions were almost unheard of after the 1950s, subtle forms of cultural tensions remained in some Bahá'í communities, and Bahá'ís may have developed more formal social relationships within communities because this insured a certain distance from persons with whom they felt uncomfortable.[76]

In any case, a trend towards greater formality seems to have been encouraged by the direction focus of Bahá'í activities for several decades. Although this has yet to be adequately studied, it appears that Bahá'í communities in the 1940s and

1950s were characterized by high levels of membership commitment to the Bahá'í Cause, but rather minimal bonds of reciprocal obligation between the Bahá'ís themselves. Bahá'ís might provide financial or other forms of assistance to each other, but this seems usually to have stemmed from an understanding that the assistance would aid someone in his or her service to the Faith. In most communities, there was little development of communal devotional activity, which might have enhanced community solidarity, and most communities were too small to offer the types of services to believers that churches could. Because of the changes in the physical boundaries of communities and the emphasis on "pioneering," Bahá'í communities tended to be smaller than in earlier decades. While the number of Bahá'í communities roughly quadrupled between 1936 and 1947, the average size of local Bahá'í communities in North America went from 30 to 15 during this period.[77] Fifteen believers came to be seen as the ideal size of a Bahá'í community; when communities exceeded this size, Bahá'ís were encouraged to move elsewhere to form new communities. In these small communities, the basic Bahá'í activities of the time—Feasts, commemorations of Bahá'í holy days, firesides, Local Spiritual Assembly meetings, and committee meetings—occupied the active Bahá'ís to such an extent that little consideration could be given to other matters.

However, in the 1960s and the 1970s the Western Bahá'í population experienced a series of significant demographic changes which changed the composition and focus of many local communities. For one, there was a relatively rapid process of suburbanization in the post-war period in North America, as middle-class families moved out of urban centers. This migration was reflected in the loss of members in urban Bahá'í communities and contributed to the growth of new communities in suburban areas, a process that is observed in the essays on Sacramento and Baltimore. However, a study of the Bahá'í population in 1976 shows that the number of Bahá'ís living in suburbs was disproportionately low. It appears that many Bahá'ís left large cities to establish new communities in small towns (under 45,000), where the Bahá'í population was disproportionately high.[78]

The major event that affected Bahá'í communities, however, was the rapid spread of the Bahá'í Faith, especially among youth, which occurred in a number of Western countries in the late 1960s and early 1970s. The Bahá'í population of the continental United States during this period increased from about 11,000 in 1963 to about 75,000 in 1976; it had reached 110,000 by 1991.[79] The rate of growth appears to have been higher in Canada, where the Bahá'í population went from 554 in 1953 to 17,724 in 1986.[80] Similar growth took place in other Western countries.[81]

This process received impetus from the growth of the counterculture, which removed social constraints from youth that might have otherwise impeded their investigation of the Bahá'í Faith and which simultaneously encouraged the study of nontraditional religious teachings. However, few of the Bahá'í converts seem to have been deeply involved in the counterculture. In the continental United States, many of the youth conversions resulted from activities on college campuses[82]; while in Hawaii, the vast majority of the converts were U.S. military servicemen who were stationed in Honolulu.[83] These persons may have been influenced by the pervasive youth subculture, but they had not dropped out of society to pursue alternative lifestyles. Like the youth described in the Sacramento article, many of the new Bahá'ís expressed their identities using the symbols and trappings of counterculture, and they seem to have developed an oral teaching that mediated those elements of the Bahá'í Faith that were most incongruent with that culture. But the message these young Bahá'ís conveyed within that subculture may have been far closer to mainstream Bahá'í thought than other Bahá'ís realized. Most of the new Bahá'ís were able to make a transition to a middle-class lifestyle with little difficulty. Those who did were probably more likely to remain active in Bahá'í communities.

A series of surveys conducted in the 1970s and 1980s illustrates this point. A 1979 study of Bahá'ís in Rhode Island found only one Bahá'í—a former Hare Krishna member—who had been part of any group identified with the counterculture.[84] Surveys of Bahá'ís in Los Angeles and in the United Kingdom conducted in the same year found that 5% and 12.1% respectively had been members of non-traditional religious groups. But most of these persons had been Christian Scientists, Mormons, or Spiritualists, groups that were not associated with the 1960s counterculture.[85] A 1985 survey of Bahá'ís who had experiences with non-traditional religious groups found persons who had been members of groups that were associated with the counterculture, such as a Kundalini Yoga Ashram and the Children of God, but they were outnumbered by former Jehovah's Witnesses and Mormons.[86] Although no reliable statistics are available, it is highly unlikely that persons who had been members of nontraditional religious groups ever comprised more than 10% of the Bahá'í population.[87] Nevertheless, anecdotes that circulate among Bahá'ís suggest that in the early 1970s a significant minority of new Bahá'ís had been involved in nontraditional religious movements. The surveys seem to indicate that those who were deeply identified with this religious subculture were less likely than others to remain active in the Bahá'í community.[88] A significant percentage of all new Bahá'ís, perhaps one-third of those in North America, became inactive or withdrew from the Bahá'í community by the late 1970s, but the Bahá'í population continues to be dominated by babyboomers, most of whom converted during this period.[89]

The growth of the Bahá'í population in the 1960s and

1970s increased the ethnic diversity of Bahá'í communities. In the United States, a significant percentage of the new Bahá'ís were African-Americans. This was true in urban areas, but the Bahá'í Faith also began to spread among blacks in rural areas of the American South, especially in South Carolina. About 20,000 persons converted there in 1970 and 1971, but the absence of established communities in these areas made it difficult to reinforce and sustain the Bahá'í identities of new converts.[90] In urban areas, new Bahá'ís were gradually socialized into a new identity through association with a community, both before and after conversion. In some parts of the South this was not possible, and many Bahá'ís there seem to have continued to regard themselves as Christians. Nevertheless, well-established communities have emerged in the "mass teaching areas," and this represents the first major penetration of the Bahá'í Faith into the rural population of North America.

In the 1960s, the Bahá'í Faith also began to spread in another sector of the rural population: Amerindians in the United States and Canada. As with rural conversions in the South and in some other parts of the world, many of these Bahá'ís seem to have developed dual religious identities; and many still practice their traditional religions.[91] There have also been some conversions of Hispanics in rural areas, primarily in the American Southwest. Because many of these Bahá'ís are migrant farmworkers, their integration into existing communities and the development of new communities among them has been problematic.

Rural conversions have changed the social base of the Bahá'í population, but, because the new converts are geographically segregated from the majority of the other Bahá'ís, this has had a very limited impact on the majority of local communities. Other demographic changes had a greater impact, especially in the larger urban communities. For example, although their numbers have been relatively small, the conversion of Hispanics in urban areas of the United States and of French-speaking persons in Canada has added to the diversity of a number of communities. The influx into the American Bahá'í population of Southeast Asian refugees—some of whom converted before they arrived and some after—has dramatically changed the demographic composition of a few Bahá'í communities, primarily on the West Coast.

The most dramatic demographic change to affect Western Bahá'í communities, however, has been the influx of Persian refugees following the Iranian Revolution of 1978-79. They spread throughout North America and Europe, and although no reliable statistics are available, it seems probable that they comprise 15% or more of the Bahá'í population in these areas.[92] Both the Iranian and Southeast Asian emigres tend to be disproportionately represented in certain large metropolitan areas, where they sometimes comprise the majority of Bahá'ís in a community.

The frequency of certain Bahá'í activities in these communities—race unity deepenings, cross-cultural workshops, language and culture classes, and the like—suggests that there have been some difficulties dealing with cultural differences among Bahá'ís. At the same time, such activities also underscore the commitment of these communities to full integration. Serious cultural tensions have emerged between Iranian and local Bahá'ís, but this phenomenon appears to have been specific to a few large urban communities. In general, Iranian Bahá'ís seem to have assimilated more easily into Western societies than non-Bahá'í Iranian immigrants,[93] and their presence, as Peter Smith and Moojan Momen have observed, has contributed to "an increased sense of international Bahá'í solidarity and cohesion."[94]

The growth of the Bahá'í Faith since the 1960s has changed the size and character of many local communities.

Although it is not possible to determine with accuracy the current average community size, we can observe that in the United States the average number of Bahá'ís in a locality went from 5.1 in 1947 to 14.2 in 1991.[95] If Bahá'í communities experienced a similar growth, the average community would have 41 members. Some of the communities in major urban centers now number several hundred, while the Bahá'í population of Los Angeles has exceeded one thousand for more than two decades. The increasing size of communities has allowed for the development of more diverse and specialized Bahá'í activities, a trend that became very visible in the 1980s.[96] A number of activities that fostered a stronger sense of community were sponsored by Local Spiritual Assemblies, including counseling services, women's support groups, Alcoholics Anonymous groups, Bahá'ís in Recovery Programs (which has chapters in many communities), ESL classes, dance and drama workshops, programs for single Bahá'ís (including at least one matchmaking service), and Youth for One World (a youth organization with chapters sponsored by local communities). These changes seem to have been more pronounced in the large metropolitan communities.

The 1980s also saw the emergence of activities that drew together Bahá'ís from various local communities around a special interest or profession. For example, the Association for Bahá'í Studies now has a number of special interest sections that have facilitated the development of networks of Bahá'ís with particular areas of expertise, and there are now organizations or informal networks of Bahá'í lawyers, physicians, publishers, computer users, short-wave radio operators, and academicians. There have also been a number of new Bahá'í journals—mostly short-lived—focusing on specialized subjects, such as literature, social issues, parenting, women's issues, and the academic study of the Bahá'í Faith.[97] It is significant that a number of these endeavors were initi-

ated not by Bahá'í institutions but by individual Bahá'ís.
Corporations owned by individual Bahá'ís have also been
formed to publish and distribute Bahá'í books, audio record-
ings, and other materials; and to initiate philanthropic
projects. This is a marked departure from the Bahá'í practice
considered normative for several decades.

Many of these activities, whether begun by individuals or
Bahá'í institutions, amount to the formation of voluntary associations within the Bahá'í community. Their impact on local communities is not yet clear, but presumably they draw
some resources away from local activities. On the other hand,
although they only involve a minority of Bahá'ís, they appear
to have fostered greater social cohesion in the Bahá'í population at an international level.

The way communities were affected by and responded to
the trends described above has varied greatly and has usually been dependent on the local conditions within and outside Bahá'í communities. Some of the diversity of the Bahá'í
experience in the West is documented in this volume. However, significant areas of Western Bahá'í history, are not represented here. It is hoped that future volumes in this series
will include articles that, for example, document the experiences of African-Americans in communities in South Carolina and Amerindians on reservations and reserves in the
United States and Canada. It is especially important that
histories be written for Bahá'í communities in continental
Europe. The focus of this introduction on North America is
no reflection on the significance of European Bahá'í history;
it is a reflection of the state of the existing literature. It is
equally important that histories of communities outside the
West be written and published.

As the study of the Bahá'í Faith develops as an academic
field, such detailed histories will become essential. There is a
huge mass of primary source material relating to the history

of the Bahá'í Faith, including community records, personal papers, newsletters, and memoirs. These materials, especially voluminous for recent decades, are scattered around the world. No single historian can hope to make use of all of these sources. Therefore, the development of a secondary literature, including well-researched local, regional, and national histories is necessary before reliable broader studies can be written. This volume is intended as a small contribution to such a literature.

RICHARD HOLLINGER
NORTH BERGEN, NEW JERSEY
JULY 1992

NOTES

1. Charles Joyner, *Down by the Riverside: A South Carolina Slave Community* (Chicago: University of Illinois Press, 1984) p. xvi.

2. The few exceptions to this tend to focus on the very early years of a community, which does not allow for an examination of continuity and change over time. See, for example, William P. Collins, "Kenosha, 1893-1912: History of an Early Bahá'í Community in the United States," in Moojan Momen, ed., *Studies in Bábí and Bahá'í History* (Los Angeles: Kalimát Press, 1982) pp. 225-254, and the treatment of several early American communities in Robert Stockman, *The Bahá'í Faith in America: Origins, 1892-1900* (Wilmette, Ill.: Bahá'í Publishing Trust, 1985).

3. For a full description of these classes, see Robert Stockman, *The Bahá'í Faith*, pp. 60-84.

4. The Friday night meetings in Chicago appear to have been intended for, and primarily attended by Bahá'ís. It was at these meetings that Bahá'ís were introduced to the "Higher Teachings"—those based on Bahá'í scriptures. These meetings are mentioned in: Attie Dealy to Maude Lamson (n.d.) and G. S. Dixon to Maude Lamson July 31, 1899. Maude Lamson Papers. National Bahá'í Archives. Wilmette, Illinois. Maude Lamson to Ibrahim Kheiralla, July 9, 1899,

July 15, 1899, and July 29, 1899. Kheiralla/Saleeby Family Papers (In private hands); and Fannie Lesch to "Brother in Faith," August 23, 1899. Portland Bahá'í Archives. There is no direct evidence that non-Bahá'ís were kept out of these meetings. But on at least one occasion persons were prevented from attending a meeting in which the final lesson (on the Greatest Name) was to be given, because they had not attended the earlier classes. (See "Only Believers were Permitted to Hear Address of Dr. Kheiralla Last Night," *Cincinnati Enquirer,* September 22, 1899, p. 2.) It seems unlikely that Kheiralla would have knowingly permitted non-Bahá'ís to attend meetings where the "Higher Teachings" were presented. The appointment of "watchmen" for the Kenosha Bahá'í meetings suggests that they had similar concerns. (Kenosha Bahá'í Community minutes, entry for June 22, 1899. Kenosha Bahá'í Community Records.)

5. See Peter Smith, "The American Bahá'í Community, 1894-1917: A Preliminary Survey," in Moojan Momen, *Studies in Bábí and Bahá'í History,* p. 121; and Stockman, *The Bahá'í Faith,* pp. 101-103.

6. "Kheiralla is Here," *The Commercial Tribune* (Cincinnati) September 21, 1899, p.5.

7. See Mírzá Abu'l-Faḍl, *The Bahá'í Proofs* (Wilmette, Ill.: Bahá'í Publishing Trust, 1983) pp. 71-78.

8. Thornton Chase, "A Brief History of the American Development of the Bahai Movement," *Star of the West,* vol. V, no. 17 (January 19, 1915) p. 263.

9. Computed from Bahá'í Membership Lists, United States, 1894-1900 (Microfilm). National Bahá'í Archives. Wilmette, Illinois. It should be noted that this list does not include the names of all of the Bahá'ís enrolled during the years covered. More importantly, it is an enrollment list—not a membership list—so it may include the names of many persons who were never active in a Bahá'í community.

10. Robert Stockman, "The Bahá'í Faith and American Protestantism, 1894-1921," (Ph.D. dissertation, Harvard University, 1985) p. 48. Stockman, *The Bahá'í Faith,* p. 110.

11. U.S. Bureau of the Census, *Religious Bodies: 1936—Separate Religious Denominations* (Washington, D.C.: Government Printing Office) Part I, Vol. II, p. 75.

12. Ibid. In 1905, a petition was circulated in Bahá'í communities that was sent to 'Abdu'l-Bahá. The petition was probably signed by the vast majority of persons who attended the meetings where it

was circulated; thus it can be used as a rough indicator of attendance at Bahá'í meetings. The names of those who signed the petition, totalling 422 persons, were listed on the tablet (letter) 'Abdu'l-Bahá wrote in response, which was printed in 1906. This is an average of eighteen persons per community. Although it is probable that the petition was not circulated in every community, it is also likely that the attendance at the meetings where it was circulated was higher than average.

13. Minutes of the Portland Bahá'í community, entry for November 25, 1906. Portland Bahá'í Archives. Membership list of the Seattle Bahá'í Assembly, April 15, 1907; minutes for the meeting of April 15, 1907; "Members of the Spokane Assembly," August 1908. Seattle Bahá'í Archives.

14. Peter Smith, *The Bábí and Bahá'í Religions: From Messianic Shi'ism to a World Religion* (London: Cambridge University Press, 1987) pp. 106-107. More detailed accounts of the establishment of these communities can be found in the following sources: Agnes Alexander, *Forty Years of the Bahá'í Cause in Hawaii, 1902-1942* (Honolulu: National Spiritual Assembly, 1974); Duane Troxel, "A Survey of the Origin and Development of the Bahá'í Faith in the Hawaiian Islands, 1900-1915" (unpublished paper); Charles Mason Remey, "The First Meetings in Paris" in "Bahá'í Reminiscences, diary, letters, and other documents by Charles Mason Remey" (New York Public Library) folio 1; "In Memoriam: May Ellis Maxwell," *Bahá'í World,* Volume VIII (Wilmette, Ill.: Bahá'í Publishing Trust, 1942); Rainer Flasche, "Der Religion der Einheit Selbstverwirklung der Menscheit: Geschichte und der Bahá'í in Deutschland," *Zeitschrift fuer Missionswissenschaft und Religionswisrenschaft,* vol. 61, no. 3 (1977) pp. 188-213; the memoirs of Alma Knobloch, Washington, D.C., Bahá'í Archives; and E. T. Hall, *The Beginning of the Bahá'í Cause in Manchester* (Manchester: Bahá'í Assembly, 1925).

15. Bureau of the Census, *Religious Bodies: 1936,* p. 75.

16. *Star of the West,* vol 10, no 8 (August 1, 1919) pp. 156-164. The number of persons on the list (1,136) has been divided by the number of localities with two or more Bahá'ís (57), resulting in an average of 19.9 per community.

17. "List of Bahais of the United States and Canada. Made at the Request of Shoghi Rabbani, March 1922," Alfred Lunt Papers. National Bahá'í Archives.

18. Stockman, "American Protestantism," pp. 33-34.

19. The time and frequency of Bahá'í meetings has been gleaned from notices and articles about local communities that appeared in *The Bahai Bulletin* (New York) and *Star of the West* between 1908 and 1910 (inclusive). Of 25 communities, 13 met on Sundays; the remainder either had meetings on weekday evenings or did not specify the time of their meetings.

The description of the meetings is based largely on instructions for the conduct of meetings that were given by Isabella Brittingham to the Portland Bahá'ís, and which she said were "widely observed in America." These are found in the minutes of the Portland Bahá'í community between the entries for March 30, 1907 and April 7, 1907. (Portland Bahá'í Archives.) As Brittingham was one of the most widely traveled American Bahá'í teachers, her observations carry considerable weight.

20. Circular letter from Charles Mason Remey in *Star of the West* vol. 1, no. 9 (August 20, 1910) pp. 2-3.

21. Ramona Allen Brown, *Memories of 'Abdu'l-Bahá: Recollections of the Early Days of the Bahá'í Faith in California* (Wilmette: Bahá'í Publishing Trust, 1980) pp. 5, 45. Marion Carpenter Yazdi, *Youth in the Vanguard: Memoirs and Letters Collected by the First Bahá'í Student at Berkeley and at Stanford University* (Wilmette: Bahá'í Publishing Trust, 1982) p. 6. Anna Monroe to Phoebe Hearst, November 9, 1911 and n.d., Phoebe Hearst Papers. Bancroft Library.

22. Yazdi, *Youth in the Vanguard,* p. 6.

23. Excerpts from letters of Helen Goodall (TS), June 20, 1904 and January 8, 1905, in private hands.

24. The involvement of entire families in communities, intra-community marriages, business partnerships between Bahá'ís, and Bahá'ís hiring personal and business employees from within the community can be seen as indicators that these communities transcended the norms of voluntary associations. This issue has not yet been systematically studied, and there is only anecdotal evidence to support this observation. However, it is possible to obtain some crude statistical evidence on family participation by examining several Bahá'í lists.

In Kenosha, the names of 86% of those who signed a petition to 'Abdu'l-Bahá in 1901 (Thornton Chase Papers. National Bahá'í Archives. Wilmette, Illinois.) appear with the name of at least one other family member, indicating that they were active as a family. For those who signed a petition to 'Abdu'l-Bahá in 1918 the figure is 94%. (*Star of the West,* vol 10., no. 8, p. 161.)

The names of 34.5% of the Chicago Bahá'ís in 1897 were listed with another family member. (Bahá'í Membership Book, Chicago House of Spirituality Records. National Bahá'í Archives.) For the 1918 petition, the figure is 48% for Chicago, and 37% for New York. (*Star of the West* vol. 10, no. 8, pp. 157-160.)

The dramatic difference between Kenosha and the other communities can be explained by the fact that this community emerged from a working-class population. It was therefore modeled after working-class social organizations which tended to have more intense social relationships, while the membership in Chicago and New York was more middle-class.

Nevertheless, the fact that there were classes for children in Chicago (*Part of the Bahá'í History of the Family of Charles and Maria Ioas*—Epilogue [n.p., n.d] [not paginated]) and a Bahá'í youth club in New York (*Bahai Bulletin,* November 1908 [not paginated]) does suggest a significant degree of family orientation. Moreover, there were well-known Bahá'í families who provided stability and cohesion to these communities: the Dodge, Harris, MacNutt, and Kinney families, in New York; the Ioas, Greenleaf, Lesch, Agnew, and Bartlett families, in Chicago.

25. [Arthur P. Dodge?], "Editorial Department," *The Bahai Bulletin* vol. 1, no. 1 (September 1908) [not paginated].

26. Jackson Armstrong-Ingram, *Studies in Bábí and Bahá'í History,* Volume Four: *Music, Devotions, and Mashriqu'l-Adhkár* (Los Angeles: Kalimát Press, 1987) pp. 197.

27. Charles Mason Remey, *Reminiscences of The Summer School: Green Acre—Eliot, Maine* (n.p., 1949) pp. 70-71, 73-75. Armstrong-Ingram, *Music, Devotions and Mashriqu'l-Adhkar,* pp. 198-202.

28. Remey, *Reminiscences,* pp. 70-71. *Star of the West,* vol. 9, no. 5 (June 5, 1918) p. 58.

29. Marie Watson to Mrs. Aseyeh Allen (copy), July 20, 1920, Aseyeh Allen-Dyar Collection. Washington, D.C., Bahá'í Archives. It is interesting to note that in this same letter, Watson cited personal inspiration in defence of a Catholic doctrine: "The Immaculate Conception is a spiritually scientific fact proved to my soul and I *know* also the *process* . . . Beware how you handle these matters. These are 'holy mysteries' not known to the merely intellectual aspect."

30. For a description of this incident, see Peter Smith, "The American Bahá'í Community, 1894-1917," pp. 189-94. Except where otherwise noted, this is the source for the information on this incident.

31. Untitled notes on the meetings of the Committee of Investigation (TS), Ella Cooper Papers. San Francisco Bahá'í Archives. *Report of the Bahai Committee of Investigation 1917-1918* (Washington D.C.: n.p., n.d.) p. 4. It is not clear, from the historical evidence, that the Reading Room group did, in fact, split off from the Chicago community. They claimed that it was their accusers (Zia Bagdadi and Corrine True) who had created the division in the community.

32. W. W. Harmon, *The Seven Principles of the Microcosm and the Macrocosm Applied to the disclosures of Baha'o'llah in the Book of the Seven Valleys* (Boston: n.p., 1915) pp. 11-12.

33. Notes on a meeting with 'Abdu'l-Bahá in San Francisco, Ella Cooper Papers. San Francisco Bahá'í Archives.

34. Smith, "American Bahá'í Community," p. 190. Interview with Walter Blakely, conducted by the author on October 25, 1985.

35. John E. Esslemont, *Bahá'u'lláh and the New Era* (New York: Bahá'í Publishing Committee, 1931) p. 86.

36. For a summary of involvement of Bahá'ís in the peace movements, see Richard Hollinger, "Bahá'ís and American Peace Movements," in Anthony Lee, ed., *Circle of Peace: Reflections on the Bahá'í Teachings* (Los Angeles: Kalimát Press, 1985) pp. 3-20. On Bahá'ís and racial issues, see Gayle Morrison, "To Move the World: Promoting Racial Amity, 1920-1927," *World Order* (Winter 1980) pp. 9-31; and Mark Perry, "Pioneering Race Unity: The Chicago Bahá'ís, 1919-1939," *World Order*, vol. 20, no. 2 (Winter 1985-1986) pp. 41-60. On Bahá'í involvement with the Esperanto movement, see Wendy Heller, *Lidia: The Life of Lidia Zammenhof, Daughter of Esperanto* (Oxford: George Ronald, 1985). No research has yet been published on Bahá'í involvement in the feminist movement, however, there were feminist Bahá'ís. Laura Dreyfus-Barney, for example, was a founding member of the International Council of Women. I am indebted to Jean L. Kling, curator of the Alice Pike Barney papers, for this information.

37. Aseyeh Allen Dyar, *Short Talks on the Practical Application of the Bahai Revelation* (Washington D.C., 1922) p. 55.

38. Remey, *Reminiscences,* p. 27-28.

39. Arthur Cuthbert, "London, England, News Notes," *Star of the West,* vol. 2, no. 2 (April 9, 1911) p. 2.

40. Armstrong-Ingram, *Music, Devotions and Ma*s*hriqu'l-A*d*hkár* pp. 261-273. Interview with Walter Blakely, October 25, 1985. Remey, *Bahá'í Reminiscences,* p. 28.

41. Thornton Chase to Ella Cooper, November 14, 1908, Ella Cooper Papers. San Francisco Bahá'í Archives. "New York," *Bahai Bulletin* (November 1908). *Star of the West* (June 24, 1910) p. 12; and (July 13, 1910) p. 16. Fisher's pilgrimage is reported in the January 1909 issue of the *Bahai Bulletin.*

42. Armstrong-Ingram, *Music, Devotions and Ma*s*hriqu'l-A*d*hkár* pp. 267-73.

43. For a discussion of this, see Mark Perry, "The Chicago Bahá'í Community, 1921-1939," (Ph.D. dissertation, University of Chicago, 1986) pp. 11-15.

44. Mariam Haney, "The American Pioneer Period," *World Order* vol. 11, no. 3 (1945) p. 92.

45. Shoghi Effendi, *Bahá'í Administration: Selected Messages, 1922-1932* (Wilmette, Ill.: Bahá'í Publishing Trust, 1974) pp. 20, 37, 79-80, 90.

46. *Reality* began as an effort to attract non-Bahá'ís to the Bahá'í Faith. (Pilgrim's Notes of Agnes Parsons, Ella Cooper Papers. San Francisco Bahá'í Archives.) As such it seems to have been supported by a number of Bahá'ís for the first few years. (See Peter Smith, "*Reality* Magazine: Editorship and Ownership of An American Bahá'í Periodical," in Juan Cole and Moojan Momen, eds. *From Iran East and West: Studies in Bábí and Bahá'í History,* Vol. 2 (Los Angeles: Kalimát Press, 1984) pp. 135-144. The founders, Eugene and Wandeyne Deuth, also started a "Bahá'í Library," with which a number of New York Bahá'ís were associated. (Wandeyne Deuth to Governor Sulzer, January 6, 1920, William Sulzer Papers. Bailey/Howe Library, University of Vermont.)

Harrison Gray Dyar, who took over the editorship in 1922, took the magazine in a more radical direction than the original editors. He was critical of Bahá'í administration, especially of the Guardianship. (See "A Brief History of the Bahai Movement," *Reality,* vol. 10, no. 3, pp. 3-4; "Unjustified Bahai Organization," *Reality,* vol. 6, no. 7, pp. 35-37; and "The Will of Abdul Baha," *Reality,* vol. 6, no. 7, pp. 16-20.) Dyar must have had an independent source of income, because he worked much his adult life as an unpaid curator at the Smithsonian Institution. (Biographical Note in the Inventory of the Harrison Gray

Dyar Papers, Smithsonian Institution Archives.) Since the publication of *Reality* magazine ended with his death in 1929, it seems probable that he was providing it with financial support. Dyar was also the proprietor of a journal on entomology.

The activities of the New History Society could not have been undertaken without the financial support of Julie Chanler. See Ahmad Sohrab, *Broken Silence: The Story of Today's Struggle for Religious Freedom* (New York: New History Foundation, 1942).

47. E. C. Getsinger to L.A. Bahai Assembly, February 1934. Local Spiritual Assembly of Los Angeles Records. Los Angeles Bahá'í Archives.

48. "Editorial—Our Change of Policy," *Reality,* vol. 10, no. 3, p. 3.

49. See Mark Perry, "Boundaries and Horizons in the Chicago Bahá'í Community, 1920-1940," (unpublished paper); and Dr. Loni Bramson-Lerche, "Some Aspects of the Development of the Bahá'í Administrative Order in America, 1922-1936," in Moojan Momen, ed., *Studies in Bábí and Bahá'í History,* pp. 267-295.

50. Local Spiritual Assembly of Chicago to the National Spiritual Assembly, May 20, 1931, National Spiritual Assembly records. Cited in Mark Perry, "An Overview of the Chicago Bahá'í Community, 1921-1939," p. 19.

51. For the affect of this on the Denmark Bahá'í Community, see Margit Warburg, "The Circle, the Brotherhood, and the Ecclesiastical Body: Bahá'í in Denmark, 1925-1987," in Armin W. Geertz and Jeppe Sinding Jensen, eds., *Religion, Tradition, and Renewal* (Denmark: Aarhus University Press, 1991) pp. 201-224.

52. Interview with Anne Stevenson, conducted by the writer on September 8, 1982. Yazdi, *Youth in the Vanguard,* pp. 72-74. It should be noted that the formation of the Berkeley community occurred before the National Spiritual Assembly's announcement of this policy.

53. This has been deduced from 49 questionnaires on "Local Bahá'í History and Records," circulated in North America in 1937. (National Bahá'í Archives. Wilmette, Illinois.) According to this survey, 34 communities (69%) had such classes. Most of the communities did not specify the length of time of these courses but of those that did, the average length was twenty-seven weeks. Twenty-eight communities (57%) indicated that Bahá'í Administration was a major focus of the classes.

54. Bureau of Census, *Religious Bodies: 1936,* p. 75.

55. "Local Bahá'í History and Record" questionnaires. Of the communities who identified their period of most rapid growth, 71% indicated that it was after 1926.

56. "Local Bahá'í History and Record" questionnaires. The questionnaires usually give a percentage in answer to this question. I converted these to numbers using the total membership of the local community, added the figures from all of the communities together, and computed the percentage (61%) from the total membership included in this survey (1,497).

57. Ibid.

58. Haney, "The American Pioneer Period," p. 92. "Committees" here refers to Boards of Counsel and the Chicago House of Spirituality, precursors to Local Spiritual Assemblies.

59. The "Local Bahá'í History and Record" questionnaires, included a question about attendance at Feast, which was usually answered with a percentage. I converted these to numbers; added up the total number who were estimated to attend Feast regularly; and divided by the total number of Bahá'ís listed in these communities, to arrive at the 56% estimate.

I have used the list of Bahá'ís on a petition sent to 'Abdu'l-Bahá in 1918 to arrive at the second estimate. The petition circulated in local Bahá'í communities for a number of weeks (Carl Scheffler, "Outline of how Supplication was drafted," *Star of the West,* vol. 10, no. 8, p. 168) and would therefore have been circulated at one or more Feasts. If anything, this number (1,124 for the United States) would be a high estimate of Feast attendance, as some could have signed at other meetings.

Much of the change between 1918 and 1936 may have resulted from changes in the definition of membership. Many of those counted on the 1916 census would probably not have been counted in 1936.

60. *The Bahá'í Centenary 1844-1944* (Wilmette: Bahá'í Publishing Committee, 1944) p. 175. The number of Bahá'ís in North America in 1943 was 4,578 (*Bahá'í News,* no. 161, p. 3.). The pioneers would constitute 5.2% of this number and 9.4% of the figure given by the 1936 census (2,584). Another, possibly more accurate, gauge of the size of the Bahá'í population in 1936 is the Bahá'í Historical Record Cards (in the Bahá'í National Archives, Wilmette, Illinois), which were filled out by North American Bahá'ís in 1935-1936. There are 1,813 of these, and the Bahá'í pioneers would comprise 13.2% of this population.

61. Ross P. Scherer, "A New Typology for Organizations: Market, Bureaucracy, Clan, and Mission, with Application to American Denominations," *Journal for the Scientific Study of Religion,* vol. 27, no. 4 (December 1988) pp. 475-498. Scherer notes that "missions" can also focus their resources on social action, but few can balance both social action and evangelical activities. The decline in social activism in the Bahá'í community during this period fits this pattern.

62. Arthur Hampson, "Growth and Spread of the Bahá'í Faith," (Ph.D. dissertation, University of Hawaii, 1980) pp. 378-82; Warburg, "Bahá'í in Denmark"; Karel Dobbelaere and Michel Voisin, "Sekten en nieuwe religieuze bewegingen in België," *Tijdschrift voor Sociologie* vol. 7, nos 1-2 (1986) pp. 395-437; Flasche, "Bahá'í in Deutschland." A useful primary source that documents the activities of Bahá'í "pioneers" in Europe during this period is Charles Mason Remey, *Journal-Diary of Bahá'í Travels in Europe,* 2 volumes (n.p., 1947 and 1949). See also Will C. van den Hoonaard, comp., "An Annotated Index of the United States European Teaching Committee Minutes. Sources for the Study of European Bahá'í History" (unpublished ms.).

63. Hampson, "Growth and Spread," pp. 222, 229. I have used the figure 11,047 as the number of Bahá'ís in 1963 ("Proposed Budget for the First Year of the Nine Year Plan," copy in my possession) and the 1936 Census figure of 2,584, to arrive at this estimate.

64. Will C. van den Hoonaard, "Canada," (draft of article for the *Short Encyclopedia of the Bahá'í Faith). Bahá'í News* (March 1947) p. 8.

According to these sources, the Bahá'í population of Canada went from 270 in 1947 to 554 in 1953.

65. Stockman, "The Bahá'í Faith and American Protestantism," p. 48-49.

66. Frank Newport, "The Religious Switcher in the United States," *American Sociological Review,* vol. 44 (1984) p. 533. Wade C. Roof and Christopher K. Hadaway, "Denominational Switching in the Seventies: Going Beyond Stark and Glock," *Journal for the Scientific Study of Religion,* vol. 18 (1979) pp. 366-67. Rodney Stark and Charles Glock, *American Piety: The Nature of Religious Commitment* (Berkeley: University of California Press, 1968) p. 195.

67. Peter Berger, "From Sect to Church: A Sociological Interpretation of the Bahá'í Movement" (Ph.D. dissertation, New School for Social Research, 1954) p. 133. The Berger survey suggests that the

number of Bahá'ís from a Catholic background in New York went down slightly from 9.7% (14) in 1937 to 7.8% (7) in 1953. However, the Berger survey was conducted at a single Nineteen-Day Feast and therefore was not a survey of the entire community. The percentages for 1937 have been computed from figures in Stockman, "The Bahá'í Faith and American Protestantism," pp. 48-49.

68. Hampson, "Growth and Spread," p. 357. The percentage of Catholic converts was still below their representation in the wider population, which was then 26%. It should be noted that this survey only included persons who converted in December 1968.

69. Peter Smith, "A Sociological Study of the Bábí and Bahá'í Religions" (Ph.D. dissertation, University of Lancaster, 1982) p. 438.

70. Morrison, *To Move the World,* pp. 32-34, 204-205. Robert Stockman, "The Bahá'í Faith and Protestantism," pp. 45-46.

71. Hampson, "The Growth and Spread of the Bahá'í Faith," p. 340.

72. T. Lane Skelton, "A Sociological Analysis of the Bahá'í Movement" (M.A. Thesis, University of California at Berkeley, 1955) p. 68.

73. Hampson, "Growth and Spread," p. 347.

74. Morrison, *To Move the World,* p. 283. Sandra Kahn, "Encounter of Two Myths: Bahá'í and Christian in Rural American South—A Study in Transmythicization," (Ph.D. dissertation, University of California at Santa Barbara, 1977) pp. 261-262. Lucille Buffin, "Fifty-Three Years with Miami, Florida Bahá'ís, 1933-1966," (unpublished paper, an earlier version of which is in the National Bahá'í Archives. Wilmette, Illinois) p. 5.

75. Mary Elizabeth Archer, "Global Community: Case Study of the Houston Bahá'ís," (M.A. Thesis, University of Houston, 1980) p. 180. Interview with Lois Willows conducted by the writer on January 2, 1985. According to Willows, the FBI agent charged with investigating Bahá'ís in Long Beach, California eventually became a Bahá'í. The writer was informed by former employees of the U.S. Bahá'í National Center that this institution was infiltrated by an intelligence unit of the Chicago Police Department in the late 1960s or early 1970s.

76. This possibility was raised by a series of conversations I had with Bahá'ís who were active in one U.S. community in the 1950s. Although these were not formal interviews, I did ask questions that were intended to uncover what types of relationships Bahá'ís had

with each other during this period. Several patterns emerged from these queries. It appears that the conduct of Bahá'í meetings was rather formal and impersonal and did not lead to the development of friendships among the members. Individual Bahá'ís did develop close relationships, over time, as a result of personal contact outside Bahá'í meetings. However, because blacks and whites in the community rarely met together socially they rarely developed close friendships. This pattern of relationships may be specific to one community, however.

77. In 1949, there were 372 Bahá'í communities in North America (*Bahá'í World,* Volume XI, pp. 525-531); there were, in 1947, 5,720 Bahá'ís (*Bahá'í News,* March 1947, p. 8). Hence the average community size was approximately 15. The Bahá'í population probably grew between 1947 and 1949, and therefore this estimate may be slightly low. According to the figures in the 1936 census, the average Bahá'í community would have had 29.3 members; the average community size according to the "Local Bahá'í History and Record" questionnaires was 30.5

78. Hampson, "Growth and Spread," pp. 308-309.

79. Ibid., p. 229. The "Proposed Budget for the First Year of the Nine Year Plan," gives the figure 11,047 for 1963. The 1991 figure comes from a statistics sheet provided by the U.S. Bahá'í Office of Public Information, dated September 1991.

80. Will C. van den Hoonaard, "Canada."

81. See Warburg, "Bahá'í in Denmark," and Margaret J. Ross, "Some Aspects of the Bahá'í Faith in New Zealand," (M.A. Thesis, University of Auckland, 1985) pp. 116-124.

82. This conclusion is based on conversations with Robert Phillips, Anthony Lee, and Jesse Villagomez, each of whom was a member of the U.S. Bahá'í National Youth Office during the period of youth conversions.

83. Interview with Lois Willows, January 2, 1985.

84. Robert Stockman, "A History of the Rhode Island Bahá'í Community, 1866-1979." National Bahá'í Archives. Wilmette, Illinois.

85. Smith, "A Sociological Study," p. 438.

86. Unpublished (and untitled) survey of selected Bahá'ís in the United States conducted by Janet Tanaka in 1985.

87. The Tanaka survey was not a random sample, and therefore cannot be used to gauge the percentage of Bahá'ís who had been

involved in non-traditional religions. However, a 1968 survey (Hampson, "Growth and Spread," p. 357) indicates that 90% of new converts stated that they were either Christians, Jews, or had been raised as Bahá'ís.

88. One exception to this might be Bahá'ís involved with Transcendental Meditation (TM), some of whom have been able to reconcile continued involvement in this movement with their Bahá'í identities. For example, at a Bahá'í conference in St. Louis in 1974, I met Bahá'ís from a community the total membership of which was active in this group. As of the late 1980s, there was a Bahá'í community in Iowa composed entirely of individuals who were studying these teachings at a TM college.

89. Hampson, "Growth and Spread," pp. 228-230. Hampson notes that, in 1976, 31% of the persons on the U.S. Bahá'í membership lists were "mail returns," —their addresses were unknown and they were not known to be active in any Bahá'í community. A similar pattern can be seen in Canada where the Bahá'í population exceeded 17,000 in 1986, but the number with known addresses was 11,500 (*Bahá'í Canada*, April 1988, p.3.)—a mail return rate of 32%.

90. Kahn, "Encounter of Two Myths," pp. 15-16.

91. A Bahá'í pioneer on a Navajo reservation in Arizona, for example, informed the author that all of the Bahá'ís there continue to participate in Navajo religious ceremonies.

92. It is estimated that 25,000 Bahá'ís fled Iran after the revolution ("NSA of US Presents Peace Statement to President Reagan," *Alaska Bahá'í News*, March 1986, p. 3.) Not all of them settled in the West, but it would appear that most of them did. In the mid-1980s, the writer was given an unofficial estimate by an employee of the U.S. Bahá'í National Center that there were 12,000-14,000 Iranian Bahá'ís in the U.S., which would be slightly more than 10%. Resident Bahá'ís in Canada have informed me that the percentage is higher in that country. Peter Smith's survey of the British Bahá'í community in 1979 found that 31.8% were Iranian. ("A Sociological Study" p. 439.) As of 1981, Iranians comprised 17% of the Danish Bahá'í Community. (Warburg, "Bahá'í in Denmark.")

93. Chantal Saint-Blanat, "Nation et religion chez les immigres iranien en Italie," *Archives de sciences sociales des religions* (July-September 1988) pp. 27-37.

94. Peter Smith and Moojan Momen, "The Bahá'í Faith 1957-

1988: A Survey of Contemporary Developments," *Religion,* vol. 19 (1989) p. 85.

95. Computed from information in *Bahá'í World,* Volume XI, pp. 525-541; *Bahá'í News* (March 1947) p. 8; and a statistics sheet provided by the U.S. Bahá'í Office of Public Information, dated September 1991. These figures include localities in which there is only one Bahá'í; the figures given above for the average community size included only localities with two or more Bahá'ís.

96. Most of the information discussed below has been gleaned from a review of bulletins from twenty U.S. Bahá'í District Teaching Committees and local Bahá'í newsletters from the following communities: Boston, Chicago, Indianapolis, Los Angeles, Milwaukee, Minneapolis, New York Portland, San Diego, San Francisco, Seattle, Toronto. I reviewed publications dating from 1985 to 1990, although it was not possible to locate copies of every publication for this entire time period.

97. Among the journals are: *Spiritual Mothering, dialogue, Wherefore, The Green Door, I Read the News Today, The Journal of Bahá'í Studies, Soundings,* and *The Bahá'í Studies Bulletin.*

STUDIES IN THE
BÁBÍ AND BAHÁ'Í RELIGIONS

VOLUME SIX

COMMUNITY HISTORIES

BAHÁ'ÍS OF KENOSHA, 1897

These are the first eighteen Bahá'ís of Kenosha, Wisconsin. Mr. and Mrs. Byron Lane are seated in the center.

A HISTORY OF THE KENOSHA BAHÁ'Í COMMUNITY, 1897-1980

by Roger M. Dahl

The Bahá'í Community of Kenosha, Wisconsin, was one of the earliest in North America, having been established in the 1890s. It is of special interest to students of American Bahá'í history because it was probably the only working-class Bahá'í community in America at that time. For several decades, the Kenosha Bahá'í community was one of the largest in the country, and it is still in existence today. The course of its history reflects the changes that have shaped the national Bahá'í community since its birth and also provides us with a glimpse of the diversity that characterized that larger community at the local level.

The city of Kenosha lies on the shores of Lake Michigan in Wisconsin, forty miles north of Chicago. In 1890, it had a population of only 6,532 and little industry. But Kenosha was a growing industrial town. By 1920, it was an important city of 40,000. Its proximity to Chicago and Milwaukee allowed it to become a manufacturing center tied to both neighboring cities.

In the 1890s, immigrants from northern Europe made up the majority of Kenosha's new citizens. By 1900, more than

1

one quarter of the population of Kenosha County was foreign born, particularly from Germany and Scandinavia. After the turn of the century, however, a second wave of immigration from southern and eastern Europe provided for most of the city's growth.[1]

Beginnings: The Bahá'í Faith was introduced in America by Ibrahim George Kheiralla (Khayru'lláh), a Syrian Bahá'í of Christian background. In 1894, he settled in Chicago and established a successful spiritual healing practice. Corollary to this practice were his efforts to convert his patients, and others, to the Bahá'í religion.[2] He may have visited Kenosha to spread the Bahá'í teachings as early as 1895,[3] but the first success there was achieved in 1897, when a Kenoshan, Byron Lane, became a Bahá'í through his Chicago friend, Paul K. Dealy. In the fall of 1897, Kheiralla began making weekly trips to Kenosha to deliver his lessons on the Bahá'í Faith, in Lane's home, to those who were interested.

These classes, known as lessons for "Truth Seekers," followed a fixed course of study. There were twelve or thirteen lessons, personally delivered in order by Kheiralla himself. The students were expected to keep all of the teachings strictly "private":

> . . . these teachings are private and you are not to mention them to anyone; they are not secret but private, and we trust to your honor. We do not ask you to take any obligation or oath. These teachings are private for many reasons. You will remember that Jesus talked to the masses in parables. . . . When [the apostles] attempted to expound the teachings He rebuked them and told them that they must not cast their pearls before swine. This was to show them that the truth was only for truth seekers. . . . So you are not to mention the teachings until you are given permission.[4]

The classes began with lessons on the mind and soul and went on to discuss various religious subjects current at the time. The last three classes dealt with the Bahá'í religion, presenting it as the fulfillment of biblical prophecy. Students were taught that Bahá'u'lláh was the incarnation of God the Father. 'Abdu'l-Bahá, the head of the Faith living in 'Akká, Palestine, was presented as the son of God, the return of Christ. At the end of the classes, students were asked to sign a confession of faith addressed to 'Abdu'l-Bahá. If they did, they were eventually given the Greatest Name,[5] the culmination of Kheiralla's instruction. Those who completed the classes were known as Truth-knowers.

Thus, the Bahá'í Faith was introduced in Kenosha not as an independent religion, but as a secret society or lodge. Those who became Bahá'ís continued to regard themselves as Christians; they were not expected to withdraw from church membership; and their faith was centered on the Bible, which they continued to study in relation to their new beliefs. They had joined an "Order" with secret teachings, much as one might join a Masonic lodge or some other fraternal organization. As Kheiralla himself explained in his early book, *Bab-ed-Din*:

> The instruction is private and the [true] name of the Order is known only to those who have taken the full course and received acceptance from the Great Head [i.e., 'Abdu'l-Bahá] of the headquarters of the Order; hence it is that our members are not publicly known and recognized.[6]

Fraternal orders were extremely popular in American cities in the late 1890s. These orders—especially Masonic lodges—frequently taught metaphysical lessons and provided an alternative social network to Protestant churches, although many individuals belonged to both. In Kenosha, in 1899, there were more than twice as many fraternal organizations as there were churches.[7] It is likely that most of the adults in Kenosha belonged to at least one of these societies. The rapid success of the Bahá'í Faith in Kenosha should be viewed in this context.

As the number of those interested in the Bahá'í teachings grew in Chicago, and in other cities around the United States, Kheiralla could no longer keep up with the demand for his services. He began to appoint other Bahá'í teachers to take on some of his classes. Paul K. Dealy was assigned to teach the Kenosha classes.[8] Beginning in early April 1898, Dealy commuted by train to Kenosha every Friday to deliver his classes in the evening. On April 18, he reported to Kheiralla that there were eighteen new Bahá'ís as a result of his work and that he was about to start a new class immediately, with seven students.[9]

Dealy reported that the older Bahá'ís in Kenosha were repeating the classes. Therefore, it seems that the meetings were not only a means of recruiting new members, but also a point of gathering for those who were already Bahá'ís.[10] With so many people repeating the classes after having taken them before, it is likely that Dealy eventually felt the need for innovation and flexibility with regard to the content of his lectures, which became in effect the first Bahá'í community meetings.

The Bahá'í community of Kenosha grew rapidly, with a total of one hundred and eighty-five members enrolled by the end of 1899. (See Table 1.) This was a predominantly working-class community. While there were a few small businessmen and professionals among the new believers, there were no Bahá'ís among the town's elite. A possible exception was the Timme family: Ernst G. Timme and his wife, Caroline, with their two daughters, Elizabeth and Lena, were Bahá'ís. Timme acted as the Kenosha assessor, justice of the peace, and county clerk. He was the Wisconsin state senator for the area, and he was an auditor in several federal departments in Washington, D.C.[11]

Most of the Bahá'í men in Kenosha were factory workers. The women were generally full-time homemakers, an indication of the relative prosperity of Kenosha laborers. In 1900, 60% of those who had become Bahá'ís were born in the United States, while 40% were foreign born.[12] Fully 87% of the foreign-born came from Sweden, Germany, England, or Denmark.[13] (See Tables 2 and 3.) But they were not all newcomers: John C. Bishop was from a long-time Kenosha family, his grandfather having settled in the county in 1838.[14] By the middle of 1900, there were more Bahá'ís per capita in Kenosha than in any other American city, about 2% of the population of 11,000.[15]

On May 26, 1899, the Kenosha Bahá'í community established its first organizational structure by electing community officers. Byron Lane was elected as the community's president. The other elected officers were: vice-president, second vice-president, secretary, correspondence secretary, treasurer, and collector.[16] There was no administrative body elected, and important decisions seem to have been made by the community as a whole at general meetings.

Even before this, in 1898, the community had collected funds in a treasury to pay for Dealy's weekly train fare. His travel expenses remained a major expense through 1899. No one contributed regularly to this fund, but the community could count on sufficient donations when there were bills to be paid.[17]

Church Opposition, 1899: Opposition to the Bahá'í teachings from at least one Christian church had developed in Kenosha by the time that Dealy assumed responsibility for teaching in Kenosha in 1898. The parents of one of the new Bahá'ís, William Heser, were Baptists from Racine, a town nearby.

Learning of their son's new faith, they pronounced it the work of the devil. Armed with their Bibles, they visited their son in Kenosha in an effort to convince him to cut himself off from the Bahá'ís. When this did not work, they sent the deacon of their church. When he too was unsuccessful, they sent the minister himself to confront Paul Dealy. There was much quoting from the Bible back and forth. But Dealy claimed that he won the debate and that the encounter had helped to confirm the faith of the Kenosha Bahá'ís and the new inquirers.[18]

By late 1899, the Bahá'í successes caused the mainstream churches in Kenosha (Baptist, Methodist, and Congregational) to take direct, public action to denounce the new religion. The churches hired a Harvard-educated Bulgarian minister, Stoyan Vatralsky, to come to Kenosha from Chicago and refute the Bahá'í teachings. Vatralsky attended some of the Bahá'í classes in Kenosha and shortly thereafter denounced the Faith in the local newspapers as "an esoteric Mohammedan sect," "the most dangerous cult that has yet made its appearance on this continent."[19] For several weeks, the Kenosha newspapers carried articles and letters from Vatralsky and from various Bahá'ís who sought to defend their Faith from attack. Meetings were held in local churches where Bahá'ís were challenged to prove that their religion was not anti-Christian. Some of these debates became quite loud and rancorous. They received a good deal of newspaper coverage.

Up to this point, the Bahá'í teachings had not been made public. They were available only to those who attended the "private" classes given by Bahá'í teachers. However, faced with this public denunciation, the Bahá'ís were forced to defend themselves by making at least some of their beliefs known, though they seem to have given out as little as possible. Their principle line of defense was to reject the charge that the Bahá'í Faith was a Muhammadan religion; to express their contempt for Islam, "the most corrupt of all religions"; and to insist that they were teaching God's truth from the Bible.[20] Kheiralla himself came to Kenosha, where at the Rhodes Opera House, he delivered a public talk explaining some of his teachings and faced Vatralsky in a public debate.

In December 1899, Vatralsky moved on to Milwaukee. However, the secrecy and anonymity which had surrounded the Bahá'í community in Kenosha had been ripped away. Despite the Bahá'í protestations of Christian credentials, the churches had made it clear to all that they found the Bahá'í Faith and its teachings unacceptable. No doubt, Bahá'ís felt under pressure to either give up their Bahá'í activities or leave their churches.[21] Bahá'ís were now known and publicly labeled. As a result, they became a more close-knit group and, as time passed, their community meetings came to replace church activities for most members.[22] Denounced by the mainline churches, the Bahá'í meetings took on the character of an alternative church, with many Bahá'í activities being similar to functions in a Protestant congregation.

During the year between May 1899 and May 1900, the Bahá'í community met at least thirty-nine times. The Christian orientation of the group is made clear by the subjects of their study. Most of these centered on the Bible: Revelation, chapters 1-22 (more than once); Ezekiel, chapters 35 and 47; Chronicles, chapter 30; and Isaiah, chapters 47 and 62. Bahá'í materials read and studied were: Bahá'u'lláh's Hidden Words, his "Tablet of El Hak," and his Tablets (letters) to Napoleon III and to the Pope; a Tablet from 'Abdu'l-Bahá to the American Bahá'ís, one of Edward G. Browne's books on the Faith, and letters from Bahá'í teachers Marion Kheiralla, Anton Haddad, and Lua Getsinger.[23]

Many people in nearby Racine, Wisconsin, were also attracted to the Bahá'í teachings. Byron Lane introduced the

Faith to that city in 1899, and he taught the first seven believers there. In March 1900, he was able to deliver a public lecture in Racine to an audience of over one hundred people. The community elected its first officers on November 8, 1899. By 1901, an additional forty people had been brought into the Faith by Fred Peterson, a Racine Bahá'í.[24]

Crisis, 1900: At the end of 1898 and during the first several weeks of 1899, Kheiralla and a number of American Bahá'ís were able to travel to 'Akká, Palestine, to visit 'Abdu'l-Bahá. This was the first pilgrimage of Western believers to be made. During this visit, tensions developed between Kheiralla and the Bahá'ís traveling with him, and between Kheiralla and 'Abdu'l-Bahá. These tensions were soon to have a profound effect on the Kenosha Bahá'í community.[25]

Almost immediately upon Kheiralla's return to America in May 1899, disagreements broke out among Bahá'ís in several communities—especially New York and Chicago. Deep divisions developed between those Bahá'ís who felt that Kheiralla, their first teacher, should be regarded as the head of the Bahá'í Faith in America, and those who felt that he had no right to such a position.

Kenosha was pulled into the growing controversy for the first time on March 8, 1900, when Kheiralla visited the city and told the Bahá'ís of Kenosha and Racine that he was not sure of 'Abdu'l-Bahá's position as the head of the Bahá'í Faith. A second meeting was held on March 9, at which Kheiralla explained his doubts. At the end of this meeting, Byron Lane remained unconvinced. He rejected Kheiralla's arguments and "announced that he himself will continue to teach that Abbas Effendi ['Abdu'l-Bahá] is the Master and he has found nothing to convince him otherwise."[26] Lane and his wife worked to keep the community loyal to 'Abdu'l-Bahá. On March 14, Mr. and Mrs. Lane presented a paper before the Racine

Bahá'ís giving reasons why 'Abdu'l-Bahá was still the "Master" and head of the Bahá'í Faith.[27]

However, it appears to have taken the Bahá'ís in Kenosha and Racine several months to make up their minds about the controversy. There were a few Bahá'ís who agreed with Kheiralla, and some who definitely rejected him. But most fell somewhere in the middle. They maintained relations with both groups and were reluctant to cut ties with either side.[28]

In April 1900, the Bahá'ís of Kenosha were studying Kheiralla's new book *Behá 'U'lláh* in their meetings. The Bahá'ís of Racine began studying the book the next month. It was not until September of that year that the Bahá'ís of Racine decided to replace Kheiralla's photograph with one of 'Abdu'l-Bahá.[29]

Kheiralla retained more support in Kenosha than he did anywhere else in the country outside of Chicago, where he lived. Several factors account for this. The Lanes moved out of Kenosha at about this time, leaving the Bahá'ís there without strong leadership.[30] Kheiralla soon began making regular trips to Kenosha to organize support for himself there.[31]

Kheiralla and his followers have indicated that about one hundred and fifty Bahá'ís in Kenosha sided with him, but this number is certainly highly inflated. Some thirty or forty members of the community remained staunchly loyal to 'Abdu'l-Bahá. Another thirty or forty repudiated him in favor of Kheiralla.[32] Of the remainder, many may have drifted away from the Faith or moved away from the area. Although community records provide no documentation, it appears from a search of the Kenosha city directories that a number of Bahá'ís moved from the city during the next few years.

Transition, 1900-1904: There is a gap in the minutes of the Kenosha community between 1900 (after the Lanes' move) and 1904. It seems likely, however, that Bahá'í meetings continued to be held during this period, even though we have no record of them. There are 115 blank pages in the minute book, and most of these have a date written on them in pencil. This suggests that meetings were held, but that minutes were not taken—or if taken, were never transferred into the minute book, which was not purchased until 1904.[33]

It is known that Kenosha formed an all-male Board of Counsel early in this period, most likely during 1900. This was a consultative body that eventually developed into the local Spiritual Assembly of Kenosha. 'Abdu'l-Bahá addressed a Tablet to the Board of Counsel some time in 1901.[34] Racine had also formed a Board of Counsel by July 1900.[35] The Kenosha Board adopted the practice of rotating the chairmanship of its meetings, as did Racine. Frank H. Hoffmann of Chicago had advised the Racine Bahá'ís in 1900, to elect their secretary and treasurer for a term of office, but to choose a different chairman for each meeting, "thereby giving all members a chance to act and avoiding distinction or criticism give every body a chance. Chicago has had a severe experience in this very thing and has suffered for it."[36]

In 1900 and 1901, 'Abdu'l-Bahá sent messages of encouragement and praise to the Bahá'ís of Kenosha. He sent Tablets to the Kenosha Board of Counsel, the Bahá'í women of Kenosha (twice),[37] and to the community as a whole. In one of these Tablets, 'Abdu'l-Bahá addressed them in words that echoed their study of biblical prophecies:

> O ye firm, steadfast and faithful Believers! . . . the Tabernacle hath been elevated upon the Hill of Might, the powers of heaven have been shaken, the corners of the earth have quaked, the sun has been darkened, the moon ceased to give light, the stars have fallen, the nations of the earth have lamented, and the Son of Man hath come upon the clouds of heaven with power and great glory, and He hath sent His angels with the sound of the great trumpet, and no one knows the meaning of these emblems save the wise and informed.

Ye are the angels, if your feet be firm, your spirits rejoiced, your secret thoughts pure, your eyes consoled, your ears opened, your breasts dilated with joy, and your souls gladdened, and if you arise to assist the Covenant, to resist dissension and to be attracted to the Effulgence! Verily, I say unto you that the Word of God has assuredly been explained and has become an evident sign and a strong and solid proof, and its traces shall be spread in the East and West, and to these all heads shall bow and all souls shall submit and kneel down with their faces to the ground."[38]

In July 1901, Mírzá Asadu'lláh, one of the Persian Bahá'í teachers that 'Abdu'l-Bahá had sent to America to support the new community in the wake of Kheiralla's defection, visited Kenosha with Anton Haddad, a Lebanese believer resident in the United States, as his interpreter. Upon returning to Chicago, Asadu'lláh advised the House of Spirituality (the administrative body there) that Kenosha was in need of a Bahá'í teacher every Sunday who could "impart to them the true teaching of Baha Ullah and otherwise look after the flocks."[39] Apparently, this was not done since, in October 1901, twenty-four Kenosha Bahá'ís signed a petition addressed to Chicago saying that they were in need of a teacher. They asked that Byron Lane be sent.[40]

Byron Lane was able to visit Kenosha every other week during 1902,[41] but it is certain that the community felt the lack of a strong resident teacher. This may account for the decline in membership and the inconsistency of the community's records during these years. Though it is not clear exactly when, the Boards of Counsel in both Kenosha and Racine stopped holding meetings and became defunct. This did not leave the Bahá'ís without organization, however, since community officers were reelected.

The financial records of the Kenosha Bahá'í community between 1900 and 1904 demonstrate on-going activities but suggest that the community had grown weaker. The number

BERNARD AND THERESA JACOBSON
with their son.

of contributors decreased in 1900, with only 50 Bahá'ís giving money to the funds that year.[42] In 1900, train fare continued to be the largest expense of the community, dependent as it was on outside teachers. In 1902, hall rent was a major item in the budget, but the rents varied considerably since the community was probably only using halls for special occasions. By 1904, most of the money was being spent on halls, and only a little for train fare.[43]

In the early 1900s, the Chicago House of Spirituality acted as a regional center for all Bahá'í communities in the Midwest. Chicago undertook to instruct Bahá'ís in the region on various aspects of Bahá'í life. In 1902, the Chicago Bahá'ís wrote to Kenosha urging that they celebrate the "Feast of the Master" on November 26, and Kenosha agreed to commemorate the occasion.[44] In 1903, Chicago reminded other communities about the Bahá'í nineteen-day fast. Kenosha replied that those who could would observe the fast.[45] The Chicago community also helped the Kenosha community relocate Miss Maud Frazine, an invalid Kenosha Bahá'í, to the home of Isaac H. Doxsey, a Chicago believer. "She would by this act be saved the humiliation of being placed in the public poor house."[46]

In 1904, Bernard Jacobsen moved to Kenosha from Chicago and quickly became the center of a reorganized community. He provided new leadership by delivering weekly lectures on the Bahá'í teachings which were summarized as being on: "the way we should live, words we should speak, the attitude we should take towards others, in order to bring about the most Great Peace, and urging us to be ready at all times to deliver the message of God's Kingdom on earth."[47]

After Jacobsen's arrival, the Kenosha Board of Counsel was reestablished. In 1904, there was a meeting of the male believers who wanted to form a board. They wrote to the Chicago House of Spirituality and to the New York Board for advice, and to 'Abdu'l-Bahá for his approval. The whole community was polled to see if it wanted a permanent Board. A temporary all-male Board was reestablished, with Bernard Jacobsen as its president and Louis Voelz as secretary. This Board replaced the community officers who had served since the collapse of the original Board of Counsel. It also had the effect of excluding Bahá'í women (such as Mrs. Saint Germain—then the community treasurer) from the administration of the community.[48]

Consolidation, 1904-1910: During the next several years, the Kenosha Bahá'ís were able to establish a regular and distinctive community life, resembling that of a small Protestant church. Jacobsen had success in activating some of the inactive Bahá'ís who had entered the Faith during the 1890s. He was also able to win over some of Kheiralla's followers in Kenosha.[49] But there were few enrollments. (See Tables 1 and 4.) It does not appear that there was any significant effort made to spread the Faith among the new immigrant population from Southern and Eastern Europe. As the Bahá'í teachings were being spread primarily by word of mouth, the lack of any believers from Italian, Polish, Russian, or Hungarian backgrounds meant that the Bahá'ís would have difficulty reaching the new immigrants. The absence of believers who had been Roman Catholics also proved to be a formidable barrier.

Isabella Brittingham established the regular observance of the Nineteen-Day Feast[50] in Kenosha, as she did in many other places. The Feast was a worship service and a social gathering, rather than a business meeting. There was no consultation. The meeting was customarily opened by one of the children, who would recite a verse from the writings of 'Abdu'l-Bahá and anoint all those present with attar of rose. The first Nineteen-Day Supper, as it was called, was held on

March 21 (the first day of the Bahá'í calendar), in 1906, with fifty-three Bahá'ís present.[51] The refreshments served at subsequent Feasts ranged from ice cream and cakes, to sandwiches, fruit, and oyster stew. In 1908-1909, the average attendance at the Feast was twenty-four.[52]

A continual stream of visitors and Bahá'í teachers passed through Kenosha during these years. This was partially due to the proximity of the community to Chicago, which was the center for many national Bahá'í events. But it also indicates the dependence of this working-class community on wealthier, better educated, and more prominent believers from outside. During seven months of 1909 alone, Kenosha had at least sixteen Bahá'í visitors, including Howard and Mary MacNutt, Roy Wilhelm, Charles Mason Remey, Edward Struven, Mrs. A. M. Bryant, Thornton Chase, and Sidney Sprague.[53] Kenosha also had an early tradition of summer picnics which drew Bahá'ís from nearby communities, such as Racine and Chicago, and later Milwaukee. The first recorded picnic was in 1905. The Racine Bahá'ís were invited, and everyone was to bring his own basket of food.[54]

In 1907, the Kenosha Board—now calling itself the Board of Consultation[55]—began a tradition of corresponding with other Bahá'í communities which continued into the 1920s. Ameen Ullah Fareed suggested that Kenosha send out a circular letter with a report of their June 30, 1907 reception for several Chicago believers recently returned from pilgrimage to 'Akká. Later, it was decided to have the report translated into Persian and sent to Eastern Bahá'í communities. It took over a year to accomplish, but by August 1908, the report had been mailed to over one hundred communities around the world. A number of responses were received, including one from Rangoon, Burma.[56]

From very early on, Kenosha participated in fund-raising activities for the Bahá'í Temple to be built in Chicago. In

1907, the Board created a Temple Fund, with Walter Bohanan as treasurer.[57] In 1908, at the request of the Chicago House of Spirituality, a Temple Committee was appointed, consisting of three men and two women.[58] By August 1908, they had raised about two-hundred dollars and had another two hundred in pledges.[59] When Chicago issued the call for the first Bahai Temple Unity convention, to be held March 20-23, 1909, Kenosha elected Bernard Jacobsen as its delegate. During the convention, Jacobsen was elected to the Executive Board of the Temple Unity, a national body. He was also elected its secretary. He served on the national Executive Board until 1914.[60]

During the early years of the community, the Kenosha Bahá'ís met in each other's homes or rented halls for special occasions. However, in May 1907, the community began renting a hall on a full-time basis. It seems to have been a second-story room above a store. Most of the money of the community was now used to pay for rent, utilities, and furnishings for the new meeting place. Several local drives were undertaken to pay for wallpaper, paint, chairs, and other furniture.[61]

Kenosha was unusual among Bahá'í communities in the United States because of the large number of children who were included as part of the community. This may, again, reflect the working-class background of most of the believers. In 1906, children were included on the Bahá'í membership list. The community established a Bahá'í Sunday school in the fall of 1907.[62] In the summer of 1908, the Board of Consultation announced that "a School of Industry has been organized that the children may learn some useful work, in accordance with instructions contained in the Kitab-el-Akdas.[63] And a school for all the children to learn the communes and prayers and simpler teachings of the Religion of GOD is under way."[64] The industrial school for children was a unique

THE BAHÁ'Í CHILDREN OF KENOSHA, WISCONSIN, c. 1909.

innovation in the American Bahá'í community. The year it was established, the school held a picnic which drew 50 children.[65] By 1910, the industrial school for girls had grown to 125 students.[66] Efforts were made to include children in the programs of Bahá'í meetings, especially Holy Day observances. In 1909, the children conducted the program for Naw-Rúz (Bahá'í New Year), March 21, and presented a musical program and recitations for the Day of the Covenant, November 26.[67]

The Society of Behaists, the organization established by the followers of Kheiralla, was also active in Kenosha during this period. They held regular Sunday meetings in 1909, which were advertised in the church column of the *Kenosha Evening News*.[68] This was the only organized group of Kheiralla's followers outside of Chicago, where Behaist meetings were held in Kheiralla's home. However, the existence of this rival group was sometimes discouraging to the Bahá'ís. In January 1904, before the community was reorganized by Jacobsen, the community drafted a letter to 'Abdu'l-Bahá which read in part:

> We are a little band of believers in Kenosha, who are trying to hold together throught [sic] all difficulties caused by the Nakazeen[69] of this town. This is their stronghold in America. We humble [sic] beg that Thou willt [sic] intercede for us that we may be strengthened through the confirmations of the Spirit, to keep our numbers together, to hold to the Center of the Covenant [i.e., 'Abdu'l-Bahá], and be enabled to draw these deniers nearer to Thee.[70]

The Behaist group continued holding their meetings in Kenosha, their only stronghold, until the early 1950s.[71]

Gender Tensions, 1910-1911: The establishment of all-male Bahá'í councils in Chicago and Kenosha in 1900, was a matter which caused some tension at the time. Only days after the election of the Chicago House of Justice, on May 15,

THE BAHÁ'Í SCHOOL OF INDUSTRY

Unique to Kenosha, Wisconsin, the Bahá'í industrial schools were organized in 1908. There was also a school for boys.

1901, a Ladies Auxiliary Board (later known as the Women's Assembly of Teaching) was organized in Chicago at the suggestion of Ella Nash and Corinne True. The Ladies Auxiliary managed to hold on to the treasury of the Chicago community, despite the election of the new all-male board.[72]

The exclusion of women from some local Bahá'í institutions was a development to which some Bahá'í women were never reconciled. In 1909, Corinne True received a Tablet from 'Abdu'l-Bahá, in response to her questions on this matter, which she construed to mean that women could now be elected to the Chicago House of Spirituality, the successor of the House of Justice.[73] However, the House of Spirituality did not interpret the Tablet to mean any such thing. The House wrote immediately to 'Abdu'l-Bahá for a clarification, but they do not seem to have received a reply. True's interpretation soon opened up a nationwide controversy over the rights of women to serve on Bahá'í institutions.[74]

In Kenosha, the women raised the issue in the summer of 1910. On July 4, the Kenosha Board of Consultation wrote to the Chicago House of Spirituality asking if they had any Tablets from 'Abdu'l-Bahá that instructed that women should be elected to local Bahá'í institutions. They explained that two ladies in their community were insisting that such Tablets exist.[75] The reply of the Chicago House of Spirituality quoted three recent Tablets from 'Abdu'l-Bahá. The first Tablet, to Corinne True, stated that men and women are equal, except for the universal (or general) House of Justice.[76] The second Tablet, to Louise Waite, stated that institutions organized for the sake of teaching could be all men, all women, or made up of both: ". . . whether assemblies for men, assemblies for women, or mixed assemblies, are all accepted and are conducive to the spreading of the Fragrances of God."[77] In the third Tablet, to the Bahá'ís of Cincinnati, 'Abdu'l-Bahá stated that since it was impossible to organize the House of Justice at the present time, a Spiritual Assembly should be organized in that city, and that it would be preferable if an Assembly of both men and women should be elected.[78]

The Chicago House concluded from these Tablets that, although local boards had originally been intended as all-male institutions, 'Abdu'l-Bahá now approved of the establishment of institutions made up of both men and women. Albert Windust, writing for the House of Spirituality, suggested:

> As your Assembly has had a Board of Consultation established for some years, it seems to me it would be wise to ask for a vote from them as to whether the majority desire to have a mixed Board of men and women before making a change. It is evident from the foregoing extract from a recent Tablet that in organizing Spiritual Assemblies of Consultation *now* it is deemed advisable by Abdul-Baha to have them composed of both men and women. The wisdom of this will become evident in due time, no doubt.[79]

Rather than do this, however, the Kenosha Board of Consultation submitted the question to 'Abdu'l-Bahá. All the men of the Board signed a "supplication" asking if the Board should be dissolved, and reelected with women as members. They pledged that they would dissolve the Board if 'Abdu'l-Bahá wished, but that their intentions had been pure at the founding of the institution, since it had been established in accordance with a Tablet revealed for the Chicago House of Spirituality some years before.[80]

'Abdu'l-Bahá, however, would not sanction the idea of dissolving the all-male Board. His reply, received March 4, 1911, explains:

> Now Spiritual Assemblies must be organized and that is for Teaching the Cause of God. In that city you have a spiritual Assembly of men and you can establish a spiritual Assembly for women. Both Assemblies must be engaged in diffusing the fragrances of

God and be occupied with the service of the Kingdom.
The above is the best solution for this problem.[81]

It is not known if the Kenosha community elected a special women's Board at this time. Neither do the records of
the community indicate when women first started serving as
members of the Board of Consultation. In Chicago, the change
came in 1912. 'Abdu'l-Bahá, while in New York, during his
journey through America, directed that the Chicago House of
Spirituality should be reorganized and a new institution,
called a "Spiritual Meeting," composed of both men and
women, be elected. This was accomplished on August 11,
1912.[82] Certainly by 1917, women were serving alongside men
on the Kenosha Board. In that year, a new "Committee of 9"
was elected, with Augusta Nelson as the assistant secretary.[83]

'Abdu'l-Bahá's Visit to Kenosha, September 15-16, 1912: In
May of 1912, 'Abdu'l-Bahá traveled to Chicago to attend the
Bahai Temple Unity convention. His visit to the United States
had received a large amount of newspaper publicity.
Kheiralla's followers in Kenosha, the Behaists, sought to use
this publicity to gain some attention for their own cause.

Mirza Shua Ullah (Mírzá S͟hu'á'u'lláh), the son of 'Abdu'l-
Bahá's half brother, Mírzá Muḥammad-'Alí, was also in the
United States at this time. Muḥammad-'Alí and his family
had rejected 'Abdu'l-Bahá's leadership of the Bahá'í community. Kheiralla and his followers, after their break with
'Abdu'l-Bahá, had associated themselves with Muḥammad-
'Alí and his faction. On May 4, 1912, Shua Ullah wrote to the
Kenosha Evening News from Pasadena, California. His letter
was published on the front page of that newspaper on May
11. It was an open letter to 'Abdu'l-Bahá which denounced
him for allegedly trying to substitute his own teachings for
those of Bahá'u'lláh. Shua Ullah claimed that only Muḥammad-

'Alí was truly following Bahá'u'lláh's teachings. However, Shua Ullah proposed a peace conference between himself and 'Abdu'l-Bahá to settle their differences. Kheiralla would also attend this conference.[84] 'Abdu'l-Bahá chose to ignore this letter.

On July 8, Kheiralla himself wrote to the *Kenosha Evening News* defending Shua Ullah's May letter and making new accusations. His letter made it clear that he supported Mírzá Muhammad-'Alí and his claims.[85] The Kenosha Bahá'ís were disturbed by these letters, but they made no public rebuttal. 'Abdu'l-Bahá, who had returned to New York, assured the believers in Kenosha in a Tablet written to them in July 1912, that such attacks would come to nothing:

> The bats fly away from the rays of the sun and hiding themselves in dark and narrow nitches they blame the sun saying "Why do not the rays of the sun reach our dark corners and cranies? And why does it not associate and affiliate with us?" What relation is there between the all glorious sun and the weak-eyed bats! What friendship exists between the nightingale of the rose garden of significances and the gloomy crows! The sun travels in its own sphere and is entirely above the fluttering blindness of the bats.[86]

On the evening of September 12, 'Abdu'l-Bahá returned to Chicago for a brief visit. The Bahá'ís of Kenosha invited him to come to their city, Mr. and Mrs. Henry L. Goodale sent the letter inviting him to stay at their house. Before leaving Chicago on September 15, 'Abdu'l-Bahá spoke to Dr. W. Frederick Nutt, who was associated with the Behaists, about Kheiralla. With great emotion, he said that he knew that Kheiralla wanted him to arrange a special meeting between the two of them. But, during his journey to America many people, great and small, had come on their own accord to see 'Abdu'l-Bahá, and he had received them all. If Kheiralla's intentions were pure, he would come with sincerity, like everyone else. Dr. Nutt accompanied 'Abdu'l-Bahá to Kenosha.[87] The visit there seems to have been primarily intended by 'Abdu'l-Bahá as a means of lifting the spirits of the Bahá'ís in Kenosha and raising the public prestige of that community in the face of opposition by the followers of Kheiralla.

The *Kenosha Evening News* highlighted 'Abdu'l-Bahá's approaching visit with a front-page article. The headlines read:

ABDUL BAHA COMING
Leader of Bahaists to Visit Kenosha Sunday and Deliver Address
Expect Great Gathering

The newspaper announced that 'Abdu'l-Bahá would speak at the Congregational Church:

While the visit of the spiritual leader of the Bahaist to this city is intended primarily to strengthen and encourage his followers in this city, the Kenosha public is cordially invited to attend the lecture and hear the exposition of the new religion and the stand it is expected to take in this country.[88]

'Abdu'l-Bahá arrived in Kenosha on Sunday afternoon, September 15, 1912. He was taken to the Bahá'í Hall, where he had a meeting with the Kenosha Bahá'ís. He spoke on Bahá'u'lláh's imprisonment and blessed the children. He was seated in the ceremonial chair which, at Bahá'í meetings, had always been left empty in his honor.

After speaking to a large audience at the Congregational Church, 'Abdu'l-Bahá remained overnight in Kenosha at the home of the Goodales. There he received many of the Kenosha believers in private conversations. On the afternoon of September 16, he returned to Chicago.[89] That day the *Kenosha Evening News* carried another front-page article describing the talk at the Congregational Church in enthusiastic terms.[90]

Decline, 1912-1920: The activities of the Kenosha Bahá'í community in the period between 1912 and 1920 are not well documented. Therefore it is difficult to discuss this history in any great detail. There are no minutes or treasurer's ledgers for the years 1911 to 1917. But it is clear that the community was slowly declining in size. There were few enrollments. Several families moved away, while some older Bahá'ís died— including the Goodales. The community maintained a local institution, called either a Board of Consultation or a "Committee of Bahá'ís." Walter Bohanan acted as its secretary until 1923.

Around 1916, a period of disunity began. It appears that this was caused by personality conflicts centered around Bernard Jacobsen, though the individual responsible is not named in the records. Louis Voelz, a member of the community later recalled that a certain Bahá'í man had "caused dissension by domineering the community and persecuting some."[91] A contemporary document, however, suggests that this division may also have been linked to disunity in the Chicago Bahá'í community.

Some Bahá'ís in Chicago had opened a reading room which offered lessons that mixed the Bahá'í teachings with those of Theosophy. Other Bahá'ís objected, claiming that this was a form of Covenant-breaking. In an investigation of the matter conducted in 1917, Walter Bohanan and Bernard Jacobsen claimed that a number of Bahá'ís in Kenosha had been influenced by Luella Kirchner (who had organized the reading room) and were sympathetic to Covenant-breakers.[92] These Bahá'ís, it was reported, likened themselves to "Lutherans," and referred to other Bahá'ís as "Catholics."[93] While these Bahá'ís are not known to have endorsed the positions of any Covenant-breakers, it does seem that they felt uncomfortable with the authoritarianism that was implied by the concept of the Covenant, at least as it was understood at the time.

These feelings may have had their roots in a reaction to the authoritarian style of leadership in the local community referred to by Voelz.

About half the Bahá'ís stopped attending meetings. In 1920, the Kenosha House of Spirituality, as the Board was then calling itself, made an attempt to persuade some of them to rejoin the community. They asked a committee to meet with the inactive Bahá'ís and encourage them to forget the past. But this attempt was not successful.[94]

The remnant of the community maintained the regular activities that had become customary in the Kenosha community, such as Feasts, Sunday school classes, Sunday meetings, and summer picnics. Prominent Bahá'í teachers continued to visit the city. The industrial school for girls continued, and the Bahá'í Hall was maintained.

The summer picnics were elaborate affairs. In August 1919, the picnic was held at the country home of the secretary, Walter Bohanan. At noon there was a meal, followed by an afternoon spiritual meeting. There were talks by Adolf P. Chapman, N. Peterson, and others. Zia and Zenat Bagdadi, of Chicago, chanted prayers and sang songs in Persian. The children recited from Bahá'í scriptures. Mr. Bagdadi spoke. And a public meeting was held in the evening.[95]

Changes in Bahá'í Administration, 1920-1929: After the passing of 'Abdu'l-Bahá in 1921, Shoghi Effendi, the new Guardian of the Bahá'í Faith, spent much of the next decade supervising the development of a uniform system of Bahá'í administration—in terms of organization, terminology, and procedure—in the United States and elsewhere. The local Bahá'í institutions in Kenosha gradually came to conform to this new system.

In 1920, Kenosha had a House of Spirituality made up of six men and three women.[96] When Jenabe Fazel (Mírzá

Asadu'lláh Mazandarání, known as Jináb-i Faḍil), a Persian Bahá'í teacher, visited Kenosha on June 19, 1920, he offered his advice on the duties of the House. This advice was the most current understanding of the matter. He listed thirteen duties of the House of Spirituality:

1. members must be firm in the Covenant;
2. members must be sincere;
3. members must be polite and humble;
4. members must have harmony and love;
5. members should not discuss politics;
6. the House should spend one half of its time instructing and teaching;
7. the children must be educated in spiritual matters;
8. the House must study the Teachings;
9. the House should look after the sick and poor;
10. there should be at least nine members on the House;
11. the House should meet at least once a week, depending on the work to be done;
12. the House should arrange one or two meetings a week where the Bahai Writings are read and talks given;
13. members should not repeat the secrets of the House outside its meetings.[97]

The House took its duty to look after the sick and poor seriously. In 1920, the Kenosha community sent a two-hundred-pound box of food and clothing to needy German Bahá'ís impoverished by World War I. The Bahá'í women also prepared Christmas baskets for the needy in Kenosha.[98] The House regularly sent flowers to those Bahá'ís who were ill and to the families of those who passed away. Also in 1920, August Rudd, a Kenosha Bahá'í moved back to Sweden to become the first Bahá'í to reside in that country.[99]

In January of 1923, Shoghi Effendi wrote a letter in English directly to the Kenosha community urging them to renew their efforts on behalf of the Faith. The style and

approach of his writing—direct, literate, and unembellished—
was markedly different from that of 'Abdu'l-Bahá:

> I am sure that every one of you, in view of the perilous state of
> the world, realizes more than ever before the urgent need for the
> full recognition by the peoples and governments of the world of
> the new Message of Salvation that the Cause of Bahá'u'lláh brings
> in this day to distracted humanity. . . . It is our task and privi-
> lege to capture gradually and persistently the attention of the
> world by the sincerity of our motives, by the breadth of our out-
> look and the devotion and tenacity with which we pursue our
> work of service to mankind. If only we discharge fully and consci-
> entiously our sacred duties, surely the Hand of Divine Power
> shall in time come to our aid and shall so shape the affairs and
> circumstances of the world as to enable us to win for the Cause
> of Bahá'u'lláh the admiration and the allegiance of all mankind.[100]

Responding to another letter from Shoghi Effendi,[101] the
Kenosha Bahá'ís held their election for their local institution
on April 21, 1923. The body was termed a Spiritual Assembly for the first time. At the election, a new means of voting
was used by which all would write nine names on a piece of
paper, and the nine who received the highest votes would
constitute the Spiritual Assembly for one year.[102] There were
also changes in the internal workings of the Assembly. For
the first time, a permanent chairman was elected. Previously,
a new chairman had been chosen for each meeting.[103] Philip
Savilles replaced Walter Bohanan as the Assembly's secretary.[104]

On October 20, 1923, a special meeting of the community
was held at the request of the National Spiritual Assembly.
At the meeting, after reading the Will and Testament of
'Abdu'l-Bahá and the Guardian's letter of March 12, 1923,
the adult Bahá'ís of Kenosha formally added their names to
the recently established national membership list. Eighteen
adults were enrolled,[105] only a small fraction of Kenosha's
earlier membership.

At the elections in 1924, the community elected ten, rather than nine, members to the Spiritual Assembly. In 1925, on a motion by Adrian DeBruin, the community unanimously returned the incumbent ten members of the Assembly to office, by acclamation.[106]

In 1920, the Kenosha House of Spirituality had appointed a teaching committee. Efforts to teach the Faith, using various techniques were carried on throughout the 1920s, but they did not result in any significant growth in the size of the community. The Kenosha Bahá'ís relied heavily on public lectures delivered by prominent outside speakers to spearhead their teaching efforts. The orientation of teaching efforts seems to have been to reach out to established organizations in the area and deliver the Bahá'í message to those groups in their own venues. The efforts were interracial. When Annie Parmerton visited in July 1920, there were blacks as well as whites among the inquirers in the crowd. Chris Jensen actively taught the Faith to the black population, attending services at black churches.[107] In 1921, Louis Gregory, a prominent black Bahá'í lecturer, visited Kenosha and spoke at the Racine African Methodist-Episcopal Church. Two black people in Racine became Bahá'ís as a result of this visit.

During 1922, there was a busy round of Bahá'í meetings in Kenosha. Four weekly meetings were being held: the Sunday children's meeting, the Sunday adult meeting, the Monday evening teaching meeting, and the Thursday evening study meeting. The women met together every other week on Thursday afternoon. There were, in addition to the weekly meetings, the Nineteen-Day Feasts, Holy Day observances, Assembly meetings, monthly Temple meetings, entertainments and socials, and fund-raising events.[108] The annual summer picnic was also an important event which drew many Bahá'ís from Chicago, Milwaukee, and Racine, as well as local non-Bahá'í friends.

In September of 1922, at the request of their national body, the Bahá'ís of Kenosha sent a letter to the Persian ambassador in Washington, D.C., signed by all of the believers, asking his assistance in stopping attacks on Bahá'ís in Iran. Kenosha also organized prayers on behalf of the Persian Bahá'ís, saying one prayer nineteen times at 6:00 a.m., for nineteen days.[109]

Also in 1922, Kenosha established a nineteen-day circular letter which it sent out to Bahá'í communities around the world. As a result, the community received replies and, for a number of years, carried on an international correspondence. In March 1923, the Spiritual Assembly reported that it had received letters from seventy-one other Bahá'í communities. In one Bahá'í month later that year, it received letters from eight communities in the United States and from Bahá'ís in Japan, Egypt, Burma, Iran, Palestine, Germany, and England.[110]

In May 1923, the Bahá'ís arranged for Faḍil-i Mazandaráni to speak at the College of Commerce, at a luncheon of more than one-hundred Jewish ladies, and at the Socialist Hall.[111] Between 1924 and 1927, the community organized three series of public lectures. The lectures were delivered every other week, by Bahá'í speakers from Chicago and other communities, for three periods of several months.[112]

However, the pace of other Bahá'í activities slowed down. By the end of 1925, it seems that the only regular meetings being carried on were the Sunday meetings, the Feasts, and the Spiritual Assembly meetings.[113] By 1925, circular letters were no longer being sent out every nineteen days; and by 1928, most of this correspondence had died out. However, between 1927 and 1929, the community did manage to send out seven circulars to other communities in an effort to raise funds for the construction of the Bahá'í Temple in Wilmette, Illinois.

Some effort must have gone into contacting believers who

JINÁB-I FADL MAZANDARÁNÍ
(seated center) with some of the Bahá'ís in Kenosha, Wisconsin.

had been active in the community in earlier years, but had not yet formally enrolled as Bahá'ís under the new administrative system. Between April 1925 and April 1926, four former members of the community were added to the membership list: Eva Russell, Carrie Gates, Rose Harmon, and Rose Russell.[114]

Fund raising for the Temple was an important activity in Kenosha during the 1920s, even though it was not a well-to-do community. In 1927, the Kenosha Assembly explained to the National Spiritual Assembly that they could not send large contributions for the Temple because most of the believers were not well off and were heavily in debt. The community had to give up their full-time hall during this year, since they could now only afford to rent it for Sunday meetings, still the most important feature of community life.[115] In 1929, in response to appeals to raise enough to begin work on the Temple's superstructure, the Kenosha Bahá'ís sold the community's piano for fifty dollars and gave it all to the Temple Fund.[116]

By 1928, the Assembly had three standing committees—the Sick Committee, the Program Committee, and the Feast Committee. The Program Committee had primary responsibility for bringing the Bahá'í teachings to the public. They were to "seek openings for public talks at various religious, social and club centers."[117] The Sick Committee continued to assist Bahá'ís who were ill or injured.

Also in 1928, a letter from the National Spiritual Assembly prompted some changes in the way Kenosha conducted its Feasts. The Spiritual Assembly decided to permit consultation by the believers after the devotional readings, giving the Feast three parts. The National Assembly suggested that contributions to the Bahá'í Fund be accepted at the Feasts, and the Assembly agreed to receive contributions to the national Plan of Unified Action immediately after the consultation.[118]

That same year, a youth group—Bahá'í Juniors—was formed. This was one of the few youth groups in the country. It was formed to accommodate the maturing Bahá'í children of Kenosha. No one could be formally enrolled as a Bahá'í until age twenty-one. But the Assembly agreed to have the youth arrange monthly social meetings for the entire community. The first entertainment was a bunco party, for Bahá'ís and their friends, with prizes and refreshments. Several more bunco parties and card parties were organized over the next year.[119]

Community Development, 1930-1939: During the 1930s, the decade of the Great Depression, the Kenosha Bahá'í community developed considerably. The city was hit hard by the failure of the economy and many Bahá'ís were unemployed.[120] Nonetheless, Bahá'ís came to rely a bit less on teachers from outside, and the community developed more distinct boundaries. The activities of the community continued to retain a Protestant flavor in their style, reflecting the background of most of the believers.

Two questions concerning Bahá'í membership came up during the 1930s which reflect a shift in the nature of the community which was taking place nationwide. In 1932, the Spiritual Assembly of Kenosha inquired of the National Spiritual Assembly whether it was permissible for Bahá'ís to belong to other churches. This suggests that some Bahá'ís were still members of churches at this time, and that others were beginning to feel uncomfortable with this practice. The National Assembly assured the Kenosha community, however, that Bahá'ís could belong to other churches and still maintain their Bahá'í membership.[121] It was not until 1935, that the Guardian of the Bahá'í Faith definitely ruled that Bahá'ís should separate themselves from church membership.[122]

On June 16, 1932, Kenosha wrote to ask the National Spiritual Assembly about involvement in politics. In a general letter to the Bahá'ís of the United States and Canada, the Guardian had recently stated that all Bahá'ís should withdraw from all involvement in political activities and association with political parties: "Let them refrain from associating themselves, whether by word or by deed, with the political pursuits of their respective nations, with the policies of governments and the schemes and programs of parties and factions. In such controversies they should assign no blame, take no side, further no design, and identify themselves with no system . . ."

One of the Bahá'ís in Kenosha, Eva Russell, was the county clerk and stood for office on the Republican ballot. The Kenosha Assembly wondered if this was no longer to be allowed. The National Assembly responded that the Guardian's instructions concerning politics "represented a spiritual ideal which all faithful believers will ponder in their hearts and not a formal ruling which the National Assembly can apply in cases such as the one brought to our attention in your letter." They indicated that the Kenosha Assembly should "not exert any undue pressure upon this particular believer."[123] However, the National Assembly later that same year came out with a stronger statement on non-involvement in politics, including holding political office, which was published in the December issue of *Bahá'í News*. The Kenosha Assembly stressed these new instructions in a letter sent to the entire community.[124]

The lecture series had always been Kenosha's primary means of bringing the Bahá'í teachings to the attention of the public. In 1931, this method was used again. The community organized 48 lectures and 25 afternoon forums. These large public meetings were supplemented by smaller study classes held on Monday and Friday nights. Kenosha had Bahá'ís within the community who were able to lead the small group meetings, but they relied on outside Bahá'ís to

STOREFRONT
set up for the Bahá'í lecture series in Kenosha, Wisconsin,
in 1931.

give talks before public audiences.[125] In 1931, Ruth Moffett was the principal speaker. During her stay in Kenosha she delivered 32 of the lectures and spoke at most of the forums, in addition to a number to talks given in local churches and clubs.

The response to Moffett was tremendous. An average of 65 people attended the lectures, and an average of 18 participated in the forums. This resulted in six new Bahá'ís and the enrollment of nine old Bahá'ís who had not been active in the community since 1918.[126] The going-away party held for Moffett on November 23, 1931, attracted 50 guests.[127] Of course, these were modest gains compared to the initial growth of the Bahá'í community at the turn of the century (1898-1900), but they represented the largest enrollment of new believers since that early period.

Throughout the 1930s, Kenosha continued its tradition of weekly Sunday meetings, supplemented by special lecture series whenever prominent Bahá'í speakers became available. By 1932, some Kenosha Bahá'ís began delivering the lectures themselves. Up until then, the Kenosha community had relied entirely on outside speakers to give public talks. Earl Parker and Louis Voelz were the first to take part in the Sunday lectures as speakers. However, most public speakers continued to come from outside, including Albert Windust (1933), Fanny Knobloch (1934), Madame Orlova (twice in 1935), and Lenore Morris (1936).

During this decade, the organization of the local Assembly became more complex and the Bahá'ís became more concerned with issues of organization and administrative procedure. For example, the Assembly voted in 1930 to arrange the Feast so that the readings would always come first and the refreshments last, eliminating the previous, less-structured practice. In 1931, the question was raised with the National Assembly whether the Feast of 'Alá' (Loftiness) should be held on February 26 or March 2. The National Assembly decided to refer the matter to the Guardian, as "this is a subject that ought to be uniformally [sic] known by all the friends."[128] In 1933, the Assembly added to the Feast a short period for an Assembly report and consultation with the community.[129] In 1935, acting on instructions of the National Spiritual Assembly, the local Assembly informed the believers that only the writings of the Báb, Bahá'u'lláh, and 'Abdu'l-Bahá could be used during the devotional portion of the Feast. The average attendance at Feasts was high, with 29 out of 48 adult, voting members attending during 1936.[130]

By the mid-1930s, the Kenosha Bahá'í community appears to have been about evenly divided between working-class and middle-class members. This was a major shift from its original composition.[131] This was partially due to the fact that some of the original working-class Bahá'ís and their children had achieved some upward mobility, finding better jobs. But it was at least equally due to an influx of middle-class individuals into the Bahá'í community.[132] Another factor may have been the decline of Kenosha as an industrial center, which would have forced working-class believers to move elsewhere to find employment.

It appears that the working-class culture of the old Kenosha community was, during this period, coming into conflict with more middle-class values, which included greater concern with public image. Open displays of religious emotion were frowned on, non-conformist ritual practices were eliminated, and a more reserved and genteel manner was encouraged, at least at public meetings. In 1934, the Kenosha Assembly voted to "inform the believers not to use vebaly [sic], the Greatest Name, in our public meetings, as applause, when visitors are present." Later, they asked the community not to turn around to see who was coming in during public meetings or to use the Greatest Name aloud unnecessarily

when the public is present.[133] The community was also asked
not to hold the Bahá'í speakers in conversation when there
were visitors waiting to meet them and ask questions.[134]

In 1934, the Assembly appointed five committees: Visiting, Publicity, Arrangements, Social, and Teaching. It is significant that two of these committees were still primarily
concerned with the pastoral functions of visiting the sick and
arranging social occasions for the community. The Visiting
Committee now also had the task of calling on believers who
were lax in attending meetings.[135] In 1935, two more committees were added, the Program Committee and the Feast Committee. However, much of the work of the community was
accomplished through individual initiative, usually through
the contributions of goods and personal services. The children's
Sunday School, which had lapsed, was reestablished, with
Eva Russell and Grace Anderson as teachers. On April 15,
1937, Kenosha became the first local Spiritual Assembly in
Wisconsin to legally incorporate.[136]

In 1937, it appears that some members of the community
wanted to eliminate the practice of anointing each believer
with attar of rose at the Nineteen-Day Feast. This had been
regular practice since the Feast had been instituted in
Kenosha in 1906. The local Assembly asked the National
Assembly about the custom and also inquired about the practice of having each believer read a passage from Bahá'u'lláh's
Hidden Words at the Feast. The National Assembly replied
that they knew of nothing in the Bahá'í teachings which
required either of these practices.[137]

In 1938, the Kenosha Assembly asked the National Spiritual Assembly whether those Bahá'ís in the city who never
attended any meetings could be dropped from the voting list,
but kept on the membership list. Here again, the Assembly
was seeking firmer boundaries. The National Asssembly replied that this question had been discussed for many years,

but that a Bahá'í must himself declare that he was no longer a Bahá'í for his status to change. The local Assembly might periodically ascertain the attitude of a believer, but "the obligation to attend the Nineteen Day Feast is a spiritual one and not an administrative duty which we can enforce."[138]

The singing of hymns had always been a regular part of Bahá'í meetings. As late as 1938, the local Assembly had encouraged enthusiastic singing at the Sunday meetings and had arranged for singing practice at the Feasts.[139] However, in 1939, the Assembly received a report from William Schend that he had learned at the National Convention that the Guardian did not approve of regular singing at meetings. After that, music was used only occasionally.[140]

In the Mainstream, 1940-1949: In the 1940s, the Kenosha Bahá'í community changed in terms of its occupational makeup. There were now more professionals and small businessmen. To a large extent, this was because the women and the youth were able to find better jobs than their parents' generation could. Also, some of the men had improved their positions over the years. Still, the community was fairly poor, and several new believers came from the working class. Tensions continued between the middle-class values and the working-class cultural assumptions found in the community.

In 1940, the National Spiritual Assembly informed the Kenosha Bahá'ís of the Guardian's ruling that local Assemblies should limit their jurisdictions to the civil city limits of their localities. This meant that Bahá'ís living outside the city limits would have to form separate Bahá'í communities. Five long-time Kenosha Bahá'ís found themselves suddenly in a new community.[141]

Despite this loss of membership, the Kenosha Assembly continued to elaborate its own administrative structure. That same year it appointed eleven committees: Teaching, Publicity, Art and Decorating, Welfare, Feasts, Anniversaries, Social, Garden of Light (children's classes), Hall Custodian, Music, and Transportation. The practice was for the Assembly to appoint a chairman for each committee, and for the chairman to then submit suggestions for members of that committee. The Assembly would then appoint the committee members from the chairman's list. Some committees were large, like the Teaching Committee, with twenty members. Others were small: the Art and Decorating Committee, the Publicity Committee, and the Welfare Committee each had only two members besides the chairman.[142]

The community's devotional life remained somewhat unconventional by wider American standards, but still Protestant in inspiration. In 1940, the Spiritual Assembly set up a new prayer campaign. Four groups of believers were organized that would each offer a prayer for nineteen days. Every nineteen days the prayer would be changed. The community prayed for teaching, healing, material needs, and for universal peace. The Welfare Committee was instructed to inform the community that they would be prayed for at the prayer meetings.[143]

The lecture series continued to be the Bahá'ís' principal means of approach to the public. Regular Sunday meetings were a fixture of Bahá'í community life. The believers made persistent efforts to reach the black population. Louis Gregory visited the city again in 1941. There were occasional lectures and programs on the question of racial harmony. In support of its lecture programs, the Kenosha Assembly would place ads or articles in local newspapers, and Bahá'í radio programs on the local station, WLIP.[144]

Music still played a role in community life, though the Bahá'ís seemed to be less comfortable with it. In 1944, Kenosha wrote to the National Assembly to ask that a recording of the Bahá'í hymn "Benediction" be produced, using a good singer, and be made available to local communities. Some Bahá'ís enjoyed singing the "Benediction" at the close of Sunday meetings, but others were afraid that a lack of good singers among the Bahá'ís might give a poor impression to visitors. Here again was the tension between the working-class need for congregational singing, on one hand, and the middle-class desire for good performance, on the other. The National Assembly replied that it was not in a position to produce such a record, as it had no music policy or procedure.[145]

The Kenosha community maintained a local Bahá'í Center at 5912 22nd Avenue. A great deal of time and labor was invested in maintaining the building. Two of the eleven committees appointed in 1940 were exclusively concerned with the Center. Beyond this, volunteers helped with such tasks as cleaning, painting, making new curtains, and eliminating the squeaks in the chairs. Christmas displays were arranged in the window of the Center in December.

In 1940, the Bahá'í children's classes, the Garden of Light, included 23 children. The Bahá'í youth remained active. That year they held an International Youth Meeting, inviting non-Bahá'í speakers of different nationalities, and one Bahá'í speaker.[146] However, by 1945, the attendance at the children's classes was down to 5 (the Voelz children, Marilyn and Ronald; the Johnson children, Jacqueline and Thomas; and Georgia Ann Halberstadt). Nonetheless, the children presented the Naw-Rúz (Bahá'í New Year) program.[147] That same year, the youth organized two programs, a youth symposium and a banquet.[148]

On December 17, 1947, the Kenosha community celebrated its fiftieth anniversary at the local Bahá'í Center. Louis Voelz spoke on the history of the Kenosha Bahá'ís, Jessie Halberstadt talked about the present. Horace Holley, secretary of the National Spiritual Assembly, spoke about the future. Floral tributes were given to those Bahá'ís who had been members of the original community. Among the refreshments was a huge golden cake, decorated to honor the occasion. The National Spiritual Assembly sent a cable of congratulations and also informed the Guardian of the celebration. On December 29, Kenosha received the following cable from the Bahá'í World Center:

> OCCASION FIFTIETH ANNIVERSARY ESTABLISHMENT FAITH KENOSHA MOVED EXPRESS DEARLY BELOVED STEADFAST DEVOTED MEMBERS COMMUNITY HEART-FELT CONGRATULATIONS WARM ADMIRATION SPIRIT ANIMATING THEIR SERVICE FAITH ARDENT HOPE EXTENSION RANGE MERITORIOUS LABOURS. SHOGHI.[149]

Continuation, 1950 to the present: The Kenosha Bahá'í community, after its early years, reached a peak in membership in 1938 (with fifty believers). After that, there was a steady decline in membership to the 18-25 range, where membership has remained to the present day. (See Table 4.) Between 1946 and 1960, there was a net loss of 20 Bahá'ís, more than half the community's membership. By the 1980s, Kenosha had the resources and the level of activity of a small Bahá'í community, even though its numbers on paper remained considerable, by Bahá'í standards.

Throughout this period the community was aging. Members were lost due to death, pioneering, and moves to other cities. The first generation of Bahá'ís passed away during these years, and the next generation moved away. Several believers left as pioneers for the Faith in Canada and Europe. The city of Kenosha was itself in economic decline, and the Bahá'í community did not recruit new and active members to offset its losses. Only one new believer was enrolled in the six years between 1964 and 1970, for example. The Bahá'í community has maintained itself since 1950, but it seems to have gone through cycles—with periods of teaching and activity alternating with periods of inaction.

From the 1950s to the 1970s, the local Spiritual Assembly maintained a full committee structure. The usual committees were Teaching and Holy Days, Welfare, Social, Feast, Library, Garden of Light, and House.[150] The Assembly maintained a modest local fund, and generally met its budget goal—which in 1969 was $35 per month. Contributions were sent to the National Fund when money was available.[151] The tradition of summer picnics was maintained. The community kept its local Bahá'í Center until October 1979, when it had to be given up.[152]

By 1956, decline in Kenosha was already obvious and the National Spiritual Assembly wrote to the community to express its concern. The local Assembly's annual report indicated that very little was happening. The National Assembly's chief concern was that there were no firesides[153] being held in the city. The community had always relied on the public lecture to introduce new people to their religion. The National Assembly suggested that fireside meetings be organized and that the Bahá'ís in Kenosha study two booklets on teaching which had recently been published.[154] However, there was little response to this appeal since Kenosha still had no firesides or deepening classes the next year.

In 1960, the Area Teaching Committee for the Central United States described the Kenosha community as a place where "the people are old and need fresh planning and assistance in setting up an active and progressive program." A traveling teacher, Thelma Jackson, was sent to the city in 1961, to deepen the community and provide teaching advice. By March, the community had started firesides and a Thursday-evening study class, which resulted in the enrollment of two new believers.

But the situation in Kenosha changed very little. In 1970, the local Assembly summed up its feelings thus:

We need one or two "alive" Bahá'í couples to move into Kenosha. We are now down to 15, but 5 members never come. One member is in his 80's and two have a heart condition. We need more young workers.[155]

During the 1980s, the community recovered a bit, but the numbers of Bahá'ís remained small, and the activities of the community were limited. Kenosha had become a typical small Bahá'í community.

Summary and Conclusion: There are some conclusions about the expansion of the Bahá'í Faith and the consolidation of its communities which can be drawn from Kenosha's Bahá'í history. The first is the important role played by proven, experienced, and talented Bahá'í teachers. From Paul K. Dealy to Bernard Jacobsen, from Ruth Moffett to Lenore Morris, the Bahá'í lecturer played a central role in sparking each new phase of expansion in Kenosha. They were also major figures in the efforts to deepen the community's knowledge of the Bahá'í teachings and maintain its unity.

The second conclusion is that one of Kenosha's major strengths as an early community was the large number of families which converted as units. Families added a richness and stability to community life that Bahá'ís in most other areas lacked. The large number of children, and later youth, strengthened the community and eventually contributed greatly to its growth in numbers. Families also insured a variety of Bahá'í activities could be organized—for children, women, youth, and so forth. There are at least ten early Kenosha families, scattered around the country and around the world, whose descendants are still Bahá'ís: the families of Louis Voelz, George Anderson, Christ Howard, Peter Nelson, Henry Benning, Alfred Anderson, John Wilcott, August Anderson, Adrian DeBruin, and Charles Carson.

Third, the Bahá'í community in Kenosha was strengthened by opposition—first from the Protestant churches, and later from the followers of Kheiralla. Although both of these episodes resulted in the loss of membership, they also defined the boundaries of the community, strengthened the Bahá'í identities of the remaining believers, and accelerated their acceptance of the Bahá'í teachings as a total and exclusive religious system. One reason that the first generation of Bahá'ís in Kenosha developed such a close and cohesive community, in sharp contrast to most other Bahá'í communities around the country (which usually functioned as voluntary societies or clubs, rather than as close religious communities), was that they had vocal opponents.

Fourth, we might note the relatively small role played by the individual teaching of rank-and-file Bahá'ís. It appears that the enrollments during the two decades of greatest growth, the 1890s and the 1930s, was caused by important teachers. The efforts of the ordinary believer were more limited and less effective. If there had been more effective teaching by each individual believer, the growth of the Kenosha community may have been more consistent.

Fifth, the Kenosha Bahá'í community was unable to move beyond the borders of its ethnic composition to reach new immigrants from Southern and Eastern Europe, especially during the early 1900s. Even the enrollments during the 1930s were of people from Northern European or American backgrounds.[156] This inability of the Bahá'ís to keep pace with the changing ethnic makeup of the city was probably a major factor in its limited growth. Kenosha did not focus its teaching activities on any specific ethnic group, except for blacks. Their proclamation and teaching activities were just aimed at the general public.

For a time, Kenosha was the second or third largest Bahá'í community in the Western world. The crisis caused by Kheiralla's defection caused a sharp decline in numbers, but the community remained sizeable by Bahá'í standards, and it maintained an active life. Reaching a low point in the

1920s, there was a brief moment of growth in the 1930s. But, this momentum could not be sustained, and Kenosha again became a small Bahá'í community. Having contributed richly to Bahá'í history, the Bahá'ís of Kenosha have now taken their place alongside of hundreds of other Bahá'í communities in the United States, among which Kenosha is now virtually indistinguishable.

NOTES

1. John D. Buenker, "Immigration and Ethnic Groups" in *Kenosha County in the Twentieth Century: A Topical History*, John A. Neuenschwander, ed. (Kenosha, WI: Kenosha County Bicentennial Commission, 1976) pp. 2-5, and Richard H. Keehn, "Industry and Business" in ibid. pp. 175-81.

2. For detailed accounts of the introduction of the Bahá'í Faith in the United States, see Richard Hollinger, "Ibrahim George Kheiralla and the Bahá'í Faith in America" in *Studies in Bábí and Bahá'í History*, Vol. 2: *From Iran East and West*, Juan R. Cole and Moojan Momen, eds. (Los Angeles: Kalimát Press, 1984); Peter Smith, "The American Bahá'í Community, 1894-1917: A Preliminary Survey" in *Studies in Bábí and Bahá'í History*, Vol. 1, Moojan Momen, ed. (Los Angeles: Kalimát Press, 1982); and Robert H. Stockman, *The Bahá'í Faith in America: Origins, 1892-1900* (Wilmette, Ill., Bahá'í Publishing Trust, 1985). The summary of Kheiralla's teachings and early activities which follows is taken from these sources.

3. Shoghi Effendi indicates that Kheiralla secured "an opening" for teaching the Faith in Kenosha in 1895 (Shoghi Effendi, *God Passes By* [Wilmette, Ill.: Bahá'í Publishing Committee, 1944]).

4. From a Truth-knower Lessons manuscript, lesson on "The Soul," p. 1. Kenosha, WI, Bahá'í Community Records, National Bahá'í Archives, Wilmette, Illinois. (Hereafter, Kenosha Community Records.)

5. *Alláh-u Abhá,* God the Most Glorious. An invocation used by Bahá'ís.

6. Ibrahim Kheiralla, *Bab-ed-Din: The Door of True Religion* (Chicago: Charles H. Kerr and Co., 1897) p. 9.

7. *Wright's Kenosha City Directory, 1899-1900*, pp. 11-19.

8. Hollinger, "Ibrahim George Kheiralla," pp. 109-110; Stockman, *The Bahá'í Faith in America*, pp. 110; Ibrahim George Kheiralla, *O Christians! Why do Ye Believe Not on Christ?* (Chicago: Goodspeed Press, 1917) p.168.

9. Paul K. Dealy to Ibrahim Kheiralla, April 18, 1898. Paul K. Dealy Papers. National Bahá'í Archives, Wilmette, Illinois.

10. Ibid.

11. Frank H. Lyman, *The City of Kenosha and Kenosha County, Wisconsin* (Chicago: The S. J. Clarke Publishing Co., 1916) vol. 2, pp. 13-14.

12. Based on the 114 (of 219 total) Bahá'ís for whom countries of birth could be identified.

13. Later, 16 of 27 (of 60 total) adults on the 1906 membership list for whom countries of orgin could be identified were foreign born. United States Census, 1900: Kenosha County, Wisc.; Bahá'í Historical Record Cards, National Bahá'í Archives.

14. *Portrait and Biographical Album of Racine and Kenosha Counties, Wisconsin* (Chicago: Lake City Publishing Co., 1892) pp. 393-94 and *Commemorative Biographical Record of Prominent and Representative Men of Racine and Kenosha Counties, Wisconsin* (Chicago: J. H. Beers & Co., 1906) pp. 323-25.

15. Stockman, *Bahá'í Faith in America*, p. 114.

16. Minutes, May 26, 1899. Kenosha Community Records.

17. Treasurer's Cash Book, 1898-1911. Kenosha Community Records.

18. Paul K. Dealy to Ibrahim Kheiralla, April 18, 1898. Paul K. Dealy Papers. National Bahá'í Archives. A draft letter from Ibraham Kheiralla to 'Abdu'l-Bahá (dated c. 1898) also mentions opposition from the clergy in Kenosha. Ibrahim Kheiralla papers. In private hands.

19. *Kenosha Kicker*, October 19, 1899.

20. Ibid., October 26, 1899.

21. Even decades later this was still a significant issue within churches in Kenosha. Meg Naysmith, a Bahá'í from Wisconsin, first heard of the Bahá'í Faith from an anti-Bahá'í sermon delivered by a minister in a Congregational Church in Kenosha. (Interview with M. Naysmith, conducted by Richard Hollinger, September 1987.)

22. For a fuller account of the Vatralsky episode, see William P.

Collins, "Kenosha, 1893-1912: History of an Early American Bahá'í Community in the United States" in Momen, ed., *Studies*, Vol. 1.

23. Minutes, May 26, 1899 to May 11, 1900. Kenosha Community Records. It is not clear from the records which of Browne's books were used in Kenosha. Kheiralla had access to four such books. See Stockman, *Bahá'í Faith in America*, pp. 43-46.

24. Minutes, November 8, 1899; November 15, 1899 to November 28, 1900; List of enrollments, 1899-1900 in the minute book. Racine, WI, Bahá'í Community Records. (Hereafter, Racine Community Records.) National Bahá'í Archives.

25. For detailed accounts of how these events affected Kenosha, see: Collins, "Kenosha, 1893-1912," pp. 239-42; Hollinger, "Ibrahim George Kheiralla," pp. 112-19; and Stockman, *The Bahá'í Faith in America*, pp. 136-93.

26. Voelz, "History of the Kenosha Bahá'í Community from 1897 to November 1933," p. 2. Kenosha Community Records. National Bahá'í Archives.

27. Minutes, March 14, 1900. Racine Community Records. Minutes, March 2, 1900 and March 9, 1900. Kenosha Community Records. Collins, "Kenosha, 1893-1912," p. 239.

28. See Richard Hollinger, "The Origins, Development, and Decline of the Behaist Sect, 1894-1955." Unpublished paper.

29. Minutes, April 6, 1900. Kenosha Community Records. Minutes, May 9, 1900 and September 17, 1900. Racine Community Records.

30. *Kenosha Evening News*, p. 1, "They Repudiate Him." Minutes, May 25, 1900. Kenosha Community Records. National Bahá'í Archives.

31. *Kenosha Courier*, November 15, 1900, "Local Notes." I am grateful to Richard Hollinger for this citation.

32. For a fuller discussion of this point, and an account of the numbers of those loyal to 'Abdu'l-Bahá and to Kheiralla, see Hollinger, "Behaist Sect."

33. Minutes, July 15, 1904. Kenosha Community Records.

34. The Tablet was translated by Ali Kuli Khan, c. December 30, 1901. The Board members addressed in the Tablet were Robert Walters, Magnus Norlander, Henry Benning, Edward Thomsen, John Anderson, Louie Schleimer, Edward Lindstrom, Arthur Lindstrom, and Charles Redeen. (*Tablets of Abdul Baha*, pp. 141-42. The Board members and translator are listed on the translation in the Commit-

tee for Editing the Tablets of 'Abdu'l-Bahá Records, National Bahá'í Archives.)

35. Racine's Board originally had seven members, but when it was reelected in November 1900, two additional members were added. Soon after that, the Racine Board (at least) adopted the rules and regulations which had been given to the Chicago Board by 'Abdu'l-Karím Tihrání. (Minutes, July 12, 1900; November 28, 1900; December 3, 1900. Racine Community Records. National Bahá'í Archives.)

36. Behais Supply and Publishing Board to Racine Assembly, September 12, 1900. Racine Community Records. National Bahá'í Archives.

37. The women named in the first Tablet were Ida Walters, Caroline Borkenhagen, Minnie Saint Germain, Elvira Benning, Mrs. L. Schleimer, Emma Lindstrom, Emma Voelz, Chersti Redeen, Wilhelmina Norlander, and Jane Parks. This may suggest that there was a women's Board of Counsel parallel to the men's Board, as in Chicago. (*Tablets of Abdul Baha*, pp. 143-45. Translations by Ali Kuli Khan, about December 30, 1901. Committee for Editing the Tablets of 'Abdu'l-Bahá Records. National Bahá'í Archives.)

38. *Tablets of Abdul Baha*, pp. 145-46.

39. Minutes, June 25, 1901. Chicago House of Spirituality Records. National Bahá'í Archives.

40. Kenosha Council Board to Chicago House of Spirituality, October 13, 1901; Minutes, October 15, 1901. Chicago House of Spirituality Records. National Bahá'í Archives.

41. Minutes, March 28, 1903. Chicago House of Spirituality Records. National Bahá'í Archives.

42. Between 1901 and 1910, the number of contributors varied between 12 and 26 per year, with an average of 16. (1903 is not included in the figures for contributors as the Treasurer's records are incomplete for that year.) Treasurer's Cash Book, 1898-1911. Kenosha Community Records. National Bahá'í Archives.

43. Ibid.

44. Now known as the Day of the Covenant, this has become a Bahá'í Holy Day which is universally observed. Chicago first celebrated the day in 1901. In 1902, they wrote to twelve other communities suggesting that they institute celebrations on November 26. (Minutes, November 15, 1902. Chicago House of Spirituality Records. National Bahá'í Archives.)

45. Minutes, February 14, 1903; Kenosha to Chicago House of Spirituality, February 26, 1903; Minutes, February 28, 1903. Chicago House of Spirituality Records. National Bahá'í Archives.

Bahá'í law requires that all believers between the ages of 15 and 70 abstain from food and drink during daylight hours. Exceptions include those who are ill, traveling, pregnant, and nursing.

46. Minutes, April 4, 1903. Chicago House of Spirituality Records. National Bahá'í Archives.

47. Circular letter from Kenosha Assembly to the Different Assemblies of America, February 21, 1906; Minutes, March 3, 1906. Chicago House of Spirituality Records. National Bahá'í Archives.

48. Minutes, May 25, 1904; June 8, 1904; June 17, 1904; July 22, 1904; August 2, 1904. Kenosha Community Records. National Bahá'í Archives. Minutes, January 21, 1903. Racine Community Records. National Bahá'í Archives.

49. See "Kenosha, Wisconsin," *Baha'i Bulletin*, vol. 1, no. 1 (September 1908).

50. The Ninteen-Day Feast is a Bahá'í community meeting which is usually held on the first day of each (nineteen-day) Bahá'í month. It appears to have started here as primarily a devotional and social event. At the instructions of Shoghi Effendi, the Feast eventually developed (in the United States, at least) as the primary community gathering, divided into three parts: devotional, administrative, and social. Despite its name, the Feast was never regarded as an occasion for regular feasting, though refreshments are always served.

51. Nineteen Day Feast Minutes, March 21, 1906. Kenosha Community Records. National Bahá'í Archives.

52. Nineteen Day Feast Minutes, May 17, 1908 through December 31, 1909. Kenosha Community Records. National Bahá'í Archives.

53. Minutes, February 2, 1909 to September 14, 1909. Kenosha Community Records. National Bahá'í Archives.

54. Louis Voelz to Andrew Nelson, August 29, 1905. Racine Community Records. National Bahá'í Archives.

55. Minutes, May 29, 1907. Kenosha Community Records. National Bahá'í Archives.

56. Minutes, July 3, 1907; September 11, 1907; January 8, 1908; June 23, 1908; June 30, 1908; August 4, 1908; August 11, 1908; November 10, 1908. Kenosha Community Records. National Bahá'í Archives.

57. Minutes September 18, 1907; September 25, 1907; October 9, 1907. Kenosha Community Records. National Bahá'í Archives.

58. They were Bernard Jacobsen, Walter Bohanan, John Wilcott, Tillie Schend, and Emma Goodale. (Minutes, November 3, 1908; November 17, 1908. Kenosha Community Records. National Bahá'í Archives.)

59. Bernard M. Jacobsen to Chicago House of Spirituality, August 28, 1908. Chicago House of Spirituality Records. National Bahá'í Archives.

60. Bruce Whitmore, *The Dawning Place* (Wilmette, Ill.: Bahá'í Publishing Trust, 1984) pp. 49-52.

61. Minutes, June 12, 1907; March 3, 1908; September 15, 1908; October 13, 1908, and Treasurer's Cash Book, 1898-1911. Kenosha Community Records. National Bahá'í Center.

62. Minutes, September 11, 1907; September 25, 1907; October 23, 1907. Kenosha Community Records. National Bahá'í Archives.

63. *Kitáb-i aqdas*, (Bahá'u'lláh's) Most Holy Book. This book contains the basic laws of the religion.

64. Circular letter from the Kenosha Board of Consultation, July 25, 1908. Minutes, August 4, 1908. Chicago House of Spirituality Records. National Bahá'í Archives.

65. Minutes, July 21, 1908. Kenosha Community Records. National Bahá'í Archives.

66. *Bahá'í News*, vol. 1 (March 21, 1910) no. 1, p. 16.

67. Minutes, November 30, 1909. Kenosha Community Records. Nineteen Day Feast Minutes, March 21, 1909. Kenosha Community Records. National Bahá'í Archives.

68. *Kenosha Evening News*, June 26, 1909; July 3, 1909; July 10, 1909, August 14, 1909.

69. *Náqidín*, Covenant-breakers. Here the term refers to the followers of Kheiralla.

70. [Kenosha Bahá'ís] to 'Abdu'l-Bahá (draft), January 23, 1904. Kenosha Community Records. National Bahá'í Archives.

71. See Hasan M. Balyuzi, *'Abdu'l-Bahá: The Centre of the Covenant of Bahá'u'lláh* (London: George Ronald, 1971) p. 527; Collins, "Kenosha: 1893-1912," pp. 239-43; Hollinger, "Behaist Sect."

72. Minutes of the House of Justice (Chicago), June 28, 1901 and January 26, 1902. Chicago House of Spirituality Records. National Bahá'í Archives.

73. 'Abdu'l-Bahá to Corinne True, July 24, 1909. Microfilm. National Bahá'í Archives.

74. Minutes, August 31, 1909 and September 7, 1909. Chicago

House of Spirituality Records. National Bahá'í Archives. Chase to Remey, January 19, 1910. Chase to Scheffler, May 10, 1910. Thornton Chase Papers. National Bahá'í Archives.

75. Bahai Assembly of Kenosha to House of Spirituality, July 4, 1910. Chicago House of Spirituality Records. National Bahá'í Archives.

76. *Baytu'l-'adl-i 'umúmí.* Tablet dated July 24, 1909. See note 73.

77. House of Spirituality to Board of Consultation, Kenosha, Wisc., July 23, 1910. Chicago House of Spirituality Records. National Bahá'í Archives.

78. Ibid.

79. Ibid.

80. Kenosha Assembly to House of Spirituality (Albert Windust), May 16, 1911. Chicago House of Spirituality Records. National Bahá'í Archives.

81. 'Abdu'l-Bahá to the members of the Spiritual Assembly and Mr. Bernard M. Jacobsen, Kenosha, Wisc., May 4, 1911. Chicago House of Spirituality Records. National Bahá'í Archives.

82. *Star of the West*, vol. 3, no. 4 (August 20, 1912) p. 16. See also, 'Abdu'l-Bahá's instructions to Howard MacNutt (who accomplished the reorganization), August 6, 1912. Microfilm collection. National Bahá'í Archives.

83. Bernard Jacobsen to Harlan Ober (postcard), February 28, 1917. Alfred Lunt Papers. National Bahá'í Archives. Minutes, October 24, 1917. Kenosha Community Records.

84. *Kenosha Evening News*, May 11, 1912, p. 1.

85. *Kenosha Evening News*, July 8, 1912, p. 4.

86. Tablet translated by Ahmad Sohrab, July 1912, at New York City. Microfilm of Translations of Tablets of 'Abdu'l-Bahá, National Bahá'í Archives.

87. Mahmúd Zarqání, *Kitáb-i Badáyi'u'l-Áthár*, vol. 2 (Bombay: Elegant Photo-Litho Press, 1921) pp. 103-104. See also Balyuzi, *'Abdu'l-Bahá*, pp. 271-72.

For a more complete account of 'Abdu'l-Bahá's visit to Kenosha, see Collins, "Kenosha, 1893-1912," pp. 243-48.

88. *Kenosha Evening News*, September 14, 1912, p. 1.

89. Louis Voelz, "History of the Kenosha (Wisconsin) Baha'i Community, 1897-1947," p. 3. National Bahá'í Archives. See also, note 85.

90. *Kenosha Evening News*, September 16, 1912, p. 1.

91. Voelz, "History, 1897-1933," p. 4 and Voelz, "History, 1897-1947," p. 4. National Bahá'í Archives.

92. Bahá'ís expelled from the community by 'Abdu'l-Bahá for various reasons.

93. Notes of the Committee of Investigation (TS), p. 6. Ella Cooper Papers. San Francisco Bahá'í Archives. San Francisco, California.

94. Minutes, June 23, 1920. Kenosha Community Records. National Bahá'í Archives.

95. *Star of the West*, vol. 10, no. 13 (November 4, 1919) p. 251.

96. Walter Bohanan to Alfred Lunt, December 5, 1920. Alfred Lunt Papers. National Bahá'í Archives.

97. Minutes, June 19, 1920. Kenosha Community Records. National Bahá'í Archives. See Smith, "The American Bahá'í Community," p. 134, for Mazandaráni's full name.

98. Minutes, October 20, 1920; November 10, 1920; November 17, 1920; December 15, 1920. Kenosha Community Records. National Bahá'í Archives.

99. He settled in Boviken, where he taught the Faith to Miss Anna Gustavssen, the first person to become a Bahá'í in Sweden. *Star of the West*, vol. 11 (1920) no. 16, pp. 270 and 276; *The Bahá'í World*, vol. 18, pp. 980-82 (Haifa: Bahá'í World Center, 1986; *The Magazine of the Children of the Kingdom*, vol. 1 (1920) no. 4, p. 22.

100. Shoghi Effendi to the Kenosha Bahá'ís, January 4, 1923. Microfilm of Original Letters and Cables from Shoghi Effendi Collection. National Bahá'í Archives.

101. Dated March 12, 1923.

102. Minutes, April 21, 1923. Kenosha Assembly Records. National Bahá'í Archives.

103. Minutes, May 7, 1928. Kenosha Assembly Records. National Bahá'í Archives.

104. Minutes, April 25, 1923. Kenosha Assembly Records. National Bahá'í Archives.

105. Minutes, October 20, 1923. Kenosha Assembly Records. National Bahá'í Archives.

106. Minutes, April 21, 1924 and April 21, 1925. Kenosha Assembly Records. National Bahá'í Archives.

107. Teaching Committee of Nineteen Bulletin, August 19, 1920. National Bahá'í Reference Library. Wilmette, Illinois. Johnathan W. Zohpy, "Invisible People: Blacks and Mexican-Americans" in *Kenosha County in the Twentieth Century*, pp. 54-55.

108. Kenosha Assembly circular letter, March 21, 1922. Kenosha Community Records. National Bahá'í Archives.

109. In 1925, and again in 1927, the Kenosha Assembly placed articles in the local newspaper concerning the persecution of Bahá'ís in Persia. (Minutes, September 24, 1922; May 20, 1925; January 4, 1928. Kenosha Assembly Records. Kenosha Bahá'í community to Persian Ambassador to the United States, September 15, 1922. Kenosha Community Records. National Bahá'í Archives.)

110. Kenosha Assembly Circular letters, March 2, 1923 and November 4, 1923. Kenosha Community Records. National Bahá'í Archives.

111. Kenosha Assembly circular letter, May 17, 1923. Kenosha Assembly Records. National Bahá'í Archives.

112. Kenosha Assembly circular letters, March 21, 1924 and September 27, 1925. Kenosha Assembly Records. Minutes, January 24, 1924; January 12, 1927; February 23, 1927. Kenosha Assembly Records. Kenosha Spiritual Assembly to Shoghi Effendi, March 12, 1924. Alfred Lund Papers. National Bahá'í Archives.

113. Minutes, December 10, 1924; December 17, 1924; and October 28, 1925. Kenosha Assembly Records. National Bahá'í Archives.

114. Minutes, 1925-1926 Membership Lists. Kenosha Assembly Records. Kenosha Assembly to National Spiritual Assembly, September 27, 1925. Office of the Secretary Records. National Bahá'i Archives.

115. Kenosha Assembly to Carl Sheffler, January 19, 1927. Office of the Treasurer Records. National Bahá'í Archives.

116. Minutes, November 6, 1929; January 29, 1930. Kenosha Assembly Records. National Bahá'í Archives.

117. Minutes, June 18, 1928. Kenosha Assembly Records. National Bahá'í Archives.

118. Minutes, May 28, 1928. Kenosha Assembly Records. National Bahá'í Archives.

119. Minutes, May 7, 1928; June 18, 1928; January 9, 1929; May 9, 1929. Kenosha Assembly Records. National Bahá'í Archives.

120. Kenosha Assembly to National Assembly Treasurer, January 10, 1932. Office of the Treasurer Records. National Bahá'í Archives. Richard H. Keehn, "Industry and Business" in *Kenosha County in the Twentieth Century*, p. 187.

121. Minutes July 1, 1932 and July 12, 1932. Kenosha Assembly Records. National Bahá'í Archives.

122. Shoghi Effendi, *Messages to America* (Wilmette, Ill.: Bahá'í Publishing Committee, 1947) pp. 4-5.

123. Kenosha Assembly to National Assembly, June 16, 1932; National Assembly to Kenosha Assembly, September 22, 1932. Office of the Secretary Records. National Bahá'í Archives.

124. Kenosha Assembly to Kenosha Bahá'ís, January 12, 1933. Kenosha Assembly Records. National Bahá'í Archives.

125. Kenosha Assembly to National Teaching Committee, February 25, 1931. Kenosha Assembly Records. National Bahá'í Archives.

126. The new Bahá'ís were: Gertrude Collins, Anna Petersen, Elinor Beemer, Carl Walline, Daniel Roszelle, and John Wosjecnic. The nine old Bahá'ís were: Charles Carlson, Matilda Carlson, Florence Borge, Molly Anderson, Elsa Meyer, Magnus Norlander, Wilhelmina Norlander, Clara Nelson, and Joseph Borkenhagen. Previously, Bernard and Theresa Jacobsen had been added to the membership list. (Minutes, March 30, 1932; April 27, 1932; 1931 Membership List. Kenosha Assembly Records. National Bahá'í Archives.)

Racine, in the early 1930s, was also having success in its teaching efforts and recorded new enrollments.

127. Minutes, November 9, 1932; November 19, 1932. Kenosha Assembly Records. National Bahá'í Archives.

128. National Assembly to Kenosha Assembly, April 7, 1931. Office of the Secretary Records. National Bahá'í Archives.

129. Minutes, September 25, 1933. Kenosha Assembly Records. National Bahá'í Archives.

130. Minutes, January 4, 1937. Kenosha Assembly Records. National Bahá'í Archives.

131. I am grateful to Richard Hollinger for this information. Using the "Feast Attendance Record," (1936) in the Kenosha Assembly Records and the 1936 Kenosha city directory, Hollinger has identified the occupations of nineteen Bahá'ís. Blue-collar workers were as follows: plasterer, carpenter, sign painter, auto worker, mason, machinist, driver, brass worker, factory employee, and laborer. The white-collar occupations were: assistant superintendent (at an insurance company), librarian, president, secretary-treasurer, investigator, draftsman, stenographer, beauty operator, and clerk. The occupation for Walter Bohanan (plasterer) was obtained from his obituary in a clipping file at the Kenosha Public Library.

This data also seems to indicate that there was a trend from unskilled to skilled blue-collar positions during the period 1900-1936, but this may be partly accounted for by the probability that unskilled workers were less frequently listed in the city directories as the population of the town grew.

132. Of the white-collar workers, two became Bahá'ís prior to 1900. (They are on the list kept by Byron Lane. Kenosha Community Records. National Bahá'í Archives.) Two were second generation Bahá'ís whose parents had become Bahá'ís prior to 1900. (Historical Record Cards for Eldon Voelz and Lauretta Voelz. National Bahá'í Archives.) The remaining white-collar Bahá'ís were neither listed on Lane's list nor on the membership list composed by 1906 (Kenosha Community Records. National Bahá'í Archives.) Therefore, they must have become Bahá'ís between 1906 and 1936.

133. Minutes, February 19, 1934; June 11, 1935. Kenosha Assembly Records. National Bahá'í Archives.

134. Minutes, January 8, 1934. Kenosha Assembly Records. National Bahá'í Archives.

135. Minutes, May 2, 1934. Kenosha Assembly Records. National Bahá'í Archives.

136. Minutes, April 20, 1937. Kenosha Assembly Records. National Bahá'í Archives. *Bahá'í World*, vol. 7, pp. 365, 373, 398.

137. Kenosha Assembly to National Assembly, June 24, 1937; National Assembly to Kenosha Assembly, July 9, 1937. Office of the Secretary Records. National Bahá'í Archives.

138. Kenosha Assembly to National Assembly, February 19, 1938; National Assembly to Kenosha Assembly, February 23, 1938. Office of the Secretary Records. National Bahá'í Archives.

139. Minutes, July 11, 1938. Kenosha Assembly Records. National Bahá'í Archives.

140. Minutes, May 2, 1939; June 10, 1940. Kenosha Assembly Records. National Bahá'í Archives.

141. Minutes, September 9, 1940; 1940 membership list (at the back of the minute book). Kenosha Assembly Records. National Bahá'í Archives.

142. Minutes, May 6, 1940; May 20, 1940; May 5, 1941. Kenosha Assembly Records. National Bahá'í Archives.

143. Minutes, January 22, 1940; May 20, 1940. Kenosha Assembly Records. National Bahá'í Archives.

144. Kenosha also provided two international pioneers during the Seven Year Plan: Flora Hottes, who moved to Bolivia in 1942, and Lauretta Voelz, who went to Regina, Canada, in 1943.

145. Kenosha Assembly to National Assembly, January 17, 1944; National Assembly to Kenosha Assembly, March 30, 1944. Office of the Secretary Records. National Bahá'í Archives.

146. Minutes, March 27, 1945. Kenosha Assembly Records. National Bahá'í Archives.

147. Minutes, April 15, 1940; March 27, 1945. Kenosha Assembly Records. National Bahá'í Archives.

148. Minutes, July 17, 1945; Kenosha Assembly to Flora Hottes, September 20, 1945. Kenosha Assembly Records. National Bahá'í Archives.

149. *Bahá'í News*, No. 205 (March 1948) p. 4.

150. However, not all of these committees were appointed every year.

151. Kenosha Assembly Progress Report, November 1, 1968-July 1, 1969; November 1, 1969. Kenosha, Wisconsin, File. National Teaching Committee Records. National Bahá'í Archives.

152. Kenosha Assembly Annual Report, 1979-1980. Assembly Records. Kenosha Archives.

153. Informal meetings held in the homes of Bahá'ís to introduce new people to the Bahá'í teachings.

154. National Assembly to Kenosha Assembly, December 28, 1956. Office of the Secretary Records. National Bahá'í Archives.

155. Kenosha Assembly Progress Report. December 1970. Kenosha, Wisconsin, File. National Teaching Committee Records. National Bahá'í Archives.

156. Bahá'í Historical Record Cards. National Bahá'í Archives.

TABLE 1
KENOSHA ENROLLMENT BY YEAR*
1897-1987

Year	Men	Women	Youth	Total
1897	9	9	NA	18
1898	24	31	NA	55
1899	53	59	NA	112
1900	18	16	NA	34
1904	1	1	NA	2
1906	1	1	NA	2
1908	1	0	NA	1
1917	1	0	NA	1
1918	0	1	NA	1
1920	3	1	NA	4
1921	1	0	NA	1
1925	0	0	NA	0
1926	0	0	NA	0
1927	0	1	NA	1
1928	1	0	NA	1
1929	2	0	NA	2
1930	0	0	NA	0
1931	2	2	NA	4
1932	7	9	NA	16
1933	0	0	NA	0
1934	1	1	NA	2
1935	0	0	NA	0
1936	1	2	0	3
1937	1	0	0	1
1938	0	0	1	1
1939	1	1	0	2
1940	1	0	0	1
1941	0	2	1	3
1942	0	1	0	1
1943	0	0	0	0
1944	0	1	0	1
1945	0	0	0	0
1946	0	2	0	2

* Sources: Membership List, 1894-1900, Kenosha Community Records; Kenosha Membership Material, 1899-1900, 1925-1945, Kenosha Community Records; Kenosha Assembly Annual Reports, Kenosha Assembly Records. National Bahá'í Archives. Wilmette, Ill.

TABLE 1 (continued)

Year	Men	Women	Youth	Total
1947	0	0	0	0
1948	0	0	0	0
1949	0	1	3	4
1950	0	0	0	0
1951	0	0	0	0
1952	0	0	0	0
1953	1	2	1	4
1954	0	0	1	1
1955	0	0	1	1
1956	0	0	0	0
1957	0	0	0	0
1958	0	0	0	0
1959	0	0	0	0
1960	NA	NA	NA	3
1961	0	0	0	0
1962	NA	NA	NA	4
1963	NA	NA	NA	1
1964	0	0	0	0
1965	0	0	0	0
1966	0	0	0	0
1967	0	0	0	0
1968	0	0	0	0
1969	0	0	0	0
1970	0	0	1	1
1971	[1 adult]		3	4
1972	0	0	0	0
1973	NA	NA	NA	5
1974	0	0	0	0
1975	0	0	0	0
1976	0	0	0	0
1977	NA	NA	NA	2
1978	0	0	1	1
1979	0	0	0	0
1980	0	0	0	0
1981	NA	NA	NA	2
1982	0	0	0	0
1983	0	0	0	0
1984	0	0	0	0
1985	0	0	0	0
1986	0	0	0	0
1987	0	0	0	0

TABLE 2
OCCUPATIONS OF KENOSHA BAHÁ'Í MEN*
1897-1941

Enrollment Year	Machinest	Factory Workers†	Professionals§	Craftsmen**	Other††	Not Known
1897	2	3	0	0	1	2
1898	5	9	1	1	2	9
1899	8	23	4	1	6	12
1900	2	6	0	0	2	9
1903	--	--	--	1	0	0
1904	1	3	0	0	0	0
1906	0	0	0	0	1	0
1908	0	0	0	0	1	0
1912	1	0	1	0	0	0
1913	0	0	0	0	0	0
1917	1	0	1	0	0	0
1920	0	0	0	0	0	0
1928	0	0	0	1	0	0
1929	0	0	1	0	0	1
1931	0	0	0	0	0	1
1932	0	1	0	0	0	3
1933	0	1	0	0	0	0
1936	0	0	0	0	0	1
1937	0	0	0	0	1	0
1939	0	0	0	0	0	1
1941	0	1	0	0	1	0

* The occupations are those of the man at the time of enrollment as a Bahá'í or the closest year. Some of the men changed occupations. These changes were often an improvement in economic standing.

† Tinner, factory fireman, presser, enameler, tool maker, stationary engineer, stockkeeper, wagon maker, tinsmith, tanner, polisher.

§ Bookkeeper, clerk, druggist, contractor, photographer, office manager, insurance agent.

** Carpenter, printer, sign painter.

†† Ship captain, barber, farmer, servant, teamster, butcher, gardner, foremen, janitor.

TABLE 3
OCCUPATIONS OF KENOSHA BAHÁ'Í WOMEN*
1897-1941

Enrollment Year	Housewife†	Professional§	Other	Not Known‡
1897	5	0	0	3
1898	14	1	2	12
1899	28	3	11	22
1900	4	1	3	9
1904	0	0	0	1
1906	0	0	1	1
1918	0	1	0	0
1920	0	0	0	1
1926	1	0	0	0
1931	0	1	0	0
1932	0	2	0	2
1936	0	2	0	0
1939	0	0	0	1
1941	0	1	0	1
1942	0	1	0	0
1944	0	0	0	1

* The occupations are those of the woman when she enrolled as a Bahá'í or the closest year. Some of the men changed occupations. These changes were often an improvement in economic standing.

† As woman is assumed to be a housewife if no occupation is given for her in the census or city directory.

§ Teacher, bookkeeper, clerk, nurse, librarian.

‡ Farmer, factory worker, domestic, dressmaker, housekeeper, boarding house, waitress.

TABLE 4
SIZE OF KENOSHA BAHÁ'Í COMMUNITY BY YEAR*
1906-1987

Year	Adults	Youth	Year	Adults	Youth
1906	60	2	1953	28	0
1916	35	NA	1954	25	1
1920	32	NA	1956	23	1
1922	26	NA	1957	21	1
1923	18	NA	1958	21	1
1925	17	7	1959	17	0
1926	20	NA	1960	16	NA
1927	18	NA	1961	15	NA
1928	18	NA	1962	18	0
1929	23	NA	1963	18	NA
1930	23	NA	1964	19	0
1931	27	NA	1965	21	0
1932	41	NA	1966	23	0
1933	40	NA	1967	24	0
1934	42	NA	1968	22	0
1935	44	NA	1969	18	3
1936	47	NA	1970	15	9
1937	48	NA	1971	13	NA
1938	50	NA	1972	20	2
1939	49	NA	1973	19	NA
1940	47	NA	1974	21	5
1941	42	NA	1975	21	4
1942	41	NA	1976	21	3
1943	38	NA	1977	18	2
1944	39	NA	1978	20	1
1945	36	NA	1979	23	1
1946	36	NA	1980	20	1
1947	29	NA	1981	21	1
1948	26	NA	1982	24	NA
1949	25	NA	1983	19	NA
1950	25	2	1985	19	NA
1951	25	3	1987	19	0
1952	26	3			

* Sources: Kenosha Assembly Minutes, 1906 Kenosha Membership List, Kenosha Records. Local Spiritual Assembly Election Forms, Letter from Kenosha Assembly to National Spiritual Assembly, Septemeber 27, 1925, National Spiritual Assembly Records. Membership Lists, 1920, 1922, Alfred E. Lunt Papers. Kenosha Assembly Annual Reports, Kenosha Assembly Records. National Bahá'í Archives. Wilmette, Illinois.

TABLE 5
CHANGES IN SIZE OF KENOSHA BAHÁ'Í COMMUNITY*, †
1920-1987

Year	Enrollments	Transfers In / Out		Deaths	Left Faith
1920	4	0	0	0	1
1921	1	0	0	0	0
1925	0	1	0	0	0
1926	0	3	0	0	0
1927	1	0	3	0	0
1928	1	0	2	1	0
1929	2	2	0	0	0
1930	0	0	0	1	0
1931	4	1	0	1	0
1932	16	0	0	0	0
1933	0	2	0	1	1
1934	2	0	0	0	0
1935	0	0	0	0	0
1936	3	0	0	1	0
1937	1	0	0	0	0
1938	1	1	1	2	0
1939	2	0	1	0	0
1940	1	0	7	2	0
1941	3	0	3	1	0
1942	1	1	1	0	0
1943	0	0	2	1	0
1944	1	1	1	0	0
1945	0	0	2	2	0
1946	2	1	1	1	0
1947	0	0	4	2	0
1948	0	0	2	0	0
1949	4	0	2	1	0
1950	0	0	0	0	0
1951	0	1	0	1	0
1952	0	0	0	0	0
1953	4	0	2	0	0
1954	1	0	4	1	0
1955	1	0	2	0	0

* Sources: Kenosha Assembly Minutes, Kenosha Assembly Annual Reports, Kenosha Assembly Progress Reports.

† These statistics are probably not complete as the records for some years were missing or incomplete. There are discrepencies between Tables 4 and 5 for a few years.

TABLE 5 (continued)

Year	Enrollments	Transfers In / Out		Deaths	Left Faith
1956	0	0	2	1	0
1957	0	0	0	0	0
1958	0	0	0	1	0
1959-60	0	0	2	0	0
1960-61	3	0	1	4	0
1961-62	0	0	0	1	0
1962-63	4	0	0	1	0
1963-64	1	0	0	1	0
1964-65	0	0	0	0	0
1965-66	0	2	0	0	0
1966-67	0	0	0	0	0
1967-68	0	0	0	1	1
1968-69	0	0	0	1	0
1969-70	0	0	0	0	0
1970-71	1	0	4	2	0
1971-72	4	1	1	0	0
1973-74	5	0	0	0	0
1974-75	0	0	3	0	1
1975-76	0	0	0	0	0
1976-77	0	0	4	1	2
1977-78	2	0	0	1	1
1978-79	1	4	5	0	0
1979-80	0	1	2	0	0
1980-81	0	1	0	1	1
1981-82	2	0	1	0	0
1982-83	0	2	0	1	0
1986	0	2	0	0	0
1987	0	2	0	0	0

BAHÁ'Í REGIONAL CONFERENCE
for Kansas, Missouri, and Nebraska, October 13, 1946, held in Garfield Park, Topeka, Kansas.

THE BAHÁ'Í FAITH IN KANSAS, 1897-1947

by Duane L. Herrmann

About the year 1900, Abraham Keihrella [sic], an Egyptian, came to Enterprise, Kansas. Mrs. Rose Hilty was residing there at the time. Mr. Kheihrella brought his wife and son from Chicago to Enterprise for a vacation. While there, he gave the Baha'i Message including ordinances and instructions. And healed some people while there. He also organized a group of forty members in Enterprise before leaving.[1]

The Beginning: The city of Enterprise was the first place in Kansas where Bahá'í activities were organized. Bahá'í classes were held there in 1897, and Bahá'ís have been in Kansas continuously ever since. Bahá'í communities that were later formed in Kansas have connections to that first Enterprise Bahá'í community.

At the end of the nineteenth century, Enterprise was much more important than it is today. A railroad town located on the Smokey Hill River, it was a commercial and industrial center for central Kansas. The river provided abundant energy for the technology of the times. A college was established there in 1888, and the first kindergarten in Kansas was also founded there. Leading national figures, including

67

BARBARA HILTY EHRSAM

Susan B. Anthony, Carrie Nation (who "smashed" a saloon on her visit), and Elizabeth Cady Stanton, visited the town during these years.

It was among the social elite of Enterprise—among its founders, in fact—that the Bahá'í Faith would be introduced. The city had been founded by Christian Hoffman, Jacob Ehrsam, and Michael Senn. All were immigrants from Switizerland. Hoffman had owned and operated a mill in Switzerland and wanted to do the same in the new country. He enlisted the help of Ehrsam to build the mill and forge its machinery. Barbara, Elizabeth, and Michael Senn had come to the United States from Switzerland with their parents in 1854 or 1855, and settled in Kansas. Elizabeth Senn married Christian Hoffman there.[2]

Barbara Senn had married Joseph Hilty, another Swiss immigrant, in Kansas in 1860. When he died in 1868, Barbara and her children, Leonard and Josephine Hilty, joined her sister and brother-in-law (the Hoffmans) who were moving to Louden Falls to build the grain mill. Barbara's brother, Michael Senn, also moved there, and together they opened the first store in the area. The new town of Enterprise was platted around the store about a year later. In 1870, Barbara Hilty married Jacob Ehrsam, who had helped to build the Hoffman mill and had later opened his own machine shop. The Ehrsams had six children, plus the two from Barbara's previous marriage. In 1890, to house the family, they built a new home that the newspaper described as the "most elegant . . . in town."[3]

With the store, the machine shop, and the mill, the Hoffman-Ehrsam-Senn families prospered and dominated the economy of Enterprise. In 1885, the newspaper delighted in the prosperity of the town, reporting that "the J. B. Ehrsam Machine Company has secured contracts worth nearly $75,000 in a single week."[4] But this material success did not satisfy

Barbara Ehrsam. Her religious speculations became well known. She was described as someone who went "from one church and dogma to another."[5] At different times, she investigated Christian Science, the Dowieites (followers of John Alexander Dowie, centered in Zion City, Illinois), and the teachings of a vegetarian who had walked barefoot from Chicago.[6] These activities "so incensed her brother-in-law John that he publicly read her from membership in the Methodist Church as one of his last acts before leaving his pulpit at Enterprise."[7]

Ehrsam's religious interests appear to have been shared by her daughter, Josephine Hilty (Kimmel). In the 1890s, she went to Chicago to complete her musical training. There she met Ibrahim Kheiralla, the famous Bahá'í teacher and accepted his teachings.[8] She probably attended Kheiralla's classes in Chicago, but she did not receive the Greatest Name there—the culmination of Kheiralla's instruction.[9] It seems that Hilty shared her discovery with her mother. Barbara Ehrsam invited Kheiralla to come to her home and offer his teachings there. He brought his wife, Marian, and his teenage son, George. Marian Browne, Marian Kheiralla's aunt, may also have accompanied them. It was the first time that Kheiralla's lessons had been delivered outside of Chicago.[10]

Kheiralla was not the first person or the last to whom Barbara Ehrsam would turn for spiritual knowledge, but his visit caused quite a stir in Enterprise and the surrounding communities. The news of Kheiralla's new teachings quickly spread to Abilene (the closest town), to Topeka (the capital city), and beyond to Lawrence, one hundred miles from Enterprise. The articles in the newspapers of these cities, in 1897, may have been the first publicity that Bahá'í activities in America ever received.

Kheiralla arrived in Enterprise in early July, 1897. By the fifteenth of the month, articles about him had appeared in newspapers across the state. The articles focused on Kheiralla's healing techniques, the unusual ideas presented in his classes, and the secrecy that surrounded them. A detailed examination of these articles is necessary to understand the public reaction to the Bahá'í teachings and the long-term impact of Kheiralla's visit.

The *Abilene Weekly Chronicle* of July 16, published at the county seat ten miles from Enterprise, carried an article under the headline:

TEACHES STRANGE THINGS
Has Wonderful Power to Heal

The article reads:

Considerable interest and a little excitement prevails in Enterprise these days over the peculiar religious teaching of one "Dr." Ibraham [sic] G. Kheiralla an Arabian, who claims not only to teach the only true religion but to possess remarkable powers as a healer of all ills that flesh is heir to.

Dr. Kheiralla has written a book in which he sets forth his peculiar religious ideas, which are to a considerable extent fanatical. By some it is called Neo-Platonism, but others pronounced a combination of Arabic mysticism, German rationalism, mesmerism, etc. He believes in the individuality of God, that the Creator is not the universe or the universe the Creator. The resultant is a modified form of Pantheism.

He has two systems of teaching, giving public lectures on Sunday evening and private lessons in which he teaches the mysteries of the religion, on Wednesday evenings. There must be no interruption, no queries and arguments. Last night a number of Abilene people heard the lecture.

An inner circle, or class formed to take the advanced course in the Kheiralla religion, already has several members, including it is said C. V. Topping, Ed Hafner, etc. Miss Josie Hilty, who knew the "Doctor" in Chicago and through whose influence he was induced to visit Enterprise, is said to have embraced the doctrine he teaches. Just what this is no one is able to find out without acceptance thereof.

The alleged performance of one or two remarkable cures, due to gifts resulting from his religious views, has added somewhat to Dr. Kheiralla's power. One of the Ehrsam boys had the colic or something of the kind and was cured by the laying on of the "Doctor's" hands, one being placed back of his head and the other on his abdomen. Another case, that of a little girl named Hilty, who has been blind from birth, is reported in which he has so far benefited her that she can now distinguish light from darkness and note the difference in colors.

Dr. Kheiralla claims to be able to cure everything and is credited with a host of remarkable cures of all kinds of chronic diseases, including consumption, kidney troubles, fevers, etc., by hypnotic or mesmeric influences, aided by medicines whose secret powers are known to him only.[11]

The book referred to in the article is Kheiralla's *Bab-ed-Din*, and the assessment of his teachings is based on the lessons published in that booklet. This article provides one of the fullest descriptions of Kheiralla's healing methods. This same article appeared simultaneously in two Topeka newspapers, one gave credit to the *Abilene Chronicle*, the other simply gave it a dateline of "Enterprise."[12]

One reason for the wide distribution of this news can be found in the headline given to this article in a Topeka newspaper. The *Topeka Daily Capital* ran the report on the top of page three with the headline: HOFFMAN'S NEW RELIGION. The subheader explains: "The people found out what ails Agricultural College Regent." C. B. Hoffman was the son of Christian Hoffman, Barbara Ehrsam's brother-in-law and the owner of the Hoffman mills in Enterprise. He was a prominent state figure with high ambitions and later became an important politician in Kansas. He eventually ran for governor of the state and narrowly lost. The reports that he was attending Kheiralla's classes caused reprints of this article to appear around the state.

On July 17, the Enterprise weekly paper published an

article headed: THE BIBLE IS NOT THE TRUTH. This article, dealing as it did with the town's most prominent families, was less critical than the Abilene article:

Dr. I. G. Kheiralla, Chicago, who is spending his vacation with the family of J. B. Ehrsam, is teaching the people of Enterprise the religion of his order. Dr. Kheiralla was sent by his Order from the Orient to this country to teach "the truth" and has a large following in Chicago where he has resided since coming to this country from Egypt. He teaches the Oneness and Singleness of God: also whence we came, why we are here and where we are going. He gives to his private pupils the key to the sealed books of the Bible which he uses to verify his teachings. He believes the truth is in the Bible but that the Bible is not the truth.

One of the strict rules of his order is that no teacher is allowed to accept any remuneration [sic], directly or indirectly, for teaching the truth; neither is any one allowed to teach unless a most thorough investigation has been made and every statement which they make can be proved.

On Sunday evenings there will be public talks given in the parlors of the Ehrsam residence, to which all are invited. The private classes which have been held twice, meet Tuesday and Friday afternoons and evenings. There are twenty-seven people taking the private teachings and another class will be formed later. A great interest is manifested by those who have begun the teachings of this religion of which so little is said, for the name of the order is only revealed to those who have taken all the teachings.[13]

This description of the classes, both in manner and content, is accurate and is again partially based on *Bab-ed-Din*. Kheiralla did not tell anyone the "name of the order" (the Bahá'í Faith) until they had completed all the classes.

This article, with additional comments at the beginning and end, was reprinted the following Friday in the Abilene weekly. The final comment, a disclaimer the Abilene editors found appropriate, read: "Nobody, however, will take much stock in a religion which cannot stand the open light of day

THE NEW EHRSAM HOUSE
in Enterprise, Kansas, c. 1890.

and Kheiralla's 'religion' is perhaps as great a fake as his alleged miraculous cures."[14] This barb, of course, refers to Kheiralla's insistence on secrecy.

This sarcastic approach can be seen earlier in a short quip that appeared in the *Reflector*, dated July 15, 1897: "It is reported that C. B. Hoffman is practicing under an Arabian doctor in the art of curing by laying on of hands. Chris will probably add this new department to the State Agricultural college when he masters it more thoroughly."[15]

Hoffman's prominence and his advocacy of radical changes at the college (now Kansas State University), located just thirty miles from his hometown, guaranteed attention for his activities. The next day, another short feature was printed in the *Daily Reflector*, but this time with a dateline of the *Lawrence Journal*: "It is reported from Enterprise, Kansas, that C. B. Hoffman, the man who has been playing hammer and eggs with the Agricultural College, is a member of a new religious sect organized out there by a gentleman by the name of Ibrahim Kheiralla, late of Arabia. The religion is said to be a conglomeration of mysticism, rationalism, and mesmerism. With wheels of that kind in his head it is no wonder Hoffman wants to grind things up."[16] The last line, no doubt, was intended as a sarcastic reference to the Hoffman family mill, as well as to the controversies at the college.

Ironically, there is no clear evidence that Hoffman actually attended any of Kheiralla's classes. His name does not appear on any of the surviving lists of students attending the classes in Enterprise. If he did attend, it is likely that he dropped out after the adverse publicity.

With the newspaper articles, it is sufficient to say that the arrival of the Bahá'í Faith in Enterprise did not go unnoticed. Kheiralla was interviewed by a newspaper reporter while in Topeka.[17] But in spite of the skeptical reception by the press in other parts of the state, it appears that Kheiralla and his family were well received in Enterprise and enjoyed a peaceful vacation. A few weeks after the initial commotion, the following lines appeared in the Enterprise paper: "Ed Hafner, Emmett Hoffman and George Kheiralla are with a camping party on Lyons Creek, near Woodbine, and will fight chiggers and misquitoes [sic] for a week."[18] This was a typical social notice.

The next week the Enterprise paper duly noted: "Dr. Kheiralla has a large class taking lectures in the new religion and the meetings are reported to be very interesting."[19] It was now just another part of the summer. Kheiralla and his family left Enterprise on August 25.

Bahá'ís in Enterprise: Rose Hilty, one of those who attended Kheiralla's classes, recalled many years later that he had left some forty Bahá'ís in Enterprise after the summer of 1897.[20] This is probably an overstatement, however. The newspapers had reported only twenty-seven persons attending classes. Kheiralla himself recalled that twenty-one people became Bahá'ís there, while twenty-two names are found on a list of Enterprise residents who wrote "supplications" to 'Abdu'l-Bahá declaring their faith in the new religion.[21] This list does not include Josephine Hilty Kimmel, but her name appears on the list of those who were invited to the classes.[22] There is also a list of people from other towns in Kansas who were invited to the classes.[23] Thus we can account for twenty-four of the twenty-seven students mentioned in the newspaper article.

It is likely that some of the twenty-seven students had dropped out of the Bahá'í classes early on. Hoffman, the college regent, may have been one of these. So it seems clear that no more than twenty-four or twenty-five people completed Kheiralla's course before he left Enterprise, though there may have been others that showed interest in his teachings. That number was soon to diminish, however.

For some reason, Kheiralla did not deliver the Greatest Name to any of those who had become Bahá'ís while he was in Enterprise. This, in itself, was not unusual; he did not always have his students receive the Greatest Name immediately after their completion of the classes. In Chicago, he sometimes waited until there was a larger group to receive it. There is evidence to indicate that some of the students in Enterprise had not taken all the lessons. Ed Haffner, for instance, was out of town for a week while the classes were being given. The newspapers had mentioned that a second class was to be organized, but if it was started while Kheiralla was in the town, he certainly did not have time to finish it. There was just enough time to complete the first class.

At the end of Kheiralla's classes, he would provide new believers in his teachings with a form letter, a "supplication" to 'Abdu'l-Bahá, which was to serve as a model for the letters they were expected to write prior to joining the community. This would often result in a link of correspondence between 'Abdu'l-Baha and the new Bahá'í. This did not happen in Enterprise. Those who may have sent letters to 'Abdu'l-Bahá received no reply. It is possible that the letters never reached the Holy Land.[24] In any case, no personal contact with 'Abdu'l-Bahá was established, and the Bahá'ís remained dependent on Kheiralla and other Bahá'í teachers.

According to Barbara Ehrsam, Kheiralla had planned to send Thornton Chase to Enterprise to provide additional instruction to the Bahá'ís and to give them the Greatest Name.[25] Chase was unable to go, but he did correspond with one of the Bahá'ís there, John J. Abramson, the son of a cousin of Jacob Ehrsam.[26] In a letter dated April 1898, Chase instructed Abramson on how to give the Bahá'í lessons.[27] He also responded to his queries about the Greatest Name, confirming that the Enterprise Bahá'ís still did not have it. In October of 1898, Elizabeth Rychener, one of those in the original class, was still looking for someone to deliver the Greatest Name to her.[28]

Two letters survive from Barbara Ehrsam, written to Kheiralla's secretary, Maud Lamson, nearly two years after he left Enterprise. On May 3, 1899, she wrote: "This is the first time I attempted to write to you, although I wished to have done so many times since I had the teachings which make a bond of unity between us." Her health explains the delay: "I have been very ill for nearly two years but have now gained much strength the last 3 weeks that I have hopes of becoming well again."[29]

She continues: "We are a little band of believers here but have no one to instruct us." She goes on to ask if the Getsingers might stop in Enterprise on their way back from pilgrimage in 'Akká to California. (Her request came too late.) Then she asks: "What became of Mr. Chase? He used to write to one of the believers here but no one has heard lately." She is also anxious to receive a copy of Kheiralla's book, which had not been published in 1897. She greatly desires a copy of it, something to study from. She concludes her letter with a gentle reminder: "You promised in the letter to my daughter to send her, also Mrs. Hilty in Enterprise, a copy of Mrs. Getsinger's letter and perhaps some of the Dr's, but we have not seen anything of the kind yet and it is nearly 5 weeks ago."[30]

Lamson's reply has not been found. But some of its contents can be inferred from the second letter that Barbara Ehrsam sent to her later in 1899. She repeated her questions about the availability of Kheiralla's book, even offering to pay in advance. It seems that Lamson had suggested that Rose Hilty come to Chicago. Ehrsam writes: "It is now impossible for Mrs. Hilty to come to Chicago, for she had a very difficult operation performed."[31] Neither could Ehrsam herself travel that distance, being also ill.

It seems that the Enterprise Bahá'ís were cut off, with few avenues of contact with other believers in the country. Her letter closes with a brief description of Bahá'í life in the town in 1899. "We live close and see one another every day. We talk much about the blessed truth and long to hear and know more . . . 'Oh God give me knowledge, faith, and love' is the desire of my heart at all times. Hoping to hear from you soon, I remain yours for the truth. [signed]   Mrs. J. B. Ehrsam."[32] No reply remains extant.

By May of 1899, Barbara Ehrsam had received the Greatest Name from her daughter Josephine Kimmel.[33] Seven other Enterprise students are listed on a September 1899 list as having received the Greatest Name, presumably also from Mrs. Kimmel. Elizabeth Rychener is listed in 1899 as one of the persons who received the Greatest Name in Enterprise, but she had actually moved to Ohio by then, providing one of the community's few outside contacts.[34] John Abramson also received it, though he is not marked in the book. These were probably all of the students from Kheiralla's classes that still considered themselves Bahá'ís by this time.

Most of the original students in the Enterprise classes had been a part of the "upper crust" of local society, and about half of them were related to Barbara Ehrsam in some way. This also characterizes the believers who remained as of 1899. These were: Barbara Ehrsam; her daughter-in-law, Mrs. Rose Hilty; Miss Julie Ehrsam; Mr. E. Ehrsam; Mrs. E. Rychener; C. B. Harding, railroad agent; his wife, Addie; and Elizabeth Frey, wife of the postmaster.[35] The community had no formal organization, there was no systematic teaching activity, and the Faith did not grow much beyond the students who had attended the original 1897 classes.

Beyond its isolation from other Bahá'í communities, there

were other factors that may have contributed to the lack of growth in Enterprise. Barbara Ehrsam, especially after the death of her sister, Elizabeth Hoffman, was the reigning matron of the city. The Bahá'í Faith had been introduced into an elite social network and could not easily spread to other sectors of the population. In 1919, one observer described the position of the Ehrsams and the Hoffmans in Enterprise society:

> These rich people naturally would feel that they were superior to the average people in Enterprise, and that the town was too small for them. Thus they would be led to seek new friends of an equal social status and new amusements in larger cities as they travelled [sic]. Whatever the explanation may be, these idiosyncrasies were bound to destroy any influence for good which these leaders might have had among the average, church people of the town, and served to deepen the wide chasm between church and non-church groups in the town.[36]

In addition, the crisis of Kheiralla's defection from the Bahá'í community in 1900, probably added to the confusion and isolation which the Bahá'ís in Enterprise felt.[37] Yet, we have clear evidence that two of the women of the early Enterprise group, Rose Hilty and Elizabeth Frey, continued to regard themselves as Bahá'ís for the rest of their lives. There may have been others, as well, but we have no evidence of their later activities. Since the Enterprise Bahá'ís remained unorganized, the records of the community are minimal.

In addition to these two, one other resident of Enterprise retained her Bahá'í association until her death. Mrs. Mary M. F. Miller and her husband returned to Enterprise in 1903. He had been the founding minister of the Methodist church years before.[38] At the time of Kheiralla's class, they had lived in Kansas City (Kansas), and her name is found on a list of individuals from various towns in Kansas (presumably to be invited to the class). She was listed as a Bahá'í in Kansas City in 1898. She and Frey were among the few Bahá'ís in the 1897 group not related to the Hoffman-Ehrsam-Senn family. She is known to have contributed to the Bahá'í Temple project.[39] In 1905, she and Rose Hilty signed a petition to 'Abdu'l-Bahá. They were the only Kansas Bahá'ís to do so, and their names appear in a booklet, published with 'Abdu'l-Bahá's reply, among those of the 422 Bahá'ís who signed the petition. 'Abdu'l-Bahá's Tablet encouraged the Bahá'ís to spiritualize their lives, be united, teach the Faith, and promote the unity of mankind.[40] Miller's obituary appeared in the Bahá'í magazine *Star of the West* when she died in 1911: "Word came to us announcing the death of Mrs. Mary M. F. Miller, Enterprise, Kansas after a stroke of paralysis."[41]

A few years before Miller's death, Rose Hilty had moved to Topeka (c. 1905-1906), though her husband did not sell their farms on the edge of Enterprise. With both of these believers gone, the only remaining Bahá'ís in Enterprise may have been Elizabeth Frey and her daughter Elisabeth Renwanz. In 1912, they witnessed the dedication of the ground for the future Bahá'í House of Worship in Wilmette, Illinois. Renwanz wrote: "In May, 1912, attracted by the presence of 'Abdu'l-Bahá, mother and I went to Chicago to see Him. Here we partook but for a moment of the great privilege of meeting the Mystery of God. We also saw him place the cornerstone of the Baha'i Temple."[42] Shortly after the trip, a contribution is recorded from her to the Bahai Temple Unity.[43]

Renwanz had not attended the 1897 classes because she was a girl of ten at the time. She seems to have learned of the Faith through her mother's teaching efforts. Helen Erickson, a long-time resident of Enterprise, remembered that religious meetings were held, when she was a child, at the home of Mrs. Frey.[44] Renwanz described her mother as one of "only two of this group [the 1897 class] who accepted Baha'u'llah as the Manifestation and to remain faithful to the end."[45] The other would have been Rose Hilty.

Hilty returned briefly to Enterprise around 1917, which

may have prompted some Bahá'í activity there. Both Frey and Hilty contributed to the Bahai Temple Unity from Enterprise that year, as did Barbara Ehrsam.[46] Hilty moved back to Topeka in 1920.

After the death of Frey (April 9, 1930) and the departure of her daughter, we can conclude that the Bahá'í community of Enterprise ceased to exist. Considering the social distance between the Bahá'ís and the rest of society and the lack of support from Bahá'ís in other parts of the United States, it is not surprising that the community was unable to grow after an initial period of interest and could not sustain itself.[47]

Topeka, 1906-1931. Rose Hilty and her family moved from Enterprise to Topeka in 1905 or 1906. Mrs. Hilty had attended Kheiralla's classes in Enterprise with her husband, but only she had received the Greatest Name and become a Bahá'í. She was able to pass on her Bahá'í identity to her daughter, Lovelia, who was blind from birth—the "little girl named Hilty" mentioned in the 1897 newspaper article as having been partially cured by Kheiralla's healing.

These were the first Bahá'ís to live in Topeka, and Bahá'ís have lived in the city continuously since their arrival. Rose Hilty states in her memoirs that she "helped to organize a group of about 12 or 14 people in the year 1912," and that, "during the years from 1918 to 1925 study classes were held." But it seems that "in time the interest lagged and only 2 or 3 loyal believers succeeded in keeping the group alive. They were Mrs. Hilty, her daughter Lovelia and Miss Bertha Hyde, who later married Prof. Kirkpatrick . . ."[48]

Considering her experience among the Enterprise Bahá'ís, it seems unlikely that Rose Hilty would have initiated any Bahá'í activities in Topeka. It is more likely that she supported the work of Bertha Hyde, the second Bahá'í to live in the city. Hyde came to Topeka in 1908 to keep house for her

THE EHRSAM-HOFFMAN-SENN FAMILY, c. 1915.

Standing on stairs: Paul Ehrsam (child), Arnold Ehrsam*. Standing: Arthur Hoffman, Miss Eberhardt, Leonard Hilty*, unknown, Elsbeth Ehrsam*, Alma Hoffman, Catherine America Hoffman, Elsbeth Hoffman, Edward Kuster, Jessie Wagner, Mable Cutler Hoffman, Lovelia Hilty (with glasses), Hattie Grosser, Anna Hoffman, Christian Hoffman, Ralph Hoffman, Jacob B. Ehrsam, William J. Ehrsam*, Vergiline Mulvane Ehrsam, Rev. Blaney (of Abilene), Michael Senn, Marie Senn Heath*, Josephine Hilty Kimmel (Abramson). Kneeling at left: Senn Heath (child). Seated: Hortense Ehrsam, Viola Hare Ehrsam, Barbara Senn Hilty Ehrsam* (in black), Iona Senn Moulton*, Barbara Ehrsam (child), Rose Hilty*, Josephine Senn*. Children in front: Julia Ehrsam Kuster*. Kneeling left (with infant): Catherine Kuster (infant), Herbert Chase, Josephine Heath (kneeling), Catherine Johntz (in front), John Ehrsam, Hal Heath, James Ehrsam, Herbert Ehrsam, Chase Ehrsam (with toy trumpet), David Mulvane Ehrsam, John Hoffman Johntz (in front), William J. Ehrsam, Jr. Those marked with asterisks attended Bahá'í classes in Enterprise in 1897. Josephine Hilty (Kimmel Abramson), Barbara (Senn Hilty) Ehrsam, Rose Hilty, and Julia Ehrsam Kuster were affiliated with the Bahá'í Faith.

widowed brother, Dr. Arthur Hyde, and his young son. She had attended Holyoke College and worked as a school teacher in the East. She was eventually to return to teaching in Topeka, finding a job as a science teacher at Central Park Elementary School.

Bertha Hyde first learned of the Bahá'í Faith from her sister, Mabel Hyde Paine, of Urbana, Illinois. Her sister had attended classes on the Faith given by Albert Vail, a Unitarian minister in Urbana who was a Bahá'í. Paine became a Bahá'í in 1915, and it is likely that her sister followed her shortly after.[49] As was common at that time, when Bertha Hyde accepted the Faith, she wrote to 'Abdu'l-Bahá to confess her new belief. A Tablet (letter) from him, addressed to her and to several other individuals, promised "a spiritual victory."[50] The date of her entry into the Faith is not known, but in any case Bertha Hyde must have been a believer by 1918, since Rose Hilty states that she was the person who organized the Bahá'í classes in Topeka in that year.[51]

During those early years, it is known that several Bahá'í teachers visited Topeka. They included Charles Mason Remey, Mary Hanford Ford, Ida Finch, George Latimer, Albert Vail, Mabel Paine, and a certain Mr. Powell. A list of these names was kept, but no other details of their activities were recorded.[52]

In 1917, Bertha Hyde joined over a thousand other American Bahá'ís who signed a petition requesting that 'Abdu'l-Bahá return to the United States. Hyde was the only Bahá'í in Kansas to sign the petition. Rose Hilty was, at the time, back in Enterprise. Also on the list appears the name "Elizabeth Rennwanz," with the Bahá'ís of Grand Rapids, Michigan.[53] 'Abdu'l-Bahá replied that he was planning his next teaching trip to India, but this never took place.

In May of 1919, Albert Vail reported to the Second Bahá'í Teaching Convention of the Central States, held in Wilmette, the news "of the new and joyous groups started this winter in Keokuk, Kansas City, Topeka and Omaha."[54] For Topeka, this is, no doubt, a reference to the new study classes. Later Rose Hilty recalled:

> During the years from 1918 to 1925 study classes were held under the leadership of Mrs. Bertha Hyde Kirkpatrick. Meetings were held at the home of Mrs. Hilty and at times also at the Universal Truth Center, 504 West 10th Street. Members of this class during this time were—Mrs. Rose Hilty, Miss Lovelia Hilty, Miss Bertha Hyde, Mr. and Mrs. L. M. Kraege, H. R. Whittlesey, Miss Susan Whittlesey, Mrs. Margaret Williams, Mrs. Etta Trump, Mrs. Nellie Amos, Mrs. Etta Gilmore, Miss Anna Boyd, Miss Jennie Boyd.[55]

Also in 1919, a Tablet from 'Abdu'l-Bahá addressed to an individual was received in Kansas. It was translated by Shoghi Effendi and sent to "Ruth Klos" in Atchison. Ruth Klostermeier was a high school student, and her father owned a hardware store in town.[56] 'Abdu'l-Bahá wrote, in part: "Thou has written that 'I am not worthy.' Who is worthier than thee? Hadst thou not been worthy, thou wouldst not have turned to God and wouldst not have wished to enter the Kingdom. Thy worthiness has guided thee until this blessing and bounty have encompassed thee."[57]

The Bahá'í community in Topeka that emerged from the activities of Bertha Hyde and the Hiltys appears to have been a loose network of individuals interested in the study of the Bahá'í teachings—most of whom also had other metaphysical interests and pursuits. There was no formal membership in the community, and many of those involved in Bahá'í activities were also active in churches and other religious movements, as was normal for the time.[58] For example, Louis M. Kraege, in addition to his job as Secretary of the Independent Telephone Company, was a prominent member of the Universal Truth Center in Topeka and served as its president. Margaret Williams, another Bahá'í, was the librarian of the Metaphysical Library. The library was housed in her home, as was the Universal Truth Center, where the Bahá'í study classes were sometimes held.[59] Rose Hilty, in time, drifted into involvement with a "Mazdean" (Zoroastrian) philosophy. She spent many hours copying "Sutras" for the well-being of the world.[60]

It seems clear that the Bahá'í study group in Topeka, during the late 1910s and early 1920s, was a part of the metaphysical culture of the city. This culture promoted an "inclusivist" approach to all religions. It is apparent that many of the Bahá'ís of Topeka did not regard the Bahá'í Faith as an organized, independent religion which required their exclusive commitment. Albert Vail, who helped to organize the meetings in Topeka,[61] was himself a practicing Unitarian minister.

As a result of these attitudes, there was little attendance at the Nineteen-Day Feast and Bahá'í Holy Day observances in Topeka. Even though fourteen Bahá'ís were listed as members of the study group, there was not enough interest to form a local Spiritual Assembly. Even with similar obstacles, the Urbana (Illinois) Bahá'í Assembly was formed in 1920. Mable Hyde Paine came to Topeka to help her sister with the Bahá'í work, but they could not do much.[62]

Some of the tension between the metaphysical approach and a more orthodox understanding of the Bahá'í teachings surfaced during the visit of Faḍl-i Mazandarání (Mírzá Asadu'lláh Mazandarání) to Topeka in 1920. 'Abdu'l-Bahá had sent Jináb-i Faḍil (as he was known) to America to travel to as many Bahá'í communities as possible. His mission was to strengthen ties among the Bahá'ís, educate them more fully in the teachings, and proclaim the Bahá'í message to the public. His successful tour was much celebrated in the Bahá'í community.[63]

The Bahá'ís had arranged for Faḍil to give a number of

public lectures in Topeka. The topics included: "Self-Mastery," "The Ideals of the New Age," and "The Teachings of All Religions Are Identical." There is no hint in any of the titles of the Bahá'í Faith as a religion.[64] Indeed, the word *Bahá'í* is not even mentioned. Nor is it found in the ads that Bahá'ís used to publicize these meetings.[65] Faḍil was scheduled to speak at Central Congregational Church in the city. The announcement in the newspaper's church section read: "CONGREGATIONAL—Central, Evening Sermon, 'The Religion and Reality of Jesus Christ.' by Janebie Fazel Masandarani [sic]."[66]

Faḍil arrived in Topeka from Lincoln, Nebraska, on the evening of December 18, 1920. He left on December 21. He stayed in the home of Mrs. Matt Weightman. While she was supportive of the Bahá'í Cause and had helped make arrangements for the visit, she could not make a firm commitment to the Faith. She was the wife of a Kansas legislator and a cousin of George Latimer, a prominent Bahá'í—frequently elected member of the Bahai Temple Unity and, later, of the National Spiritual Assembly. A reception for Faḍil was held in the Weightman home on the evening of his arrival. The ministers of two important churches in the neighborhood were invited: Rev. Klup of the First Methodist Church and Rev. Rayhill of Central Congregational.[67] It was the latter in whose church Faḍil was to deliver the evening sermon in his church the next day.

A newspaper article published just after Faḍil's arrival states: "Professor Fazel, who is a Christian, has two purposes in his tour, that of lecturing on the doctrines of universal peace, universal religion, which is the Christian religion . . ."[68] The article contains a number of other details about Faḍil which are accurate and could only have been provided by the Bahá'ís.

The impression given out that Faḍil could be considered a Christian was soon dispelled by Faḍil himself. After the reception at the Weightman home, his sermon at the church was hastily cancelled. His talk on the reality of Christ was later delivered at a theater rented by the Bahá'ís.[69] The reason for the cancellation is not recorded, but it seems likely that Rev. Rayhill, a new and inexperienced minister, had learned more about the religion of Jináb-i Faḍil.

An article published the day after the reception is virtually identical to the one mentioned above, except that it clearly states that Faḍil is a Bahá'í: "Persecution by the Turks was the lot of Professor Masandarani [sic] when he accepted his Faith, known as the Baha'i movement."[70]

One of Faḍil's talks was given at the Metaphysical Library, where he was well received. One member of the audience commented: "I have always felt that too many missionaries are sent to the Orient, but am delighted to realize that now missionaries are coming from the Orient to give us knowledge and wisdom."[71] The president of the organization, also a member of the Bahá'í study group, announced to all that the "Library contains a *full* set of Bahai literature and a good deal for sale; that anyone can borrow or buy or come there and read their books."[72]

Rose Hilty had returned to Topeka in time for Faḍil's visit. She and her daughter, Lovelia, had helped to organize it.[72] His lectures resulted in more public exposure than the Bahá'í Faith had ever had in Topeka. Bertha Hyde's report to the National Teaching Committee, which had organized the trip, summarized the results: "The meetings I think were well attended when one considers that they were held just a week before Christmas. (Sunday, the 19th, three meetings were held; in the morning at the Metaphysical Library on the 'Master Key to Self-Mastery'; in the afternoon at the Orpheum Theater on 'The Teachings of all Religions are Identical'; and in the evening again at the Orpheum on 'The Religion and Reality of Jesus Christ'.) . . . Mr. Vail talked personally with a number and left a list with me whom I shall consult with the idea of starting our meetings again. That, I am sure, is very important, and we want prayers for our success. The Monday meetings were at the Elks Club on 'The Ideals of the New Age', and at 8 pm in the Library of Washburn College on 'Modern Education in Persia.'"[73] It is notable that Bahá'í meetings had been discontinued some time before Faḍil's visit.

If Bertha Hyde succeeded in reestablishing the study group, it did not last long. In 1921, Dr. John Kirkpatrick was dismissed from Washburn College for advocating greater democracy on campus and more power for students and faculty.[74] Arthur Hyde, Bertha's brother, resigned in protest. Brother and sister left for Michigan. Although Bahá'í classes may have been held in Topeka until 1925, and Albert Vail continued his assistance, the Bahá'í community was without leadership. At the National Bahá'í Convention in 1926, Corinne True reported that she had visited the Bahá'ís of Topeka. The need for follow-up teaching and consolidation was emphasized. There is no evidence of any Bahá'í activities in Topeka in the late 1920s, and it was not until the 1930s that such activities were revived.

After leaving Topeka, Arthur and Bertha Hyde kept in touch with John Kirkpatrick. In 1924, John and Bertha were married, but religion remained a point of difference between them. Kirkpatrick was an ordained minister of the Congregational Church. He decided to investigate his wife's religion, but the virulent and distorted information he received from Neale Alter, a missionary colleague in Syria,[75] turned him against the Bahá'í Faith for the rest of his life and divided the family. Still, he could not completely dismiss the Bahá'í religion.

In 1930, Kirkpatrick was dying. He and his wife, Bertha Hyde Kirkpatrick, returned to Topeka to be near his family and his doctor. Although confined to bed, he remained mentally alert. He and his wife began to add to their reading and discussion a collection of Bahá'í scriptures her sister was gathering, which was eventually published as *The Divine Art of Living*. Through these writings, he began to understand that his opposition to the Faith was unfounded.

One day, his wife later recounted, "he signified his desire for pencil and paper. Slowly his weakened hand, unable to hold the pencil without aid, formed the almost illegible words, 'one thing only, to be a good . . .' then for a moment there seemed a great influx of strength and spirit as with firm hand he completed the sentence with the word—BAHAI in large clear letters. . . .Those were my husband's last words."[76] He died on January 31, 1931, a newborn Bahá'í.[77]

Resurrection: Topeka, 1933. No Bahá'í activities resulted from the Kirkpatricks' return to Topeka in 1930. However, three years later the community was reorganized through the efforts of Orcella Rexford and her husband Dr. Gayne Gregory. Rexford was a professional lecturer who made her living giving talks on such topics as color, diet, and health. Her travels provided her with an opportunity to spread the Bahá'í teachings throughout the country.

May Brown, who attended her lectures in Topeka, recalled:

> In about late August 1933 a man came to visit our goat dairy as we were the only ones in town that had an "A" rating. My husband, Paul Brown, had made a nice goat barn, room for cooling and bottling milk in connection with the milking shed, etc. . . .
>
> This man looked things over and asked a few questions, in answer to which he made the following proposition: his wife, Orcella Rexford, would be in town for several days giving lectures on health and if we could furnish them goat milk for the time they were here, she would give us free tickets and reference books she had for sale. As we had plenty of goat milk we agreed.
>
> Orcella's lectures were very interesting and very dramatic . . . After a few nights of lectures Orcella announced that on Sunday

she would give a lecture on religion. Well, being faithful members of the Seabrook Congregational Church, we did not go to that lecture. Then the next night when we went again to her lectures, everyone was telling how shocking her Sunday lecture was. She even said Christ had returned.[78]

The Browns attended the next lecture on religion and became interested in the Bahá'í Faith. At the end of the lectures, they joined twenty-six other people who indicated that they wanted to start a class on the Bahá'í teachings.

Ruth Moffett, a Bahá'í from Chicago, came to Topeka for two weeks as their resident teacher. "She held a series of meetings at the Herron Studio, 625 Kansas Ave. Three meetings a day were held there until Nov. 5 covering a period of 15 days. Forty-six lectures in all were given covering prayer services, conferences and luncheons. At the end of these series twenty-six people made declaration of their intention to go on with the study of the Bahá'í Movement."[79]

Moffett returned later in the month and a meeting was held in the home of Mr. and Mrs. L. M. Kraege. The Kraeges were long-time Bahá'ís who had been members of Hyde's study class in the 1920s. At this meeting, Moffett organized new classes under the name "Baha'i Fellowship."[80] She brought her own "Book of Life" for the new believers to sign, affirming their belief. She could remain this time for only two days, but promised to return in the spring.

The Topeka Baha'i Fellowship started a library of Bahá'í books. In February of 1934, a delegation from the group visited Rose Hilty, now an invalid, to obtain information from her about the early days of the Faith in Kansas. Shortly after this, Hilty donated all of her Bahá'í books and magazines to the Bahai Fellowship. These included a complete set of *Star of the West* which she had collected and preserved through the years. Hilty died a few months later.

At this point, the status of the Baha'i Fellowship was

somewhat ambiguous. Those involved clearly regarded themselves as Bahá'ís, and they had signed Moffett's book, but their names do not seem to have been on any national Bahá'í membership list. At Riḍván (April 21) of 1934, they elected a local Spiritual Assembly, at Moffett's behest. At the meeting, however, the community first gathered and elected officers. Then committees were organized. After that, they elected the Assembly. This was a continuation of some elements of the Bahá'í practices of the early 1920s, which the Kraeges may have remembered, but it was out of step with the Bahá'í Administration of the 1930s. The Bahá'ís of Topeka clearly saw the local Assembly as an instrument of the Bahá'í community, and not its governing body. Notification of the election of the Assembly and the election of community officers was sent to the Spiritual Assembly of the Bahá'ís of Chicago. (Chicago had acted as a regional center in the 1920s.) The Chicago Bahá'ís replied with their congratulations, but news of the elections never reached the National Spiritual Assembly, so the Local Spiritual Assembly of Topeka was not recognized.

Some years later, members of the Topeka group explained how the election of the Assembly had come about: ". . . it is generally thought that we were prematurely organized. As a study group, we were given to understand that were we organized this would sort of put us on the map, so to speak, and many Bahá'ís passing through Topeka would most likely stop over to give us some help, but this has not been the case."[81]

During the following year (1934-35), at least two Bahá'í traveling teachers visited Topeka, Mamie Seto and Ali Kuli Khan. There was some press coverage of Khan's visit.

In preparation for the Riḍván election of 1935, the National Teaching Committee sent a representative to Topeka to insure that the Assembly was properly formed and recognized. Dr. Morris was in the city from April 9 to April 11. One of her tasks was to have the members of the Baha'i

RUTH MOFFETT (second from left)
with the Bahá'ís of Topeka, Kansas, c. 1935.

Fellowship Group sign Bahá'í declaration cards in order to establish a definite membership list. May Brown later recalled that: "We all became Baha'is again."[82] Twenty-one people were willing to sign the new cards. From this base, the local Assembly was elected. Moffett returned to oversee the Assembly election. The elected members were: Mr. Paul Brown, Mrs. Irena Stevens, Mrs. Mae Minor, Mrs. Irma Coburn, Mr. Louis Kraege, Miss Ruth Stevens, Mrs. Amos, Miss Tegart, Mrs. Mae Stone.[83]

During Moffett's visit, she had spent much of her time with individuals who had not signed the declaration cards offered by Morris a couple of weeks before. She eventually allowed four of these "undeclared Bahá'ís" to vote in the election. This caused resentment among some of the other members of the group, since they felt that these people had no real commitment to the Faith. One of the four was elected to the Assembly and became its treasurer, however, which indicates that the resentment was not unyielding or universal. The conflict on the Assembly was serious enough, however, that the treasurer had resigned her office by June. She gradually stopped attending Assembly meetings, and eventually refused to associate with any of the Bahá'ís at all.

Those on the other side of the conflict felt that the problems were all the treasurer's fault. According to one member of the community, she "undertook to run everything—until we were smashed . . ." Most of the Bahá'ís became inactive as a result of these problems. By the end of the year, there were only six or seven believers coming to meetings. The recording secretary of the Assembly later reported: "After the hurricane was over, six or seven of the original workers shook off the debris and quietly began to hold steady—and build . . . Now for a number of months, since August [1935]—we've been gaining our former peace and harmony and have made nice progress."[84]

Despite the optimistic face put on the situation in the secretary's report, deep problems remained in the Topeka community. In April of 1936, shortly before the annual election, the community asked a series of questions in a letter to the National Spiritual Assembly. Some of these were: 1) Should non-participating Bahá'ís have the same voice as those who have been involved all along? 2) Should Bahá'ís antagonistic to the community have the same rights as those who are working together? 3) What should be done when someone wants to withdraw from the community? 4) Who is the teacher for this area, and how do we get her to come here?[85] Most of the questions had to do with the relatively new concept of Bahá'í membership. The issue of the proper boundaries of the community would continue to be an issue for some time.

In reply to these questions, Horace Holley, the Secretary of the National Spiritual Assembly, explained that all Bahá'í communities would face tests as they grew, that individuals could not be arbitrarily removed from the membership list for non-attendance or disinterest. If the Assembly wanted to verify its membership, it could gently express that intention in preparation for the annual election and request that each member on the rolls indicate his preference for membership or not.[86]

Apparently, the advice was taken because a new membership list appeared for the 1936 election with several names omitted. Nonetheless, conflict continued among the Bahá'ís in Topeka. It appears that the central problem was that some Bahá'ís regarded the Bahá'í community as primarily a metaphysical study group and little more, while others—responding to the guidance of recent Bahá'í teachers—had come to see the Bahá'í Faith as a distinct religion with an established organization which required their exclusive commitment. And there were Bahá'ís who fell somewhere in between.

After the election of the Topeka Assembly in 1936,

Emogene Hoagg was asked by the National Spiritual Assembly to visit the city to help resolve the problems of the Bahá'í community. Hoagg was a longtime Bahá'í and an important Bahá'í administrator. She had managed the International Bahá'í Bureau in Switzerland from 1928 to 1935 at the request of the Guardian of the Bahá'í Faith.

On October 7, 1936, Hoagg arrived in town to learn that the Assembly had not met since its election and her earlier communications had been ignored. She organized study classes to "deepen" the community, but they were poorly attended. She remained in Topeka for four weeks, but found that she could not repair the situation. She reported to the National Spiritual Assembly that the circumstances "would be ludicrous, if not so tragic. Just like children quarreling." Hoagg decided that the community was hopeless. None of the Bahá'ís, she reported, except for Paul and May Brown, had any understanding of the Revelation. Nor had they given up earlier pursuits which she found incompatible with the Bahá'í teachings. They were "children so far as understanding the teachings is concerned. Too, so many things have been taught that have to be unlearned."[87] Clearly Hoagg disapproved of the work of some earlier Bahá'í teachers. She felt that the atmosphere was so impossible that the only solution was to dissolve the Assembly and start over. According to Hoagg, there were several people—including Mrs. Weightman—who were interested in becoming Bahá'ís, but would not join because of the conditions in the community. Nothing could be accomplished under the present circumstances.[88]

The chairman of the National Teaching Committee, with whom Hoagg corresponded, was reluctant to endorse dissolving the Topeka Assembly. With twenty-one Bahá'ís on the rolls, he felt that she should be able to find nine who could carry on the local body. The complications she found in Topeka were similar to those that had arisen in other cities after certain teachers had been sent there.[89]

Hoagg finally succeeded in gathering eleven of the Bahá'ís in the city together to consult on the situation. (No mean feat in itself.) The consensus was that the Assembly should be dissolved. This decision was ratified at the next Nineteen-Day Feast, and a letter sent to the National Assembly. This was the beginning of a flurry of correspondence between the Topeka Bahá'ís, the National Assembly, Emogene Hoagg, and the National Teaching Committee. By the end of January 1937, the National Assembly had decided that "the Cause will best be served by recognizing the dissolution of the Spiritual Assembly of the Bahá'ís of Topeka." An updated membership list was requested.[90]

Two lists of Bahá'ís were sent in rapid succession, one before the final letter was received and one after. The first list contained only eight names; the second, eleven. Apparently, three members were only willing to be on the list if there was to be no Assembly. After the second list was received, the Topeka Bahá'ís were advised that they should reelect their Assembly at Riḍván. They refused. An annual meeting was held on April 21, 1937, however, and fourteen Bahá'ís attended—more than the eleven on the membership list. The boundaries of community membership were still not clear. The meeting elected officers for the community for the next six months. The Bahá'í community was now a study group, as it had been before. In October, officers were elected again, for six months.[91]

In April 1938, the Assembly was reelected, with a representative of the recently created Regional Teaching Committee for Kansas and Missouri present. The official membership list now carried thirteen names.[92]

The New Bahá'í Community, 1938-1947: After the Assembly was reestablished in 1938, Bahá'í activities in the town were carried on in a steady and organized way. Study classes were held each week; Feasts were held regularly; and, the Assembly held its meetings once a month (to study a topic also). Records were kept of each activity and stored in the infant archives. All of these meetings were scheduled in advance for the entire year, and a calendar of events was distributed at the annual meeting. At that meeting, the community historian summarized events of the past year.

One former Bahá'í, a member of the 1933 study group, asked to be reinstated to membership, and two new believers joined the community. All three became active Bahá'ís.

The son of one of the new members later recalled the Bahá'í study classes that his mother attended. He was too young to go to school, so he played under the dining room table which the ladies sat around and would often fall asleep there.[93]

In 1940, a letter was received from the National Spiritual Assembly to all local Assemblies regarding a message recently received from the Guardian. It was time to clarify Assembly boundaries and jurisdictions. The Guardian explained that the boundaries of an Assembly's jurisdiction in every city must correspond to the legal city limits. Bahá'ís living in suburbs and surrounding areas were to be regarded as living in separate Bahá'í communities.[94] In Topeka, the application of this principle caused five members of the Assembly to become isolated believers scattered around Shawnee County (outside the city limits): in North Topeka, Seabrook, and Wakarusa.[95]

In 1941, the Bahá'ís residing within the city limits of Topeka elected their Assembly without the Shawnee County Bahá'ís. That summer, one Assembly member moved to Chicago; and two longtime members who had weathered the storms of the 1930s found this latest change too much and withdrew from the Faith. This brought the community down to nine members. In December, one of the nine died. The

Assembly was lost, the community reverted to "study group" status, and no election was held the next April.[96]

During 1942, however, there were six new enrollments into the Faith: one a youth (a nephew of a Bahá'í), three spouses of Bahá'ís (two lived in the county), and an entirely new couple. It looked as if the Assembly could be restored. But that December, two of the older Bahá'ís died, which meant there would not be nine adult members to form an Assembly. To insure the restoration, the Schulte family of North Topeka moved inside the city limits on April 15, 1943.[97] It was a sacrifice, but the Assembly was reelected.

Eventually, the city annexed the Seabrook neighborhood, and the Browns, who lived there, were once again a part of the Topeka Bahá'í community. They were immediately elected to the Assembly. Most of the community now consisted of stable families. Many of their children became Bahá'ís, then married, and several of their spouses also joined the Faith.

The Bahá'ís of Topeka gradually began to participate in regional and national Bahá'í activities. From 1944 to 1953, a Topeka Bahá'í was always elected as the Kansas delegate to the National Bahá'í Convention in Wilmette. Several others attended the National Convention each year, and some served on the Regional Teaching Committee. Topeka Bahá'ís regularly attended area conferences. A Bahá'í Center was rented in downtown Topeka for many years, and most Bahá'í activities were held there. This was the site of the early Kansas State Conventions.

Eventually, Bahá'ís came to live in other towns and cities across the state. In 1935, a couple moved to Wichita from Topeka. Another family moved to nearby Burlingame in 1943. A Bahá'í with no connection to Topeka was living in Elwood, in the northwest corner of the state, that same year. In 1945, a Topeka Bahá'í married and moved to Fort Leavenworth. Kingsley received its first Bahá'í resident in 1948.

RACE AND WORLD UNITY CONFERENCE

held on April 18, 1945, at the Kansan Hotel in Topeka, Kansas. About half of those present were Bahá'ís.

Just before Riḍván 1945, the Topeka community held its largest Bahá'í teaching effort to date. A "Race and World Unity" meeting was held on April 18, at the Kansas Hotel. Over thirty-five people—black and white—attended; only about half were Bahá'ís. It was a remarkable event for the time and place.

The next year, the Regional Teaching Committee sponsored the largest all-Bahá'í conference ever held in Kansas. Because of its historic nature, it remained a highlight for those Topeka Bahá'ís who attended. Forty adult Bahá'ís, plus several Bahá'í youth and a number of children attended from Kansas, Missouri, and Nebraska.[98] The Topeka Bahá'ís were impressed and delighted to see so many fellow believers gathered in their hometown. Several of those who attended were family members of early Bahá'ís, making the event all the more special. It was visible evidence that efforts to build a Bahá'í community in Kansas had borne fruit.

To the Present:[99] By the end of the 1940s, a conscious, self-perpetuating, and new Bahá'í community had taken shape in Kansas where there had not been one before. The expansion of the community continued in the 1950s. The first Bahá'í wedding took place on October 21, 1950. Bahá'ís established themselves in Emporia (1953), Scott City (1953), Oakley (1955), as well as Manhattan, Hope, and Parsons (1956). Overland Park, Greenleaf, and Merriam were opened to the Faith in 1957, along with Kansas City, where no Bahá'ís had lived since the turn of the century. Local Spiritual Assemblies were formed in Wichita (1955) and Kansas City (1958).

During the 1960s, new Bahá'í communities spread around the state, and two more Assemblies were formed. Bahá'í marriage was made legal by an act of the state legislature, and a Summer Institute was established. The next decade witnessed an explosion in the size of the Kansas Bahá'í community.

New Bahá'í communities emerged in dozens of towns, and Assemblies were formed in nine new cities. The first Kansans were appointed as members of the Auxiliary Board of the Continental Board of Counsellors.

Growth continued in the 1980s. More towns were opened to the Faith, and eight new Assemblies formed. Some Assemblies have been lost, but progress is evident in restoring some that have lapsed and stabilizing their membership.

The Bahá'í Faith is now well established across the state of Kansas, in about one hundred localities. Most counties in the state have resident Bahá'ís, and nearly every town with a population of ten thousand or more has a Bahá'í community. Many Kansas Bahá'ís have gone as pioneers to foreign countries and several have been elected to National Spiritual Assemblies in those countries. Two Kansans have been elected to the Universal House of Justice, the supreme Bahá'í body in Israel. It is not likely that the Kansas Bahá'í community will ever fade away or return to obscurity.

NOTES

1. This is the report of an interview of Mrs. Rose Hilty, the first Bahá'í of Topeka, with the Topeka Baha'i Fellowship. At the time of the interview, in 1934, the fellowship had been recently established, and Mrs. Hilty was seventy years old. She died within the year. Her recollections were all that the Bahá'ís knew of the beginnings of the Kansas community for the next fifty years. ("History of the Membership in the Topeka Baha'i Community," compiled by May Brown [n.d.] p. 1. Topeka Bahá'í Archives.)

2. Christian Hoffman, "A Brief Life-sketch of Christian Hoffman," unpublished ms., Enterprise Public Library. Edward G. Nelson, *The Company and the Community* (Lawrence, Kan.: Bureau of Business Research, School of Business, University of Kansas, 1956) p. 193.

3. *Enterprise Journal*, October 24, 1890.

4. *The Anti-Monopolist*, May 29, 1885.

5. Nelson, *Company*, p. 312.

6. F. C. Havinghurst, "The Social Development of Enterprise, Kansas" (Master's Thesis. Kansas State University, 1919) p. 39.

7. Nelson, *Company*, p. 312.

8. *Abilene Weekly Chronicle*, July 16, 1897, p. 1.

9. Josephine Hilty was given the Greatest Name in Enterprise in July of 1897. (Membership Book. Chicago House of Spirituality papers, National Bahá'í Archives.) Since the classes that were given in Enterprise were not completed until the end of August, and the Greatest Name was not given to Kheiralla's students until they had completed all the lessons, it seems likely that Hilty had finished his course in Chicago. She is listed in Kheiralla's "Supplication Book of Students in Miscellaneous States" as being the first Bahá'í resident of St. Louis.

On Kheiralla's use of the Greatest Name (*Alláh-u abhá*), see Peter Smith, "The American Bahá'í Community, 1894-1917: A Preliminary Survey," in *Studies in Bábí and Bahá'í History,* Volume One (Los Angeles: Kalimát Press, 1982) pp. 90-91; Richard Hollinger, "Ibrahim George Kheiralla and the Bahá'í Faith in America," in *From Iran East and West: Studies in Bábí and Bahá'í History,* Volume Two (Los Angeles: Kalimát Press, 1984) pp. 103-105, 110; and Robert H. Stockman, *The Bahá'í Faith in America: Origins, 1892-1900,* Volume One (Wilmette, Ill.: Bahá'í Publishing Trust, 1985) pp. 9-11.

10. Hollinger, "Ibrahim George Kheiralla," p. 109. Marian Browne is listed in the Chicago Membership Book (National Bahá'í Archives) as having received the Greatest Name in August 1897. Since Kheiralla was the only one who gave instruction in its use, and he was in Enterprise until August 25, Browne may have been a part of the party.

11. *Abilene Weekly Chronicle* (Abilene, Kansas) July 16, 1897, p. 1. Rose Hilty, Barbara Ehrsam's granddaughter, and the mother of the "little girl named Hilty" referred to in this article, later recalled that Kheiralla had healed people in Enterprise, but she made no mention of him treating her daughter. ("Topeka Bahá'í Community," p. 1.)

12. *Topeka Daily Capitol*, July 14, 1897, p. 3. The weekly newspapers in Enterprise and Abilene credited with the article carried a date two days later (July 16, 1897), but they are the same article. It may be that the weeklies were distributed earlier in the week than the dates printed on them, just as some periodicals are today dated a week or a month before they arrive at the newsstands.

13. *Enterprise Journal* (Enterprise, Kansas) July 15, 1897, p. 1.

14. *Abilene Weekly Chronicle*, July 23, 1897, p. 1.

15. *Abilene Weekly Reflector*, July 15, 1897, p. 6.

16. *Abilene Daily Reflector*, July 16, p. 2.

17. *Topeka Daily Capitol*, September 3, 1897. Clipping in Ibrahim G. Kheiralla papers, in private hands. This article makes no reference to the Bahá'í teachings.

18. *Enterprise Journal*, August 12, 1897, p. 5.

19. Ibid., August 19, 1897, p. 5.

20. See note 1.

21. Ibrahim Kheiralla, *O Christians! Why do Ye Believe Not on Christ?* Chicago: n.p., 1917) p. 169. Supplications lists, National Bahá'í Archives.

22. "Names and Addresses of people to be notified concerning the classes." Ibrahim Kheiralla papers, in private hands. A check appears by her name on this list, which seems to indicate that she had already taken the course of lessons at the time the list was made up.

23. One name is checked off, Mrs. M. F. Miller of Kansas City. (Ibid.) Her husband was a former resident of Enterprise, and it seems likely that she attended the classes there, though it does not appear that she became a Bahá'í until 1898. (*Enterprise Push*, March 1, 1911. Supplications lists.)

24. Letters to Ibrahim Kheiralla from 'Abdu'l-Karim Ṭihrání, in Egypt, indicate that hundreds of letters from American Bahá'ís to 'Abdu'l-Bahá were sent through him. Most of these letters do not now appear to be in the Bahá'í World Center Archives.

25. Barbara Ehrsam to Maude Lamson, May 3, 1899. Maude Lamson papers, National Bahá'í Archives.

26. Abramson had come to live with the Ehrsam family in 1888, "after a few years in Palestine with a missionary." He was a boy of fifteen at the time, and he spoke German, English, and Arabic fluently. This would have provided Abramson with an opportunity to converse with Kheiralla and his son George in their native language. From Enterprise, he went to college in Cedar Rapids, Iowa, returning to Enterprise to work for Ehrsam's machine factory. By 1902, he was a stockholder in the company and on the board of directors. He later married Josephine Hilty, and they moved to California. (Nelson, *Company*, p. 293.)

27. Thornton Chase to J. J. Abramson, April 1898. Thornton Chase Papers. National Bahá'í Archives. Wilmette, Illinois.

28. Elizabeth Rychener to Maude Lamson, October 27, 1898. Maude Lamson Papers. National Bahá'í Archives.

29. Barbara Ehrsam to Maude Lamson, May 3, 1899. Maude Lamson papers.

30. Ibid.

31. Barbara Ehrsam to Maude Lamson, n.d. (late 1899). Maude Lamson papers.

32. Ibid. The phrase "O God give me knowledge, faith, and love" is taken from a prayer that Kheiralla gave to his students.

33. Barbara Ehrsam to Maude Lamson, May 3, 1899. Maude Lampson papers.

34. Supplication lists. National Bahá'í Archives.

35. United States Census, 1900.

36. Havinghurst, "Social Development," p. 39.

37. On the defection, see Peter Smith, "The American Bahá'í Community," pp. 96-99 and Richard Hollinger, "Ibrahim George Kheiralla," pp. 116-22.

38. *Enterprise Push*, March 1, 1911, p. 1. Obituary of Mary M. F. Miller.

39. Bahai Temple Unity Ledger Book, October 2, 1909

40. Tablet of 'Abdu'l-Bahá, "To the beloved of God in General in America (Upon them be Baha Ullah)," translated by Ali Kuli Khan, January 3, 1906, at Cambridge, Mass. Topeka Bahá'í Archives.

41. *Star of the West* (April 28, 1911) p. 9.

42. "Elizabeth Frey Renwanz Recollections." National Bahá'í Archives.

43. Bahai Temple Unity Ledger Book, dated June 10, 1912.

44. Helen Erikson to Duane L. Herrmann, October 23, 1980. In possession of the author.

45. "Renwanz Recollections."

46. Bahai Temple Unity ledger books. National Bahá'í Archives.

47. See also, Duane L. Herrmann, "Enterprise: Second Oldest . . .?" *Bahá'í News* (March 1987) pp. 6-7.

48. "Topeka Bahá'í Community," p.1.

49. Garetta H. Busey, "Mabel Hyde Paine," in *Bahá'í News* (October 1979) p. 7.

50. Tablet of 'Abdu'l-Bahá addressed to several Bahá'ís in the West, July 24, 1919. Bertha Hyde Kirkpatrick papers. National Bahá'í Archives.

51. "Topeka Bahá'í Community," p. 1.

52. Ibid., pp. 1-2.

53. *Star of the West* (August 1, 1919) p. 161.

54. Ibid. (July 13, 1919) p. 132.

55. "Topeka Bahá'í Community," p. 1.

56. *Atchison City Directory*, 1917.

57. *Star of the West* (January 19, 1920) p. 319. This is the only Tablet to an individual Kansas Bahá'í to be published. Other Tablets were received by Fred Hale of Wichita, Mr. P. Dyer (through Fred Hale), and Edward Clark of "America [Americus?], Kansas."

58. It was not until much later, in the mid-1930s, that the Guardian of the Faith asked Bahá'ís in the United States to withdraw from membership in churches and other religious organizations. See Shoghi Effendi, *Messages to America* (Wilmette, Ill.: Bahá'í Publishing Committee, 1947) pp. 4-5.

59. *Topeka City Directory*, 1921.

60. Numerous letters to Rose Hilty of various dates in the 1920s from a source that has been obliterated are in possession of the author. Courtesy of Constance Downs, granddaughter of Rose Hilty.

61. At the second Bahá'í Teaching Conference for the Central States in May 1919, he reported a "new and joyous" group started in Topeka. (*Star of the West* [July 13, 1919] p. 132.)

62. Interview of Sylvia Parmalee, conducted by the author on September 2, 1983.

63. *The Bahá'í Centenary: 1844-1944* (Wilmette, Ill.: Bahá'í Publishing Committee, 1944) p. 166.

64. *Bulletin "A", Teaching Committee of Nineteen* (January 1921) p. 4. National Bahá'í Archives.

65. *Topeka Daily Capital*, December 19, 1920.

66. *Topeka State Journal*, December 20, 1920, p. 2.

67. *Bulletin "A"*, p. 4.

68. *Topeka Daily Capital*, December 19, 1920, p. 10c.

69. *Bulletin "A"*, p. 4.

70. *Topeka State Journal*, December 20, 1920, p. 4.

71. *Bulletin "A"*, p. 8.

72. Ibid., p. 8.

73. Ibid., p. 4.

74. James F. Zimmerman, "The Washburn Story," unpublished ms. (c.. 1960). Washburn University Archives, Topeka, Kansas.

75. S. Neale Alter to John E. Kirkpatrick, January 28, 1924 (written from Hama, Syria). In private hands, courtesy of Sylvia Parmalee.

Alter remained a long-time opponent of the Bahá'í Faith. His antagonistic thesis on the Bahá'í Faith was completed in 1923, at the University of Edinburgh.

76. Mabel H. Paine, "Tribute to Bertha Hyde Kirkpatrick," unpublished ms., p. 3. In private hands, courtesy of Sylvia Parmalee.

77. Bertha Hyde Kirkpatrick returned to her home in Olivet, Michigan. There she helped organize Louhelen Bahá'í School. For years she was the secretary of the School Committee. She was a contributor to, then an editor of, *Star of the West* magazine, and also served as an editor for several volumes of *The Bahá'í World*. She died in 1948, in Michigan. See also, Duane L. Herrmann, "Bertha," *Herald of the South* (July-September, 1991), pp. 46-48.

78. May Brown, "About the Baha'i Faith in Topeka," unpublished ms. (1982), p. 1-2. In private hands.

79. "Topeka Baha'i Community," p. 2.

80. Ibid., p. 2.

81. Maude Tegart, Secretary of the Topeka Bahá'ís, to Horace Holley, December 14, 1936. National Bahá'í Archives.

82. Interview with May Brown conducted by the author (1970s).

83. "Topeka Bahá'í Community," p. 4.

84. Mae Minor to National Spiritual Assembly, April 3, 1936. National Bahá'í Archives.

85. Ibid.

86. National Spiritual Assembly to Spiritual Assembly of the Bahá'ís of Topeka, Kansas, April 8, 1936. National Bahá'í Archives.

87. Emogene Hoagg to National Teaching Committee, May 7, 1936. National Bahá'í Archives.

88. Emogene Hoagg to National Teaching Committee, December 28, 1936. National Bahá'í Archives.

89. Ibid.

90. National Spiritual Assembly to Maude Tegart, January 15, 1937. National Bahá'í Archives.

91. "Topeka Bahá'í Community," pp. 5-6.

92. Ibid., p. 7.

93. Interview with Keith Schulte, conducted by the author in October 1986.

94. See *The Bahá'í World,* vol 9, (Wilmette, Ill.: Bahá'í Publishing Trust, 1945) pp. 28-29.

95. "Topeka Baha'i Community," pp. 4-10; *Topeka City Directory,* 1935-1940.

96. "Topeka Baha'i Community," p. 10.

97. Ibid., p. 11.

98. *Bahá'í News* (January 1947) p. 16. Conference photo.

99. This section is condensed from Duane L. Herrmann, *Ninety Years in Kansas—The Bahá'í Faith: 1897-1987* (Topeka, Kan.: Buffalo Press, 1987).

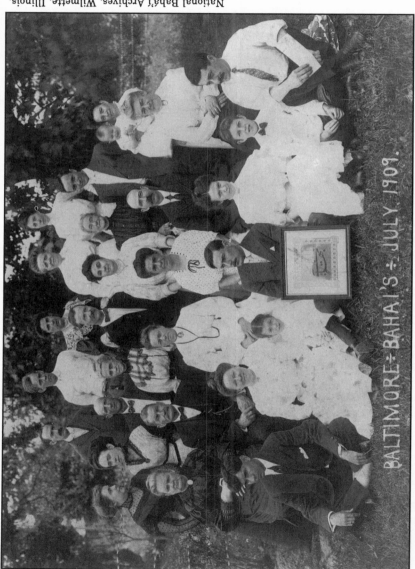

BAHÁ'ÍS OF BALTIMORE

holding a framed copy of the Greatest Name in front, July 1909.

THE BAHÁ'ÍS OF BALTIMORE, 1898-1990

by Deb Clark

In 1899, Hazel Clarke was six months old and deathly ill. Her mother, Kate Kidwell Clarke, had been to the doctors at Johns Hopkins Hospital, but they were unable to do anything for the baby. She would not eat. One day, as Kate was returning home from the doctor's on the streetcar, a woman sitting next to her saw her sobbing and said, "You seem to be upset."

"Yes," answered Kate. "My baby is dying and nothing can be done."

"Have you tried praying?" asked the woman.

Kate Clarke was a devout Christian. "Yes, I have," she replied. "Nothing helps."

The woman said, "I know a remarkable woman who may be able to help you. You must go see her at 895 Park Avenue." The woman wrote down the address and handed Kate the piece of paper.

Kate got off the streetcar near Park Avenue and found 895, where a sign in the window read "Battee Institute of Self Knowledge." She went up the front steps and knocked on the door. When she was let inside, she explained the problem. Pearle Doty held the baby and prayed for her. When she was finished and had handed the child back to her mother, Kate thought she saw a slightly healthier glow in the child. By the time Kate got home, Hazel wanted to eat.

The next day she was fully recovered.[1]

111

The Beginnings of the Baltimore Community: The early Bahá'ís of Baltimore remembered Pearle Doty as the first Bahá'í in the city and the unofficial leader of the community during its first years. Born Pearle Battee in Alexandria, Ohio, in 1868, she moved to Mulberry Street in the Mount Vernon area of Baltimore, the city where her father, Elisha Battee had been born in 1835.[2] She found work as a professor in 1892, but her calling was as a faith healer.

Pearle Battee began her practice as a phrenologist, treating people's infirmities by reading the markings and bumps on their heads. At the time, this was a fairly common alternative form of healing, based on the belief that the mind and body are a whole entity. This practice opened in about 1893, at 111 Franklin, where Battee resided during her first year in Baltimore. It was a neighborhood of artists. The Charcoal Club on the corner of Howard and Franklin was frequented by artists, musicians, and writers, who would also meet in each other's homes to discuss the events of the day.[3]

Henry (Harry) Archer Doty, born September 18, 1874, to Aristippus Doty and Josephine Charlotte Carpenter in Charleston, South Carolina, was the fifth of eleven children, and the first son to survive. His father was a military man and a school principal, a descendant of Edward Doty who arrived on the Mayflower in 1620.[4] At the age of twenty, Harry Doty moved to Baltimore to work in a laboratory. He lived on Greenmount Avenue in the Old Town area, which would have been central to both Mount Vernon and Johns Hopkins Hospital, where he may have been employed.[5]

While he may have been planning a career as a physician, he did not pursue this. After about a year in Baltimore, he moved to 111 Franklin, the same house—probably a boarding house—where Pearle Battee lived, and he was employed as a bookkeeper. Doty must have been fascinated by Battee, an older woman with an exotic healing practice; and, apparently, she by him. In April of 1896, only a year and a half after Doty came to town, Pearle Battee gave birth to their son, Henry Battee Doty.[6] Harry Doty let his family know, at that point, that he and Pearle were married and that he was publishing a magazine called *Self Knowledge*.[7] By 1897, Harry was working as a phrenologist along with his wife, and the two of them had incorporated their business as Doty and Doty.[8]

Elisha Battee moved in with Pearle and Henry Doty sometime during 1897, and the Battee Institute of Self Knowledge became official. It was located at 895 Park Avenue, a very fashionable street of brownstone houses with finely worked dark wood interiors and marble steps.[9] Clearly, the Doty family was doing well. The neighborhood was inhabited by professionals: doctors, judges, and lawyers. There were several bookstores nearby, including one owned by a poet, and a corner drugstore where young couples could go to drink a soda.[10]

Harry Doty managed the Institute, Pearle Doty was the principal, and Elisha Battee was healer and teacher. The Institute touted its monthly magazine, *Self Knowledge*, as a publication "devoted to the unfolding of the Divinity in humanity."[11] A half-page advertisement for it read: "The aim of this Institute is to unfold the highest possibilities on all planes of consciousness. All diseases of mind or body successfully treated by right understanding of the laws of being and proper application to individual needs. Phrenology and mental science healing taught and practiced."[12]

A year after Pearle Doty had healed her baby, Kate Clarke tried to return to the Institute of Self Knowledge, but it was no longer there.[13] She did not realize that the Dotys had moved a block away to 808 North Howard Street.[14] Sometime during 1900, both Harry Doty and Elisha Battee either died or moved out, and the child, Henry Battee Doty, who was then only five years old, was living with his father's parents.

Pearle Doty continued as a metaphysician until she died in about 1903.[15]

Pearle Doty may have attended Bahá'í classes in New York delivered by Ibrahim Kheiralla, an important Bahá'í teacher, as early as 1897. Her name appears on a list put together that year of people who were to be invited (or had previously attended) these classes.[16] Her name and the name of her father, Elisha Battee, also appear on a list of those who completed Bahá'í lessons in Baltimore in 1898. But the fact that Doty's name is on a similar list for New York suggests that she originally took the classes there.[17]

By 1901, fifty persons had been attracted to the Faith in Baltimore. The majority of these Bahá'ís were women, and most were from a working-class or professional middle-class background.[18] Those who became Bahá'ís during this period formed the nucleus of the early Baltimore Bahá'í Community. However, most of them do not appear to have remained active in the community for long after Pearle Doty's death.[19] Bahá'ís moved to Baltimore from other localities, which helped to sustain the community in its early years.

Some Early Bahá'ís of Baltimore: Charlotte Brittingham Dixon of Princess Anne, Maryland, began a spiritual quest which took her to Chicago in 1896. She had a feeling that there was something in that city that she should know about. So when it was time to return to Maryland in 1897, and she still had found nothing, she resisted. She later wrote: "I besought God most earnestly, often lying on my face on the floor, that I should not be allowed to leave Chicago, without finding someone who knew of this Revelation."[20] One day, while she was praying, a woman rang the doorbell asking for something, and Dixon let her in. As they talked, the woman suggested that she seek out a Mrs. Reed, who was teaching the gospel in the slums. That afternoon, Dixon tried to find Mrs. Reed, but was told that she was out of town. She returned the next day, and the day after, only to be turned away again. On the third day, a neighbor heard her asking for Mrs. Reed and said, "Woman, God sent you here; you are not seeking Mrs. Reed. We have the greatest message since Christ."[21]

The neighbor told Charlotte Dixon that she had recently accepted the Bahá'í Revelation and directed her to Ibrahim Kheiralla, who was giving lessons on the new religion. She attended his classes in Chicago, accepted the Faith, and returned to Maryland, believing herself to be the first Bahá'í there. She wrote to her brother and sister-in-law in New Jersey about the Bahá'í teachings and convinced them to travel to New York to take Kheiralla's classes. She also taught the Faith to at least six other relatives in Maryland, as well as her daughter and sister in Philadelphia.[22]

Dixon's sister, Evalina Brittingham, lived in Baltimore, and it may have been through her that the Faith was introduced into that city. Her name appears among the fifteen Baltimore Bahá'ís listed in the Supplication Book for the year 1898, while Charlotte Dixon's name appears in 1897. The Supplication Book records the names of those who completed Kheiralla's classes and who wrote letters of "supplication" to 'Abdu'l-Bahá confessing their faith. A checkmark placed after Dixon's name indicates that she received the Greatest Name from Kheiralla, his final initiation into Bahá'í membership. However, there are no check marks after the names of the Baltimoreans whose names appear in 1898.[23] Brittingham was an active Bahá'í in Baltimore during 1900.[24]

Edward Struven is also listed on the 1898 list. His parents were from Bremen, Germany, a city with close ties to Baltimore throughout the nineteenth century. Baltimore was the largest tobacco export harbor in America, and Bremen was the largest tobacco import harbor in Europe.[25] Edward lived with his parents, Rosa and Dietrich Struven, on Thames Street in Fells Point, until he left to study at Cornell University in Ithaca, New York. His younger brother, Howard Struven, learned to make things with his hands and built a greenhouse when he was only eleven years old.[26] Later, he worked as a shipbuilder and lost a finger in an accident.[27]

Edward Struven learned of the Bahá'í Faith in Ithaca from Lua Getsinger, an important Bahá'í teacher. He considered himself to be a Bahá'í immediately, and his brother accepted the Faith in 1899. The Struven brothers remained active Bahá'ís for many years.

Baltimore has always been a city of divided neighborhoods, separated by class, race, or ethnicity. In 1890, with a population of about 430,000, Baltimore was more than two-thirds white and about one-sixth black. About 12,000 foreign immigrants arrived between 1879 and 1900. Sixty percent of the new arrivals were German, between twenty and twenty-five percent were Irish; and Britons, Russians, Poles, and Austrians made up five percent each.[28]

The chief industries were canning and the production of men's clothing. Trade, transportation, and service industries were also important.[29] Industrialization brought more jobs, but many of them were in sweatshops full of low-paid workers, mostly recent immigrants and their children—Jews, Lithuanians, and Bohemians.[30] The sweatshops, particularly the coat tailors, were usually found in houses in East Baltimore.[31]

The Bahá'í community was comprised of people from a variety of backgrounds who lived in different parts of town. Several Bahá'ís lived in South Baltimore, which was inhabited mostly by working-class blacks and whites. William B. Stoffel, a railroad inspector, and Charles Lampe, a machinist, lived there. Catherine A. Anderson, also lived in South Baltimore near the Camden Station.[32]

Fells Point, in East Baltimore, was a docking area, as well as a home for the sweatshops, and many new immigrants were to be found there. Bahá'ís in Fells Point included Winnifred Watson, and Elizabeth Emmell, who worked in a lunchroom and was married to a musician. Nellie C. Babbit, who lived in Mount Clare in southwest Baltimore, was married to a painter. On the other side of town, in an area known as Goose Hill in west Baltimore, were Ann E. Stansbury and Mary E. Powell, the wife of a conductor. Later on, Howard Struven had a home in this area where he entertained 'Abdu'l-Bahá during his trip to Baltimore.[33]

Although the Bahá'ís of Baltimore were not in favor of any formal organization at this time, they held meetings and were in contact with 'Abdu'l-Bahá.[34] They were addressed by 'Abdu'l-Bahá in several Tablets (letters) written to America and mentioned in others. In one Tablet translated around 1900, 'Abdu'l-Bahá praised Mrs. Emmell and Mrs. Powell for having meetings in their homes.[35]

Although Baltimore was a large Bahá'í community during the first few years of the century, nearby Washington, D.C., appears to have been the center of more Bahá'í activity. Several prominent Bahá'í teachers lived there, including Lua Getsinger, Laura Barney, and Charles Mason Remey. 'Abdu'l-Bahá wrote often to the Bahá'ís of Washington and urged them to assist the Baltimore community. In one Tablet, addressed to Remey, he said that "every week, two or three of the Washington friends should go to Baltimore and endeavor to help and encourage the friends there."[36]

Whether or not such regular contact was established is unclear, but there is evidence that Baltimore Bahá'ís received some support from the Washington believers. When Sarah Jane Farmer was staying with Washington Bahá'ís and holding Bahá'í meetings there in 1901, for example, she also met with the Bahá'ís of Baltimore.[37]

At least one Baltimore Bahá'í, Frederick Woodward, moved to Washington, D.C., in 1902. 'Abdu'l-Bahá instructed him to "receive proofs from Mirza Abul Fazl [Mírzá Abú'l-Faḍl]," the famous Bahá'í scholar he had sent to America to instruct the believers in the teachings.[38]

Abú'l-Faḍl's visit to Baltimore received a great deal of press coverage. One article, in the *Baltimore Sun* of February 1, 1902, announced the visit and styled him the "High Priest of Behaism." The *Sun* reporter had visited Abú'l-Faḍl in Washington, where he was living at the time. In Baltimore, Abú'l-Faḍl spoke to over one hundred people at a public meeting held at 1041 North Eutaw Street, "the headquarters of the cult." Colonel Nathan Ward Fitzgerald, of Washington, D.C., conducted the evening lesson and quoted scripture to support the "Beha'i claim that Christ had returned." The article reported that Mírzá Asadu'lláh, another Persian teacher, and his interpreter, Niaz Effendi Kermani, had held a conference in Baltimore two weeks before. When the reporter saw them in Washington, they were speaking to two inquirers from Virginia.[39]

The article went on: "Washington has recently become a seat or center of the new religion in this country, and several prominent believers and teachers are now there. Among these is Mrs. Lua M. Getsinger, a well known resident of the capital." It recounted a short history of the Bahá'í Faith, starting with the Báb, and explained that the Bahá'ís use a "remarkable" method of "propaganda." First they agree with you that your religion had divine origins, but then they add that "every perfect man comes to the point where he is no longer in complete harmony with the surroundings which his forefathers prepared." The article reported that there were about seventy professed believers in Baltimore. However, the census reported only twenty-eight Bahá'ís in 1906, and that figure may be high.[40]

Transition and Organization: Pearle Doty, remembered by the Bahá'ís as the "leader" of the community in Baltimore in the early days, died sometime in 1903. 'Abdu'l-Bahá wrote a consoling Tablet to the Bahá'ís of Baltimore saying that they should not sigh in grief over her death: "I hope her noble son may seek the Path wherein his mother walked and may become better and more illustrious; nay, rather, the lights of his love may also take effect in his grandparents." He went on: "As to ye who are friends of that bird of the meadow of guidance, ye must, after her, have such unison, love, association and unity that it may make things better and more favorable than they were during her days."[41]

Another Tablet from 'Abdu'l-Bahá, addressed to Mason Remey, says: "Thou hast written concerning Baltimore. Convey respectful greetings on my behalf to Miss . . . and say, 'Exert thyself as much as thou canst in order that thou mayest illumine Baltimore, lay there an eternal foundation and ignite a lamp whose rays may shine through cycles and ages.'"[42]

In 1904, much of the city of Baltimore burned down in a great fire that lasted two days and spread over one hundred and forty acres. Something caught fire in a dry goods firm that stood between Hopkins Place and Liberty Street. Most of the reconstruction of the city was finished by 1906.[43] However, the disruption may have contributed to a decline in Bahá'í activity.

It was Edward Struven who lived in Catonsville in Baltimore County, outside the city limits, who held the Bahá'í community together after Doty's passing. The believers continued to meet in each other's homes, as before. They received correspondence from other Bahá'í communities, but avoided any organization and kept no records. They did, however, send Struven to Chicago as a representative for the first Bahai Temple Unity convention held March 22-23, 1909. That same year Struven reported to the *Bahai Bulletin* (published in New York) that: "Due to this lack of numbers and the many duties and family cares and ties of our brothers and sisters, our regular Tuesday meetings average between 6 and 9 in attendance. Then because of our proximity to Washington and principally for the reason that none of us have arisen to the actual work of teaching, our progress has been very slow."[44] In 1906, the Washington Bahá'í community paid the train fare for Baltimore Bahá'ís to travel to a lecture given by Lua Getsinger in Washington.[45]

When Struven returned from the Chicago convention, he brought a new spirit with him. It was then that the Baltimore community decided to "form an organization to help the Cause along, believing that as a body more work could be done, and correspondence attended to properly, besides keeping a record of meetings."[46] Acting as temporary chairman of the newly formed Baltimore "Assembly," as it was known, Edward Struven appointed a committee of four: Joseph Hope, Gertrude Stanwood, Howard Struven, and Maud Thompson, and Edwin B. Eardley as secretary, to frame a new constitution and by-laws for the community. The by-laws were approved on May 4, 1909. It was then decided to write to 'Abdu'l-Bahá telling him that Baltimore had organized in this way, and that it was intended as a temporary organization until the laws of the *Kitáb-i Aqdas* (Bahá'u'lláh's "Most Holy Book") were adopted. The letter expressed the community's appreciation that unity in Baltimore was achieved through the efforts of the Washington friends, whom 'Abdu'l-Bahá had instructed to support the Bahá'ís of Baltimore. They asked 'Abdu'l-Bahá to be Honored Head of their assembly and to select other honorary members if he so desired. The letter was signed by twenty-five believers.[47]

The by-laws called for spiritual meetings of the community to be opened by the members repeating the Greatest Name, followed by a prayer read by the chairman of the meeting. Unity feasts were to be held every nineteen days, and other meetings held on Tuesday evenings and Sunday afternoons. At the end of each meeting, those present would decide who would lead the next meeting. Parliamentary procedure was to be followed when business was conducted. Community officers were to be elected every six months, in March and September. All the meetings were to close either with the recitation of a passage from the Hidden Words of Bahá'u'lláh or a prayer, or both, and then all should repeat the Greatest Name. It seems that the community tried hard to prevent any one person from assuming leadership and that they adhered to the procedures they had adopted.[48]

A few weeks after organizing their group, the Baltimore community wrote to other Bahá'í assemblies to inform them of the names and addresses of their own officers. Believers from Washington continued to support activities in Baltimore. For example, Fanny Knobloch was a regular visitor who read lessons by 'Abdu'l-Bahá at her meetings. Pauline Hannen, another Washingtonian, frequently attended Holy Day celebrations and spoke at other Bahá'í gatherings. The community used booklets on the Bahá'í teachings written by Hooper Harris, Isabella Brittingham, and Paul Dealy.[49]

In 1909, Baltimore Bahá'ís included: Edward Struven, who now worked for the Maryland Viavi Company and lived in Catonsville; Margaret (Maud) E. Thompson, the wife of a clerk, who also lived in Catonsville; Estelle Lowndes was the associate manager of the Maryland Viavi Company. One of her neighbors, Anna McKhust, was also a Bahá'í. Gertrude Stanwood, an artist, and Sadie C. Ambrose, a dressmaker, lived only a few blocks from Pearle Doty's old home, and may have become Bahá'ís as a result of her efforts.

Other Bahá'ís were: Edwin H. Eardley, and his wife Louisa, and his sister, Beatrice (Eardley), all of whom lived together. The women ran a hat shop (L & B Eardley Company) from their home on O'Donnell Street in Highlandtown. Edwin Eardley worked as a draftsman and served as the secretary for the community, recording the minutes in a beautiful script. Charles W. Mann was a clerk living near Patterson Park, and Joseph W. Grant ran a grocery store in the same area. Charles L. Lampe was a pipefitter living in South Baltimore. Winnifred E. Watson was still in the community, employed as a buyer and living in fashionable Bolton Hill. Mary E. Lane lived there also. Joseph Hope, a stenographer, lived just east of the Jones Falls, near the Old Town Mall, formerly Jones Town, the oldest settled area of Baltimore.[50]

The Bahá'í community established three funds: The Kappes Fund, to send to Miss Lillian Kappes, a Bahá'í from northern New Jersey, living in Iran at the request of 'Abdu'l-Bahá to assist the Bahá'ís there; the Temple Fund; and a fund for traveling expenses (railway fare for visiting delegates) the disbursement of which was left to the treasurer's discretion.[51]

The Bahai Temple Unity was, at that time, the national executive committee elected by delegates from local Bahá'í communities. The raising of funds for the construction of the Temple was the subject of much local discussion. Various means were devised to raise money, such as the donation of a quilt made by a Baltimore Bahá'í. A room was donated by Miss Dorr in Washington where visiting Baltimore friends could pay a contribution, in lieu of rent, to be turned over to the Temple Fund. Also, Cincinnati sent twenty-five "blessing boxes" in which money could be put for various blessings "as they come to mind," like wishing wells. This money was also sent to the Temple Fund.[52]

Howard Struven was twenty-seven years old in 1909 when 'Abdu'l-Bahá asked him to travel around the world with Mason Remey to visit Bahá'í communities and teach the Faith. The Assembly in Baltimore gave him a letter, signed by twenty-three believers, to deliver to 'Abdu'l-Bahá when he arrived in 'Akká. He left on July 20, and the community invited Washington believers to a farewell gathering for him. About this trip, Shoghi Effendi later wrote: "Mason Remey voyaged to Russia and Persia, and later, with Howard Struven, circled, for the first time in Bahá'í history, the globe, visiting on his way the Hawaiian Islands, Japan, China, India and Burma."[53]

In early September, Howard Struven wrote from Denver to tell of teaching successes, and from San Francisco to say he would be sailing on November 17. Both he and Mason Remey sent letters with news of their trip which were published in *Star of the West* and *Bahai News*, and which Remey later compiled into a book. By February 1910, the two had visited Japan, China, and Singapore, and were teaching in Burma.[54] Struven later told some Baltimore Bahá'ís that he had prayed while Remey lectured, and that when they arrived in the Holy Land, 'Abdu'l-Bahá had embraced him and praised him for his efforts.[55]

'Abdu'l-Bahá gave Struven a letter to carry back with him to Baltimore. It read: "O Ye Merciful Assembly . . . He became the cause of the glory of the believers of Baltimore and imparted happiness and joy to the friends and maidservants of the Merciful. He sacrificed everything in the Path of the Kingdom and imparted life to many souls."[56]

Before leaving on his global trip, Struven had spoken enthusiastically about the Washington Sunday School, and urged the Bahá'ís to start a similar one in Baltimore. Other believers took up the task. Grace Mann offered her home at 1920 Orleans Street, and Maud Thompson offered her services in gathering children. Pauline Hannen also helped. One thousand invitation cards were printed up to advertise the Sunday School, which had its first meeting September 19, 1909. Five children attended, aged five to twelve, as well as one sixteen-year-old youth.

The community also planned a public meeting for which

a newspaper advertisement was prepared. The ad read: "Can the religions of the world be united? If so, on what basis? Free lecture by Howard MacNutt of Brooklyn, New York, Sunday afternoon, Oct. 24, 1909, 3 P.M., Florist Exchange Hall, Franklin and St. Paul Streets." Two hundred invitations were printed for Bahá'ís to give to friends who "would be likely to attend."

Also in 1909, the Assembly noted that Mrs. Carline, originally from Baltimore but now living in Washington, had reported on her "successful meeting of colored people held during the week."[57]

Howard Struven returned to Baltimore in September of 1910, and he and Edwin Eardley were elected as delegates to the Bahai Temple Unity convention held in Chicago. The Assembly supplied them with letters of credential, and Edwin left with a number 9 chalked on his suitcase.[58]

In 1910, the Bahá'í funds were again divided into categories: general use, the Temple Fund, a translator, and for the convention in Chicago. During the summer, a series of outdoor meetings were planned at the home of Rose Struven, Howard and Edward's mother, on Sundays. The speakers were to be Pauline Hannen, Mirza Ahmad Sohrab, Hooper Harris, Mons. H. Dreyfus, Joseph Hannen, Lua Getsinger, Ameen Ullah Fareed, Howard MacNutt, and Mason Remey.[59] All except Fareed were members of the Washington or New York communities.

One day in 1911, Eusibia Day Dorrida and her neighbor went shopping at a public food market in the city. For Dorrida, this day was to be a turning point in her life. When she returned home to unload her purchases, she discovered among her vegetables a little printed pamphlet, one inch square, announcing that the Lord of Ages had come and inviting her to a meeting. She went to the meeting and that same day accepted the truth of the Bahá'í Faith.[60]

In 1911, Edwin Eardley was the delegate to the Bahai Temple Unity convention.[61] Howard Struven was the alternate. While in the Chicago area, Eardley visited the Bahá'ís in Kenosha, Wisconsin.[62] The convention sent greetings to the Peace Congress which was held in Baltimore on May 6, 1911. In August, Howard Struven was sent as a delegate to the first annual conference of the Persian-American Educational Society in Washington, and was on the Hall Committee. His brother Edward attended also. Perhaps beginning to demonstrate its independence from Washington, the Assembly told Joseph and Pauline Hannen, who had been asked to come to Baltimore to conduct Bible studies, that they need not come any longer.

Both Struven brothers married in 1912. Edward married Estelle Lowndes, his former coworker, and they moved to her house on North Avenue. He was now employed as a mechanical engineer. Howard married Ruby (Hebe) Moore, Lua Getsinger's sister.

'Abdu'l-Bahá in Baltimore: Although 'Abdu'l-Bahá visited Baltimore only briefly, his stay there was extremely important to the Bahá'ís there, and anecdotes about his visit became an important element of the community's heritage. When the Bahá'ís heard of 'Abdu'l-Bahá's planned trip to America, they began to prepare for his arrival. Five days before his ship was to arrive in New York, the Baltimore Bahá'ís were expecting his imminent visit to their city. The *Baltimore Sun* announced: ABDUL BAHA COMING. The article stated that he would speak on Sunday, April 21, at the First Independent Christ's Church (Unitarian).[63] They must have been disappointed.

'Abdu'l-Bahá apparently made his plans day by day. When the believers realized that he would not be coming immediately to Baltimore, some of them traveled to New York to see him. According to an oral tradition in the community, Edward Struven rode the rails to get there. When he arrived, he was dishevelled from his trip. 'Abdu'l-Bahá had him sit down and offered him a bowl of Persian rice. When he finished eating it, 'Abdu'l-Bahá gave him another one.[64]

The biggest day in the life of the Baltimore Bahá'í community began at Camden Station on November 11, 1912, when, accompanied by a party of seven—including two translators and a secretary, 'Abdu'l-Bahá arrived at 11:00 a.m. from Washington, D.C. He went to the fashionable Hotel Rennert at Saratoga and Liberty Streets, where he met the press and took a short rest.

When he got to the Unitarian Chapel on Hamilton Street at noon, "the hall had been filled for a while before the hour set for his address, with followers, Johns Hopkins professors, and many business and professional men." 'Abdu'l-Bahá stood on the platform, "enveloped by a long black robe, with an oriental cap upon his head." The interpreter was Dr. Fareed, a Persian Bahá'í.[65]

The *News American* account of 'Abdu'l-Bahá's talk included a three paragraph summary which focused on the parts of the talk concerned with the unity of religion and the difference between its essentials and accidental aspects. However, his remarks in their entirety, as recorded by Jack Solomon, a stenographer, also specifically referred to the lecture he had delivered the day before to a largely Jewish audience in a Washington synogogue.[66]

The report in the *Sun* included illustrations depicting 'Abdu'l-Bahá in five different aspects, under the headline: PERSIAN PHILOSOPHER IN STRIKING POSES. The accompanying article was entitled: WOMEN KISS HIS HAND. Although the headlines seem rather sardonic, the contents of the article appear to be accurate. 'Abdu'l-Bahá was escorted from the train station to a waiting automobile by six people, surrounded by a crowd of well-dressed women. He greeted each of his followers as they were presented to him by his interpreter, Dr. Fareed. The article continues:

> At the lecture he wore a robe of black with triangular insert of light tan in front reaching from hem to neck.
>
> A striking-looking man of about 70 years, he's of average height, with a strong rugged face covered with a short white beard. His cheekbones are high, his eyes bright and flashing.

The article explained that ʻAbduʼl-Bahá was distinguishable from his companions in that he wore a white turban, while they wore black ones.

> The lecture was delivered in Persian in an impressive manner. His voice was low-pitched, but at times increased in volume. He spoke a few minutes before pausing to let the interpreter translate.
>
> He used frequent gestures, the favorite one being an inclusive swing of both arms to show the universality of the doctrine he propounded. He also frequently leaned over the reading desk and looked at his hearers.
>
> "God is one, we are his children, submerged in the sea of his kindness," was his theme. He said all divine religions had two parts, the essentials, which dealt with morality and ethical standards, and the non-essentials which change with time and place. In proof of this, he compared the teaching of Moses and Christ, both of whom he styled "His Holiness." He declared that the penal code announced by Moses was necessary for the Israelites travelling through the wilderness, but was repealed by Christ. Theological dogmas which, he said, had crept into religions were useless and should be forsaken. Those differences, he declared, were the cause of the world's bitterness and strife, and their elimination would bring about universal peace and love. . . .
>
> After the lecture he declared that the nations of the world looked to America as the leader in the world-wide movement and declared the situation of this country not being a rival of any other power and not considering colonization schemes or conquests, made it an ideal country to lead in the movement.

The article reported that there were six thousand Bahá'ís in the United States (almost certainly an exaggeration) and that there were a dozen or so believers in the doctrine in Baltimore.[67]

There is a story told by the Bahá'ís of Baltimore that relates how two Catholic priests had sneaked into the chapel during 'Abdu'l-Bahá's talk. They are supposed to have hidden themselves in a doorway behind the stage where he was speaking. As he lectured, so the story goes, 'Abdu'l-Bahá walked over and shut the door on the priests.

After the talk, 'Abdu'l-Bahá went to Howard and Hebe Struven's home, at 1800 Bentaloo Street in West Baltimore, a row house facing a courtyard. 'Abdu'l-Bahá stood in the courtyard with his arms outstretched and said, "Many friends have I in Baltimore."[68]

Maud Thompson missed 'Abdu'l-Bahá's talk because she had spent the morning walking out to a farm east of Baltimore to get a fresh, live chicken to make for lunch. When all the visitors were at the Struven house, Maud was in the kitchen busily preparing the meal. 'Abdu'l-Bahá called to her from the living room. She went into the living room and saw that everyone was seated, and no chairs were empty. She thought she saw a twinkle in 'Abdu'l-Bahá's eye when he pointed to the floor near his feet and motioned her to sit down there. Not only was Maud Thompson a stout woman, but she was tightly laced in a corset, and sitting on the floor was no small task.[69]

Ursula Shuman Moore was living with the Struvens in 1912, also serving as community treasurer.[70] In a letter to her sister, Louise Shuman Irani, composed the day after 'Abdu'l-Bahá's visit, she wrote:

> Yesterday, the 11th he came over to our house in Baltimore and had dinner with us at our table! Did you ever dream that this

would come to pass. He came to Baltimore about twelve o'clock and spoke at the Unitarian Church, and then they came out to our house and we had dinner for him. Many of the Washington believers came over too and many of the Baltimore believers came up. We had about 55 or 54 to feed. Had a grand chicken dinner, with rice and celery, peas, ice cream and cake, and vegetable soup. He said we had given him a *good* dinner, a *fine* dinner, and that he ate much. When I brought in the big platter of chicken and set it before him at the table he said, "Oh, chicken!" and seemed to be much pleased with it. He said everything was cooked well. We had him and the Persians in his party sit down first, 12 at the table, and served them, and then we had four relays and every body had something. They all seemed so glad to be there and enjoyed themselves so much. I was so glad for Mother could be near him and see him. I introduced Mother to him, and he took her hand and said, "Oh, your Mother!" and looked at her very kindly. I told him she had been and was sick, and that we asked that she might be well. He said "In Shalah." [God willing.] So I hope she will get well soon now. They did not stay very long, as they left on the (3 o'clock) train. It surely was a great privilege to have him in our house, and something that we will always remember.[71]

Consolidation, 1912-1934: Laura L. Drum was Baltimore's delegate to the sixth annual Bahai Temple Unity convention in 1914, although she was a member of the Washington Bahá'í community. She reported at the convention on Baltimore's response to the newly inaugurated system of monthly contributions to the Temple Fund.[72]

In 1919, when the American Bahá'ís received the Tablets of the Divine Plan from 'Abdu'l-Bahá, they learned that he had grouped the various states into regions. These Tablets charged the American Bahá'ís with spreading the Bahá'í Faith all over the country, and all over the world. Maryland, being a southern state, was part of the southern region, whose headquarters were established in Washington, D.C.[73]

After the passing of 'Abdu'l-Bahá, the Baltimore community wrote to the new Guardian, Shoghi Effendi, on March 31, 1922, expressing love, gratitude, and their willingness to serve the Faith.[74]

In 1926, there were thirteen adults and seven "junior" Bahá'ís in Baltimore.[75] They met steadily in one or two of the believers' homes until they decided to rent Maccabees Hall at 522 Park Avenue, for ten dollars a month. Their meetings were open to "strangers" and believers. Among their visitors was at least one black man, John Chase.[76]

Louis Gregory, a prominent black Bahá'í teacher, spent a week in Baltimore in 1927, from January 11 to 17. He finished up his visit at Morgan College, a black institution, where he spoke to a group of black ministers.[77] It was around this time that Aleen Lock, in Washington, D.C., made it known that she thought black Bahá'ís would be happier if they organized their own separate Nineteen-Day Feasts. There were some blacks who either withdrew from the Faith or hesitated to join it because of this. The repercussions were felt years later in Baltimore. In the 1950s, the president of Morgan College, which had been established as a school for blacks, told a friend who was investigating the Bahá'í teachings that his wife had been interested during the 1920s, but had changed her mind when she heard about these remarks in the Washington community.[78]

Several public meetings were held in 1930. On January 26, Albert Vail, a Bahá'í teacher who was also a Unitarian minister, spoke to some two hundred people at the First Unitarian Church on the topic "What is the Kingdom of God?" On March 19, Ali Kuli Khan, a well-known Persian Bahá'í teacher, visited the Assembly and spoke on the relation of the Bahá'í Faith to other religions. Meetings and study classes usually featured readings from recent translations of the Bahá'í scriptures, letters from the Guardian, reports of Bahá'ís who had attended conferences, and notes of travelers who had been to the Holy Land. Sometimes the Bahá'ís studied biblical proofs, or held classes on public speaking techniques.[79]

The community followed set procedures for all of its meetings, following agendas that were similar to the order of church services. A "Program for a Public Meeting" and a "Program for the Spiritual Board Meeting" were kept in the back of the Baltimore Minute Book, and seem to have been established in 1929. The public meeting was to open with a hymn, the Invocation found on page 3 of the blue Bahá'í prayer book, then another hymn. There followed a short history of the Cause, a prayer for Guidance (page 37 of the blue prayer book), a lecture, and then questions. After that came announcements of future public meetings and a healing prayer (from page 28 of the prayer book). The meetings closed with the Benediction, a widely used Bahá'í song.[80]

The Spiritual Board meetings were supposed to open with the prayer on page 99 of the blue *Bahá'í World* volume. Then the minutes were to be read, followed by committee reports and the evening prayer on page 23 of the Bahá'í prayer book. This was followed by new business, a prayer for protection (page 45) and a healing prayer (page 28). During the 1930s, many of the meetings were held in East Baltimore, perhaps at the home of the Mann family or of Beatrice Eardley.

In February of 1931, during the Great Depression, the Baltimore Assembly took an audacious step: They took out a bank loan in order to pay for Howard Colby Ives to come on a teaching trip to their community. He conducted "deepening" classes for the Bahá'ís and probably was invited to their homes for private gatherings with friends and relatives.[81] Bahá'í classes continued to be held twice a week in 1932, on various Bahá'í books, including *Some Answered Questions, Bahá'u'lláh and the New Era, The Dawn-Breakers*, and the *Kitáb-i-Íqán*. These efforts appear to have been intended to prepare the

SIXTH ANNUAL BAHÁ'Í WORLD YOUTH SYMPOSIUM

c. 1930. Standing (l. to r.): Unknown, Hilda Seidman, Bill Dorrida, Birdie Eardley, Lois Revell, Maude Thompson Amendt, Raymond Rouse, Anne Hatter, Mrs. Rouse, unknown, Harrison Langrell, Mildred Elmer. Seated (l. to r.): Jessie Mann Stallings, Mildred Hipsley Long.

community for reorganization in accordance with new guidelines from the National Spiritual Assembly. This reorganization was taking place in a number of Bahá'í communities at about this time.

The new Assembly elected in April of 1932 consisted of seven women and two men. Local committees, comprised of one or two Bahá'ís each, were formed to oversee study classes, Feasts and publicity, and attendance. On April 28, Ives prepared a report for the National Convention on the progress the Baltimore community had made since his stay there.[82] On May 3, 1932, there were then fifteen Bahá'ís in the city.

The Assembly began to require that new believers study the Will and Testament of 'Abdu'l-Bahá and *Bahá'u'lláh and the New Era* and acknowledge their understanding and complete acceptance of the tenets of the Bahá'í Faith. This was in compliance with new procedures suggested by the National Spiritual Assembly. For the first time, on February 1, 1933, the local Spiritual Assembly of Baltimore voted on and recorded the enrollment of a new member: It was Hazel Clarke Langrall, whose mother had taken her to Pearle Doty for healing when she was a baby, back in 1898.[83]

Langrall had serious health problems and had been told by her doctors that she only had a brief time left to live. This was the second major health crisis in her life, and it spurred her on a religious quest that would lead her to the Bahá'ís again. She learned of the Faith through Eusibia Dorrida, her neighbor on the 2800 block of Allendale Street, where Marguerite Dorrida Hipsley also lived.[84] At the time she entered the Faith, she did not know that her mother had taken her to a Bahá'í for healing when she was an infant. When she learned about the incident, she liked to say that she had been a Bahá'í all her life.[85]

Marguerite Dorrida Hipsley, whose mother had been a Bahá'í since 1911, had always been a strong-minded person.

She was a women's suffrage activist and an advocate of women's rights. She was a member of the Methodist Church before becoming a Bahá'í, but she was dissatisfied with it. Besides her mother, her sister and brother were all Bahá'ís, and they posed questions to her that she would carry to her minister. Once she asked him about the return of Christ. The minister replied, "Oh, he isn't going to come in our day."

"But he has to come in *somebody's* day! Why not our day?" Hipsley exclaimed. When the minister could not provide a satisfactory answer, she left his church and was soon actively involved in the Bahá'í community.[86]

The diversity of the Bahá'í community increased during the 1930s. Ann Hatter, a descendant of Menno Simon, founder of the Mennonites, and Paul Sadowitz, a Jewish man who had been interested in the Faith since the 1920s, became Bahá'ís. The community also developed good relations with the Theosophists and the World Federalists.[87]

Grace Mann was appointed by the Baltimore Assembly as a committee of one in March of 1933, to order sixty copies of *The Goal of a New World Order*, the Guardian's recent letter to the Bahá'ís of America. The letter was to be made known to every believer. The number of copies purchased suggests that there were many persons in Baltimore who considered themselves Bahá'ís, or who had at one time been affiliated with the Faith, but who were not included on the membership list under the new and stricter standards that had been adopted in 1932.

The year 1933 was the first for which minutes were recorded in Baltimore during the summer months. Previously, the Assembly had only met from September through spring. A youth committee was formed during this year. Further, the Assembly had a stamp made which read: "This is authentic Bahá'í literature" which they stamped in all Bahá'í books, including those they donated to libraries. An attempt was made to have the public library in Baltimore file Bahá'í materials under the heading "Bahá'í Faith," rather than under "Bahaism."[88]

Much of the effort of the community was directed towards the recruitment of new believers. In March 1934, the Bahá'ís rented a regular hall to be used for lectures and as a reading room. It was located on North Avenue, near St. Paul Street. The community furnished it with a new leather living-room suite and lamps. They placed a painted sign in the window which read: "Bahá'í Centre and Reading Room, open from 11 to 4 P.M. excepting Saturday and Sunday" and held public meetings about every other month in an effort to reach the public. Visitors were reported at the meetings, some of whom seemed interested. The official community membership list was sixteen strong.[89]

Martha Root, the internationally known Bahá'í teacher, visited Baltimore in 1936, and she stayed at the YMCA. The title of her lecture at the University Club at 800 Charles Street was "My World Travels in the Interest of Universal Peace."[86]

Mildred Elmer took a trip to Chicago to visit her relatives there and attend the World's Fair in 1936. While there, she saw the Bahá'í Temple under construction in Wilmette. Returning to Baltimore, she found that her brother was acquainted with the Bahá'ís. He took her to a fireside (an informal introductory meeting) at the home of Hazel Langrall on a Friday evening. She continued to attend firesides every Friday for a few years. At last, she wrote a letter to the Assembly in Baltimore saying that she would like to become a Bahá'í. On the evening that the Assembly met to consider her enrollment, Mildred nervously waited outside the room, wondering what the outcome would be. She was accepted into the community, and two years later she was elected to the Assembly.[91]

BALTIMORE BAHÁ'Í CENTER
is seen behind Mildred Elmer (l.) and Marguerite Dorrida Hipsley.

Hazel Langrall's son, Clarke, declared his acceptance of
the Bahá'í Faith in 1940, at the age of sixteen. He had spent
much time at Green Acre Bahá'í School, where he had worked
at Stanwood Cobb's camp. He was one of only about six Bahá'í
youth on the entire East Coast.[92]

Also in 1940, the Baltimore Assembly decided to find a
larger Bahá'í Center in a more central location. Mildred Elmer
and Clarence Percival located a site at 527 North Charles
Street, on the first floor of a fashionable brownstone building. Volunteers renovated the flat that became the new Center.[93]

A Jewish woman, Faith Amberg, became a Bahá'í in 1942.
She had been a Bahá'í for only a year or two when she died,
leaving her estate—two buildings on Gwynn Oak Avenue
and a large sum of money—to the Bahá'í community. Gwynn
Oak was a broad, tree-lined street, and the two houses were
only a few blocks from the county line, across which was the
exclusively white Woodlawn area.[94] In the 1940s, the area
where Amberg lived was predominantly Jewish.

In order to inherit the estate, the local Spiritual Assembly of Baltimore had to incorporate, and it did so in 1945. As
stipulated in Amberg's will, a sum of money was sent to the
Guardian of the Faith to be used for the completion of the
Shrine of the Báb in Israel. The Guardian wrote to the community in his own hand, thanking them. He said: "Your responsibilities are great as you now are more independent
than most Bahá'í communities from a financial point of
view."[95] The Assembly also gave two thousand dollars to the
Green Acre Maintenance Committee, probably from the
Amberg estate.[96]

Growth and Diversity, 1934 to the present: Since slavery times,
Baltimore had been a segregated city. Jim Crow laws adopted
after the Civil War excluded blacks from public facilities that
whites used and segregated the schools, jobs, stores, restau-

rants and neighborhoods. Albert James became a Bahá'í in 1934, in Tennessee and moved to Baltimore in 1937, where he remained the only black Bahá'í until after World War II. Roland Mann, a Bahá'í who lived in all-white Highlandtown, helped James find a job.[97]

Still it was very difficult for the Baltimore Bahá'ís to make contact with the black community. In February of 1936, they had made an effort to do so by sponsoring an illustrated lecture on the Bahá'í Temple, entitled "The Temple of Light," at Morgan College, and also at the Enoch Pratt Free Library.[98] Fred Amendt and Maud (Thompson) Amendt made aggressive efforts to teach the Faith to African-American people. They also lived in Highlandtown, on Kenwood Avenue.[99]

It was not until after the war, however, that the strict barriers of race and class began to weaken. More diverse types of people entered the Bahá'í community, which until then had been fairly homogeneous. The early believers were a closely knit group, like a family, still "enamoured with 'Abdu'l-Bahá—thrilled with having met him. . . . The Administration was important, but not as important as later on."[100]

During the 1950s, a few Persian Bahá'ís came to study in Baltimore, especially at Johns Hopkins University. There were also some black women, nurses, who came into the Faith. A women with an orthodox Jewish background, Betty Feldman, moved into Baltimore County, and she was the only Bahá'í there during this period.[101]

In the summer of 1958, Eugene Byrd, a dentist who practiced in Baltimore, started out for Chicago with his wife. They stopped in Pittsburgh on the way to pick up their sons who had gone to the YMCA camp there that summer, because the one in Baltimore was for whites only. When the family arrived in Chicago, they found that their motel reservations would not be honored because they were black. Eventually, they found accommodations at the Sheridan Hotel in Evanston. Their Chicago friend, Herbie Nipson, the executive editor of *Ebony* magazine, suggested that they drive up to visit the newly completed Bahá'í House of Worship in Wilmette, not far from where they were staying.[102]

Back in Baltimore the Byrd family continued to investigate the Faith. They regularly attended Friday night firesides at the home of Alma Heise, who lived in an all-white neighborhood in Baltimore where blacks might be arrested if found on the streets after dark. After a year and a half, they entered the Faith.[103]

The Friday fireside conducted by Alma Heise and Bill Burgess resulted in seven enrollments in 1956, four in the city of Baltimore and three outside. Heise and Burgess were the only Bahá'ís present, and conducted the fireside as a team inviting two or three friends to their gathering every Friday night. Sometimes seekers heard of the meetings on their own and asked to be invited. The firesides were very informal occasions. The Bahá'ís would prepare in advance the point that they wanted to cover, but their delivery was conversational, seemingly spontaneous, and not overly serious.

In 1960, the first functioning Bahá'í group was formed in Baltimore County. Two years later, an Assembly was elected in the county, with Howard Struven as one of its members. The county Assembly was active and helped organize Bahá'í events in the city.

In 1963, the Supreme Court overturned state laws that sanctioned racial discrimination. The *Baltimore Sun* ran a series of articles interviewing prominent Americans on their views on race and prejudice. Taking advantage of the opportunity, the Baltimore Bahá'ís organized a proclamation week, with four public meetings and publicity on radio, on television, and in the newspapers. This resulted in much interest in the Faith.[104]

The Byrds attended the National Bahá'í Convention in Wilmette, as delegates in 1963. They were planning to participate in Martin Luther King's march on Selma, Alabama, in protest of racial segregation. They found a group of Bahá'ís at the convention who also intended to join the march, but they were waiting for the approval of the National Spiritual Assembly before going ahead. At the last minute, the National Assembly gave its blessing, and the Byrds participated in the march.[105]

The Bahá'ís of the county and city of Baltimore jointly secured the first official proclamation of World Peace Day as the third Sunday in September, designated by the mayor. Under the direction of the National Spiritual Assembly, the communities planned a meeting to commemorate World Peace Day on September 15, 1963. Nine hundred people attended the event that evening at the Lyric Opera House in Baltimore, despite a heavy rainstorm. The audience was both black and white, with slightly more blacks than whites in attendance.[106]

On that same day, in the afternoon, four black children had been killed in a racially motivated church bombing incident in Birmingham, Alabama. Robert Quigley, then vice-chairman of the National Spiritual Assembly, set the tone of the meeting when he asked the audience to silently remember the slain children. McHenry Boatwright, an eminent African-American baritone, sang the Bahá'í prayer "Blessed Is the Spot," "prolonging the closing phrases, repeating one several times, as he felt the hearts of his listeners drawn to the prayer."[107] Lerone Bennett, Jr., senior editor of *Ebony* magazine spoke at the meeting. Although he was not a Bahá'í, he quoted from Shoghi Effendi's *Advent of Divine Justice* and the Bahá'í book *Race and Man*. In an eloquent speech, he acknowledged that the Bahá'í Faith proclaimed the brotherhood of all races. William Sears, the Bahá'í Hand of the Cause, told the history of the Faith and the Bahá'í teachings of racial unity. Boatwright returned to the stage and accompanied himself at the piano for the Negro spiritual "He's Got the Whole World in His Hands." The audience was moved to tears.[108] During the week after the program, which attracted wide media attention, some fifteen hundred phone calls were received at the Baltimore Bahá'í Center.[109]

The ethnic composition of the Gwynn Oak Avenue area, where the Bahá'í Center was located, changed from predominantly Jewish to black during the 1960s. Of the two buildings left by the Amberg estate, one had to be sold to raise money to renovate the other which began to serve as the Bahá'í Center. A Bahá'í couple, Bill and Martha Dorrida, lived there as caretakers and acted as the social epicenter of the community. Martha Dorrida died in 1966, and Bill (later known to many Bahá'ís as Uncle Billy) moved in with the Radpour family in Baltimore County. Some of the other early Baltimore Bahá'ís passed away during the 1960s.

Two days after the assassination of Martin Luther King, on April 6, 1968, riots began in Baltimore that lasted for three days and resulted in 6 deaths, at least 300 injuries, 420 fires, and 350 looted stores.[110] Much of the destruction took place around Pennsylvania Avenue and Gay Street, and the riots discouraged suburban shoppers from coming into the city.

The focus of Bahá'í activity in the Baltimore area also moved outside the city. Fred Lee, a Bahá'í in the county, was much involved with youth activities. In the early 1960s, he had urged the Baltimore City Assembly to sponsor a Boy Scout Troop, and in 1964, he hosted a youth conference on his farm, with 123 youth camping out for the weekend. During the late 1960s, youth began entering the Bahá'í Faith in the Baltimore area in significant numbers.

The Baltimore County Bahá'ís organized a booth at the

SOME BALTIMORE BAHÁ'ÍS

who attended the St. Louis Bahá'í Conference, 1975. Top row, l. to r.: Kiser Barnes, Pamela Prosser, Michael King, Gordon Jacky, Debbie King (with baby). Third row, l. to r.: Parvis Ighani, Anne Z. Ighani, Barbara Maschal, Marlene Jacky, Betty S. Feldman. Second row: W. DuBois Johnson, Mabel L. Byrd, Eugene D. Byrd, Kathyrn A. Cleveland. Front row: Danny Prosser, Jacky child (in back), Angela Prosser (in front), Matthew Maschal, Mildred Elmer, Marguerite D. Hipsley.

Maryland State Fair in Timonium in September 1968, and again in 1969. Called "It Works," the booth was built of acrylic, with panels and counters. It attracted youth from upper-middle-class Dulaney High School, who began attending firesides.[111] The firesides were so successful that declarations of faith became a regular feature every Friday evening. Young people began to enroll in the Faith so regularly that the Bahá'ís would consider the fireside a failure if there were no enrollments one week.[112]

The county community organized Sunday morning study classes to teach the new youth more about the Bahá'í Faith and actively worked to get them involved in Bahá'í activities. There were overnight conferences in Bahá'í homes, and a great deal of energy was expended to make sure that all youth could attend. Many of the youth became pioneers (missionaries) for the Faith in Mexico, Finland, the Caribbean Islands, and other places., and some were among the first mass teachers in the Carolinas.[113] A strong Bahá'í Club developed at Towson State University.

The Baltimore County Assembly incorporated in 1970, and three years later the National Spiritual Assembly authorized the division of the county into east and west communties. Baltimore County West incorporated in 1974. Later, the Baltimore County East community split again, forming the Cockeysville Bahá'í community, which considered itself the successor of the original Baltimore County Assembly. The Baltimore County Central Assembly did not incorporate until 1986. The east County split left many believers isolated, and the two new communities did not agree on their boundary for some time. Both communities experienced a decline in activities.

The Bahá'í community in the city of Baltimore remained weaker than the communities in the county, and more transient. Bahá'í college students, sometimes four or five at a

time, would live in Baltimore while going to school. They
were actively involved in the Bahá'í community while they
were in the city, but then would move on after their studies
were over.

In 1974, soon after installing cast iron bars on the win-
dows of the Bahá'í Center for security, the local Assembly was
held up at gunpoint while conducting a late-night meeting.

After the Islamic Revolution in Iran in 1979, there was
an influx of Persian Bahá'ís. The first to arrive were high
school and college students. Later, their parents and other
relatives joined them as refugees from the brutal persecution
of Bahá'ís in Iran. The older generation, unable to pursue
their careers, knew little English and had little money. They
needed the help of the Bahá'í community to get settled.

By the end of the 1980s, there were four local Spiritual
Assemblies in the Baltimore metropolitan area. Each of these
Bahá'í communities contained a widely diverse ethnic mix.
The local Assembly in Baltimore was made up of four Per-
sians, three blacks, and two whites. There were about sev-
enty believers on the rolls in the city, but most were inactive.
The Bahá'ís were largely middle class. The Baltimore County
Central Bahá'í community had achieved a good level of unity
and participation. Most of the Bahá'ís were Persian, with
Persians outnumbering Americans on the Assembly. The west
County community had about thirty believers—including
seven Persians and seven African-Americans—and held consistent proclamation activities. The Cockeysville Assembly
was revived in 1987, with a majority of Persians in the community, many of whom were refugees.

The Bahá'í community of the Baltimore area has a long
history which reaches back to 'Abdu'l-Bahá's visit to
America, and before. Originally closely tied to the Washington, D.C. Bahá'í community, it developed its independence and gave birth to new Bahá'í communities in outly-

ing areas. It stands today as an example of racial and cultural unity that is unusal in Baltimore.

NOTES

1. Interview with Clarke Langrall, December 1987, conducted by the author.

2. *Baltimore City Directory,* 1893 (Baltimore: R. L. Polk and Co., 1893). United States Census, Baltimore. Index to the 1860 Federal Population Census of Ohio, vol. 1, p. 64.

3. Meredith Janvier, *Baltimore in the Eighties and Nineties* (Baltimore: H. G. Roebuck and Son, 1933) pp. 169-71.

4. Ethan Allen Doty, *The Doty-Doten Family in America* (Brooklyn, NY: n.p., 1897) p. 819.

5. *Baltimore City Directory,* 1894 and 1895.

6. United States Census, 1900.

7. Doty, *The Doty-Doten Family,* p. 837.

8. *Baltimore City Directory,* 1898.

9. *Baltimore City Directory,* 1898.

10. Janvier, *Baltimore,* pp. 169-171.

11. *Baltimore City Directory,* 1898, p. 2015.

12. Ibid., p. 2014.

13. Interview with Clarke Langrall.

14. *Baltimore City Directory,* 1899.

15. Ibid., 1900, 1901, 1902, and 1903.

16. "List of Persons to be Notified Concerning the Classes," Ibrahim Kheiralla papers, in private hands.

17. "Supplication Book—Baltimore," and "Additional Names for the New York List." Albert Windust papers. National Bahá'í Archives, Wilmette, Illinois.

18. I am grateful to Richard Hollinger for providing this information. Mr. Hollinger has conducted research on the class origins of the Bahá'ís: A list of persons who signed a petition sent to 'Abdu'l-Bahá in 1901 (Thornton Chase Papers, National Bahá'í Archives) includes the names of 53 from Baltimore. After collating this list, with the names of Baltimore Bahá'ís on the "Supplication Lists—Baltimore," it was possible to identify the occupations of eighteen persons using

the *Baltimore City Directory* for 1900. The "List of Persons to be Notified Concerning the Classes" was used to identify the addresses of some of those on the other lists. In some cases there were no listings for Bahá'í women, but their husbands were listed. In these cases, the husband's occupations were used, because these would have determined the social status of the women. In several instances, there was more than one person of the same name listed in the directory, and no address could be located to identify the specific person who was the Bahá'í. In these cases, the occupations could not be used.

The occupations were as follows: bookkeeper, carpenter, clerk, conductor, confectioner, draftsman, inspector, laborer, machinist, painter, sailmaker, seamstress, student, teacher (3), teamster, and waitress. The fact that the names of most of the Bahá'ís could not be found in the city directory, however, suggests that a significant percentage may have been unskilled laborers, who would not have been likely to have a listing.

19. In 1909, a letter sent to 'Abdu'l-Bahá from Baltimore was signed by twenty-five believers. This is less than half the number who signed the petition to him in 1901. (Minutes, April 1909, pp. 2-9. Baltimore Bahá'í Archives.)

20. Robert Stockman, *The Bahá'í Faith in America: Origins, 1892-1900* (Wilmette, Ill.: Bahá'í Publishing Trust, 1985) p. 119 quoting Charlotte E. Brittingham Dixon, "How I Became a Believer and Was Given the Bahai Revelation by and through Visions," National Bahá'í Archives.

21. Ibid.

22. Ibid. p. 129.

23. "Supplication Book—Baltimore."

24. "Minutes of the Bahá'ís of Baltimore City," March 29, 1910, p. 23. National Bahá'í Archives. (Hereafter, Minutes, Baltimore)

25. Dieter Cunz, *The Maryland Germans* (Princeton University Press, 1948) p. 236.

26. *Baltimore News American*, April 23, 1974.

27. Interview with Nancy Lee, conducted by the author in September 1987.

28. Carl Bode, *Maryland* (New York: W. W. Morton and Co., 1978) p. 152-53.

29. Ibid., p. 153.

30. Ibid., p. 154.

31. *Third Annual Report of the Bureau of Industrial Statistics of Maryland, 1894* (Baltimore: Sun Book and Job Printing Office, 1895) p. 80.

32. *Baltimore City Directory*, 1898, 1899, and 1900.

33. *Baltimore City Directory*, 1898 and 1900.

34. Page one of the Minute Book (April 27, 1909) reads: "Previous to the organization of the Bahá'ís of Baltimore, it was the custom to hold meetings at any of the believers' homes, but since the convention held in Chicago, March 22-23, 1909, it was thought best to form an organization, believing that as a body, more work could be done . . .

"In view of the fact that for years, the believers were not in favor of any order whatever, this decision [i.e. to organize] was reached in perfect harmony."

35. *Tablets of Abdul Baha Abbas* (Chicago: Bahai Publishing Society, 1915) vol. 2, pp. 444-45. Names from Windust notes.

36. *Tablets,* vol. 2, p. 459.

37. Sarah Jane Farmer diary, entries for February-March 1901. Sarah Jane Farmer Papers. National Bahá'í Archives. I am grateful to Richard Hollinger for this information.

38. *Tablets,* vol. 2, p. 250.

39. *Baltimore Sun*, February 1, 1902, p. 7

40. Ibid.

41. *Tablets*, p. 444 (translated July 9, 1905).

42. Ibid., p. 469.

43. *Baltimore Magazine*, October 1987, p. 53.

44. *Bahai Bulletin*, 1909.

45. Financial Statement for December 1906. Records of the Spiritual Assembly of the Bahá'ís of Washington, D.C. Washington, D.C., Bahá'í Archives. I am grateful to Richard Hollinger for this information.

46. Minutes, Baltimore, April 1909, p. 1.

47. Ibid., May 1909, pp. 2-9.

48. Ibid, pp. 3-5.

49. Ibid.

50. *Baltimore City Directory*, 1909.

51. Minutes, Baltimore, May 1909, p. 7.

52. Ibid., June 8, 1909, p. 12; July 6, 1909, p. 14.

53. Shoghi Effendi, *God Passes By* (Wilmette, Ill.: Bahá'í Publishing Trust, 1944) p. 261.

54. *Star of the West*, vol. 1 (1910) no. 2, p. 2.

55. Interview with Fred Lee, conducted by the author in September 1987.

56. *Star of the West*, vol. 1 (1910) no. 9, p. 1 (translated June 17, 1910).

57. Minutes, Baltimore, October 1909.

58. Minutes, Baltimore, 1911, p. 44.

59. *Star of the West*, vol. 1 (1910) no. 6, p. 12.

60. Interview with Mildred Elmer, conducted by the author in September 1987. Minutes, Baltimore, 1911, p. 44.

61. *Star of the West*, vol. 2 (1911) no. 4, p. 3.

62. Ibid., p. 15.

63. *Baltimore Sun*, April 6, 1912.

64. Interview with Mildred Elmer, conducted by the author on January 29, 1988.

65. *Baltimore News American*, November 12, 1912, p. 13.

66. "Talk of 'Abdu'l-Bahá" (ms.), Dorrida Library, Baltimore County.

67. *Baltimore Sun*, November 12, 1912, p. 9.

68. Interview with Mildred Elmer, conducted by the author in September 1987.

69. Interview with Albert James, conducted by the author in February 1988.

70. *Star of the West*, vol. 4 (1913) no. 3, p. 52.

71. Quoted in Allison Vaccaro and Edward E. Bartlett, "'Abdu'l-Bahá in Baltimore," *Bahá'í News* (February 1982) pp. 3-4.

72. *Star of the West*, vol. 4 (1913) no. 13, p. 52.

73. Ibid., vol. 7 (1916) no. 12, p. 113.

74. Minutes, Baltimore, Baltimore Collection. National Bahá'í Archives.

75. Minute Book, pp. 150-51.

76. Ibid., 1926, p. 56; ibid., 1931.

77. Ibid., January 12, 1930, p. 71.

78. Interview with Eugene Byrd, conducted by the author in January 1987.

79. This information was gleaned from the Baltimore Minute Book for the years 1930-32.

80. Baltimore Minute Book, p. 143.

81. Minutes, Baltimore, 1931, pp. 101-102.

82. Ibid., April 28, 1932, p. 114.

83. Ibid., February 1, 1933, pp. 122-23.

84. Interview with Clarke Langrall, conducted by the author in December 1987. *Baltimore City Directory*, 1930-1935.

85. Interview with Mildred Elmer, conducted by the author in September 1987.

86. Interview with Penny Trusty, conducted by the author in January 1987.

87. Interview with Albert James, conducted by the author in January 1988.

88. Minutes, Baltimore, February 1933, pp. 121-22.

89. Ibid., March 1934.

90. *Baltimore Sun* article, n.d. Interview with Penny Trusty, conducted by the author in January 1987. *The Bahá'í World*, vol. 7, p. 89.

91. Interview with Mildred Elmer, conducted by the author in September 1987.

92. Interview with Clarke Langrall.

93. Interview with Mildred Elmer.

94. Gwynn Oak Park in Woodlawn was rocked by race riots in 1963.

95. Shoghi Effendi to Baltimore Bahá'í community, February 28, 1946, Baltimore Bahá'í Archives.

96. *Bahá'í News* (1947) no. 196, p. 1.

97. Interview with Albert James, conducted by the author in January 1988.

98. *Bahá'í News*, vol. 9 (1936) p. 4. Morgan State College (now University) was established as part of a system of higher education in Maryland for African-Americans.

99. Interview with Albert James, conducted by the author in November 1987.

100. Interview with Mildred Elmer, September 1987.

101. Interview with Betty Feldman, conducted by the author in September 1987.

102. Interview with Eugene Byrd, conducted by the author in January 1988.

103. Ibid.

104. *Bahá'í News* (1963) no. 386, p. 12.

105. Interview with Eugene Byrd.

106. *Bahá'í News* (1963) no. 386, p. 12.

107. Ibid.

108. Ibid.

109. Ibid.

110. Duane Hickman, "One Hot Fourth of July," *Baltimore Magazine* (October 1987) p. 106.

111. Interview with Lynn Fremd, conducted by the author in December 1987.

112. Interview with Fred Lee, conducted by the author in September 1987.

113. Interview with Lynn Fremd.

'ABDU'L-BAHÁ IN ENGLAND
at the Clifton Guest House, Bristol, September 1911.

THE DEVELOPMENT AND INFLUENCE OF THE BAHÁ'Í ADMINISTRATIVE ORDER IN GREAT BRITAIN, 1914-1950

by Phillip R. Smith

As I have argued elsewhere, the Bahá'í Faith began in Great Britain not as an independent religion, but as a millenarian movement that sought to hasten the approach of the coming millennium by spreading the ideas of racial, religious, and global unity that had been proclaimed by Bahá'u'lláh.[1] The first Bahá'ís formed a loose inclusive movement with no requirements for membership, no official organization, and no distinctive ritual practices. Many remained practicing and active members of Christian churches or cultic groups. Often they had little contact with other Bahá'ís. What united these individuals was a belief in the coming millennium and a devotion to the person of 'Abdu'l-Bahá.

The life of millenarian movements is generally short. For most, the crisis comes when the promised millennium fails to arrive, or when their leaders die or lose charisma. The Bahá'í Movement in Great Britain managed to avoid dissolution on the death of its charismatic leader by transforming itself into a formal religion. The principal instrument of this transformation was the development of an effective administrative structure. This structure served the dual function of binding

153

LADY BLOMFIELD

together the movement's members, once their charismatic focus had been removed, and of allowing religious beliefs and practices to become standardized. The purpose of this essay is to trace the development of this administrative structure among the British Bahá'ís and to show how this structure enabled the inclusive Bahá'í Movement to be transformed into the exclusive Bahá'í Faith.

The Early Years. The first Bahá'ís in Britain were held together by their admiration for the teachings and personality of 'Abdu'l-Bahá. They had no formal organization: they simply met together as friends to discuss the Bahá'í teachings. As in any social group, there were dominant personalities. These persons assumed leadership, rather than being given it officially; and their authority was informal.

The dominant personality and unofficial leader of the British Bahá'ís throughout the early years was undoubtedly Ethel Rosenberg. Rosenberg was the first Englishwoman to become a Bahá'í in her native land, but her position did not stem solely from this fact. She made two visits, in 1901 and 1904, to the Holy Land. There she conversed at length with 'Abdu'l-Bahá and with members of his family. She also learned Persian, and so she was able to read and help with the translation of Bahá'í scriptures. This made her an invaluable source of information to the British Bahá'ís at a time when very little Bahá'í literature was published. She was also very clearly trusted by 'Abdu'l-Bahá, who sent her on important teaching missions to the United States and to France.

There were, of course, other individuals who assumed prominent positions in the early community. Mary Virginia Thornburgh-Cropper was the first avowed Bahá'í to reside in the British Isles and the person who had introduced Ethel Rosenberg to Bahaism.[2] When Lady Blomfield became a Bahá'í in 1907, her wealth and social status automatically guaranteed her prominence. Eric Hammond, whose book of Bahá'í scripture and history was published in 1909, was probably the leading Bahá'í man of the period.

These leading personalities, along with a few others, related to one another in an informal way. They met in one another's homes to study; and later they hired halls to hold public meetings. They published books and pamphlets about the Bahá'í Cause. However, these were probably the collective actions of individuals, rather than the result of corporate decisions. There is no evidence of any formal organization. These early Bahá'í activities were limited to London.

Eventually, there developed a small group of Bahá'ís in Manchester. One of these, Sarah Ann Ridgeway, had become a Bahá'í in the United States in 1899. But most of the group had been introduced to the Bahá'í teachings by Edward Hall, and he became their unofficial leader. Although Ethel Rosenberg corresponded with the Bahá'ís of Manchester, and visited them in January 1911, there seems to have been little cooperation between the two groups. There is some evidence of tensions between them over the next twenty years.

These groups, plus a few isolated individuals like Daniel Jenkyn of St. Ives, Cornwall, made up the Bahá'í Movement in Britain. We can conclude then that this movement was organized very informally, and largely dependent on the actions of a few individuals. While some of them must certainly have discussed their activities with others, there is no evidence that an individual's actions needed group approval, or that there was any formal arrangement for group decision-making. There were personalities who seemed to have prestige or influence, but their leadership of the community was based on a variety of factors which never included democratic elections.

The Bahá'í Councils. As time passed and both the number of Bahá'ís and the range of their activities grew, there developed the need for a more formal organization. The first evidence we have of this formal organization is the Bahá'í Committee that met during 1914. This committee gives us clear evidence of Bahá'ís working together, making joint decisions, raising funds, and laying down rules, long before the advent of the Administrative Order introduced by Shoghi Effendi, the future Guardian of the Bahá'í Faith.

Although the committee kept and read minutes, no record of them can now be traced. The only firm evidence that we have of the committee's existence and activities are copies of agendas for three meetings held in 1914, which were sent to Lotfullah Hakim by the secretary, Arthur Cuthbert.[3] These agendas reveal that the Bahá'ís were engaged in a range of activities and that the committee operated under normal business procedures.

One topic on the agendas was the proposed publication of leaflets and books. Also under consideration was the financing of meetings and the question of paying the expenses of speakers at these meetings. The conduct of people who attended such meetings was also a matter of concern. On one occasion the issue of "clapping at meetings" was discussed, and at another time the issue of "undesirable persons at private meetings" was raised. The appearance of the item "Finance" or "Encouragement of Financial Support" on all three agendas clearly shows that, even at this early stage, some sort of fund for the administration of the Cause had been established.

As early as 1914, therefore, the British Bahá'ís were organizing themselves and their activities in a way that was very similar to that under which they would later operate as Spiritual Assemblies formed at Shoghi Effendi's instruction. The very membership of this Bahá'í Committee was similar to that of the assemblies to be formed later. All of the known members of the Bahá'í Committee,[4] with the exception of Cuthbert and Hakim, were later to serve on Spiritual Assemblies. There was, therefore, a continuity of organization in Britain spanning the periods of 'Abdu'l-Bahá's and Shoghi Effendi's leadership, and not a sudden imposition of administrative structure as some writers have suggested.

The Bahá'í Committee of 1914, however, did not itself span these two eras. It ceased to meet after 1916. Although no official explanation can be found, it is possible to speculate on the reasons for its demise. One reason may have been the problems caused by the war, including lack of communication with 'Abdu'l-Bahá. However, if this were the only reason, one might reasonably have expected the committee to resume its functions once hostilities ceased and normal communications were restored. This it did not do.

A more likely cause of the committee's lapse is the disharmony that existed among the members of the British Bahá'í community. As already stated, the Bahá'ís were dominated by strong personalities, and none of them had any real authority over the others. They were accustomed to thinking and acting independently; and, there is evidence that their personalities sometimes clashed.

Divisions and disagreements among the Bahá'ís are often mentioned by Esslemont in his letters. In December 1915, he wrote:

> I am sorry to hear that there is not more unity between Mrs. Holbach[5] and the London Bahá'ís, but I hope that on both sides prejudices and whatever else keeps them apart may be outgrown. We are all but babes in Bahaism and must be very charitable to each other's weaknesses.[6]

Later that month he referred in another letter to his own correspondence with Mrs. Holbach:

I had a nice letter from Mrs. Holbach enclosing one from Mr. Hall of Manchester. Mr. Hall seems depressed and feels that the London Bahá'ís have given him the "cold shoulder."[7]

Two years later, he is still concerned about the divisions among the British Bahá'ís:

Oh! If only the friends in this country could be more united, could cultivate the "sin-covering eye," be less conscious of each other's faults, and more conscious of the wonderful Power of the Holy Spirit.[8]

These comments suggest that the British Bahá'ís were probably not at that time ready to work together, to allow their individual wishes and opinions to be overruled by the decisions of the majority. The committee of 1914 does not appear to have been elected by the Bahá'í community, nor does it appear to have been granted any authority by 'Abdu'l-Bahá. Unlike the American Bahá'ís, who had been set the task of building a Bahá'í Temple, the British Bahá'ís had no single project to unite them. Therefore, the Bahá'ís would not necessarily have felt bound to any decision the committee made. Whether there was some crisis or dispute that brought these divisions to a head and resulted in disbanding this Bahá'í council cannot now be determined with any certainty.

Whatever the reason, the Bahá'í Committee ceased to meet, and the community returned to its former state for the next few years. It was 'Abdu'l-Bahá himself who encouraged the committee to reform and once again to guide and direct the activities of the movement in Britain. 'Abdu'l-Bahá clearly believed that the Bahá'í Movement needed to be organized.

The instruction to revive the Bahá'í Committee was given to Esslemont by 'Abdu'l-Bahá during the former's visit in Haifa in 1919. Although Esslemont left Haifa in January 1920, it was not until almost a year later that he was able to report to Hakim that the new council had at last met:

On Tuesday we had the first regular meeting of the new Bahá'í
Council. There were present Miss Rosenberg, Mrs. Thornburgh-
Cropper, Miss Gamble, Mrs. George, Miss Herrick and Mr.
Hammond, of the old members, and the new members were Mrs.
Coles, Miss Grand, Miss Musgrove, Mrs. Crosby, Mr. Simpson
and myself. We met at Miss Grand's flat, and the meeting was
very harmonious. I think that we all felt that it marked the
beginning of a new era in the history of the Cause in this country.
The meeting was arranged in accordance with the advice given by
Abdul Baha through me that the old members of the council who
were still able to act should add to their number a few new ones
whom the friends approved and they should then work together.
There has been no regular meeting of the council since 1914, I
think, but now we have decided to meet regularly at least 3 times
a year, while a special meeting can be called at any time, when it
is considered advisable.[9]

It seems that this council did manage to meet during
1921, and made several decisions about distributing, approv-
ing, and publishing Bahá'í literature. They also maintained
funds for the movement. Having been formed at the direct
request of 'Abdu'l-Bahá, the body seems to have had greater
authority and cohesion than the first committee. By October
1921, Esslemont was able to report that the Council was
beginning to work as a collective body:

I think we are making a little progress towards greater Unity in
the Council itself, although we are a long way from the ideal in
that way yet.[10]

We can see then, that towards the end of 1921, a formal
administrative organization was already beginning to emerge
in Britain. The fact that 'Abdu'l-Bahá not only approved of
this organization, but was instrumental in its development, is
an important factor to bear in mind. The process of organizing
the Bahá'ís had begun, and it was soon to be accelerated
under the influence of the successor to 'Abdu'l-Bahá, Shoghi
Effendi.

The Guardianship of Shoghi Effendi. 'Abdu'l-Bahá died on November 28, 1921. The Bahá'í Movement, centered as it was on his charismatic authority, was thrown into temporary crisis and confusion. In his Will and Testament, 'Abdu'l-Bahá appointed his grandson, Shoghi Effendi Rabbani, as the Guardian of the Bahá'í Movement. From that first period of confusion, the new Guardian led the Bahá'ís into a period of stability and growth which resulted in the movement becoming established as a separate religion in the West. As Vernon Johnson has observed:

> Shoghi Effendi gave to Baha'i a precision of historical understanding, doctrinal formulation, and institutional organization which had not yet been fully achieved in the religion.[11]

> Under Shoghi Effendi the Baha'i faith became truly the Baha'i World Faith.[12]

The process of transforming the movement into a religion was one that Shoghi Effendi began immediately. Until that time, many Bahá'ís had remained active within their previous religious communities, and in contemporary Bahá'í literature one finds references to Christian Bahá'ís, Muslim Bahá'ís, and Zoroastrian Bahá'ís. 'Abdu'l-Bahá himself continued to attend Friday prayers at the mosque in 'Akká right up to the week that he died. He observed the Muslim, as well as the Bahá'í fast. Indeed, he was accepted by many as an exemplary Muslim.[13]

The behavior of Shoghi Effendi was very different. From this assumption of office, he refused to attend prayers in the mosque and observed only the Bahá'í fast and prayer rituals. By his actions, he demonstrated his belief that Bahaism was already a separate religion. His task over the next fifteen years was to ensure that all Bahá'ís came to the same realization.

The first stage of this task was to unite and organize the

A BAHÁ'Í GATHERING IN LONDON, c. 1925.

Bahá'ís themselves. From the very beginning of his Guardianship, Shoghi Effendi began the task of providing for the Bahá'í Movement an efficient, democratically based, administrative organization. To a large extent, it was this organization that transformed the inclusive movement into an exclusive religion.

In his first communication to the Bahá'ís throughout the world, Shoghi Effendi urged them to form Spiritual Assemblies in every locality where there were nine or more believers, and wherever possible to elect a National Spiritual Assembly. He quoted extensively from both 'Abdu'l-Bahá and Bahá'u'lláh to demonstrate that the concept and the duties of these assemblies were derived from their writings, and not from himself. However, elaborating the details of this system was certainly to become the work of the Guardian. He made it clear to the Bahá'ís of Britain, even in this first communication, that the presentation of the Bahá'í message to the world could no longer be left to individual initiative and interpretation.[14]

Shoghi Effendi requested that the new national bodies should be established as a matter of urgency. The British Bahá'ís seem to have responded to his request, despite the fact that their activities were at a low ebb. As early as May 1922, Esslemont was able to write of the progress they were making:

> The election of the new Assembly is now in progress. Ten members are being elected from the London group and these 10 with Mr. Hall and myself will constitute the National Assembly for Great Britain.[15]

Later, he reported that the first meeting of the "new Bahai Spiritual Assembly" was held in London on June 17, 1922.[16] Although he was unable to attend the first meeting, Esslemont did go to the second meeting in July 1922, and reported that it was "very harmonious." He lists the ten members elected

BAHÁ'Í UNITY FEAST
held in London, England, during 1923.

from the London group, and it is significant to note that seven of them had served on the Bahá'í Council that had been formed in 1920. Shoghi Effendi was not imposing a new structure upon the movement, but merely continuing a process that had already begun. The main effect of his leadership was to give the Assembly an authority that it had not had before. This authority came from the outline of their duties as defined in the writings of 'Abdu'l-Bahá and Bahá'u'lláh, and from the fact that they were now democratically elected. These changes were being made not only in Britain but throughout the world.

This transition was from a time of individual action and personal interpretation to a period of much more centralized control over the presentation of the teachings. Leadership of the community was in the future to be based on democratic support, and not merely on the strength of personality. Individuals would not only have to gain the support of their fellow Bahá'ís for any teaching initiative, but would be restrained by the community if they could not gain that support. To effect these changes in the administrative system would take several years, but the British community did attempt to follow Shoghi Effendi's instructions.

Local Assemblies were soon established in Manchester, Bournemouth, and London. The National Assembly was also reelected each year, with the number of members being fixed at nine after 1922. However, even in the simple matter of these elections, there were new rules to follow and simple mistakes were made.

In 1927, Ethel Rosenberg visited Haifa and discovered that the delegates at each annual convention had been wrong to elect the members of the National Assembly only from among their number. She immediately wrote to the Assembly in Britain to inform them of the error:

... Shoghi Effendi says, all the 19 delegates must clearly understand that they must select from the whole body of the believers
in Great Britain and Ireland those 9 whom they consider the
most fit and suitable members to constitute the National Assembly. Therefore it will be necessary to supply each of the 19 delegates with a complete list of all those believers in Great Britain
and Ireland.[17]

As with all communications from the Guardian, or from
his secretary, the National Spiritual Assembly was quick to
follow his advice. The National Assembly of 1927 was, therefore, the first to be elected in accordance with the Guardian's
new instructions. However, as two people tied for position as
the ninth member of the Assembly, they decided that for that
year the Assembly should consist of ten members. Within a
month, they received another letter from the Guardian:

I feel sure that next year, the number of members should be
strictly confined to nine, and a second ballot is quite proper and
justified.[18]

In the same letter he appears also to be concerned that
the Reverend A. H. Biggs, who was a Unitarian minister from
Altrincham, should have been elected to the National Assembly:

I trust the choice of the Rev. Biggs signifies his unreserved acceptance of the faith in its entirety—a condition that we must increasingly stress in the years to come.[19]

This instruction began to point the British Bahá'ís in the
direction of greater exclusivity. At this time, there still remained no initiation, nor even interview, that one had to go
through before being added to the list of those Bahá'ís eligible
to vote for Assembly members. Indeed, in London anyone who
attended several meetings was automatically added to the list
of London Bahá'ís.[20] Also, most British Bahá'ís at this time

seem to have retained the belief that theirs was an inclusive movement, and not a religion. These beliefs and practices help to explain how a Christian minister could be elected to the National Assembly as late as 1927.

Despite the misunderstandings that we have listed above, the British Bahá'ís did attempt to carry out the duties that the Guardian had laid upon the first Assembly in 1922:

> I need hardly tell you how grateful and gratified I felt when I heard the news of the actual formation of a National Council whose main object is to guide, co-ordinate and harmonise the various activities of the friends.[21]

During the 1920s, the National Spiritual Assembly organized and coordinated a variety of activities, including public meetings, the publication of books, and the presentation of the Cause at the "Conference of Living Religions within the Empire" that was held in 1924. It also maintained contact, albeit intermittently, with both the Guardian in Haifa and other Bahá'ís around the world.

However, it would be wrong to infer from this activity that all was well within the community or that a full transition to the new Administrative Order had been achieved. There were problems with this new organization from its very beginning, and by the end of the 1920s, the Bahá'í Movement had all but disappeared from the British Isles.

Problems and Difficulties. The main problem that the British Bahá'ís had to face was the decline in their numbers. This is the same problem faced by virtually all millenarian movements when the promised millennium does not arrive or their charismatic leader is removed. For many, being a Bahá'í had simply meant being a follower of 'Abdu'l-Bahá. On his death, these Bahá'ís may have had difficulty finding a focus for their admiration and devotion. This resulted in an almost immediate falling away of activity and interest, even as early as May 1922.

> There is little news about the Cause in England. Mrs. George's meetings seem to be the largest now. At Lindsay Hall there are only a very few except on special occasions when people are rounded up by postcards![22]

There were, undoubtedly, some Bahá'ís who found it impossible to accept the new situation. They had been able to accept the decisions and authority of 'Abdu'l-Bahá whom they regarded as a Christ-like figure. However, now they not only had to accept the authority of his grandson, the twenty-five-year-old Guardian, but they also had to recognize the authority of an Assembly elected of their equals. Some were never able to do this, and others took many years to do so. As late as April 1926, Shoghi Effendi wrote to the British National Assembly to express his pleasure that one of the London Bahá'ís had ". . . at last complied with my request and written to the London Assembly acknowledging their authority."[23]

In addition to getting ordinary Bahá'ís to acknowledge the importance of Assemblies, Shoghi Effendi seems to have had some difficulty in getting even the members of the National Spiritual Assembly to do so. One of the persistent problems the Assembly faced was achieving a quorum. In May 1926, its members wrote to the Guardian requesting permission for substitutes to attend Assembly meetings. They received this reply:

> I realise the special and peculiar difficulties that prevail in London and the nature of the obstacles with which they [the National Spiritual Assembly] are confronted. I feel however that an earnest effort should be made to overcome them and that the members must arrange their affairs in such a way as to ensure their prompt attendance at 9 meetings which are held in the course of the year. This is surely not an insurmountable obstacle.[24]

It was, nevertheless, an obstacle, and it may have been exacerbated by the continued personality clashes among members of the Bahá'í community. The difficulties that prevailed during the previous decade seem to have been overcome for a while in the early 1920s, partially due to the skillful chairmanship of both the London and National Spiritual Assemblies by George Simpson. However, towards the ends of this decade the problems began to surface once more.

A glimpse of the conflicts that arose is given by Ruth White in her account of a visit to London in April 1928. White was an American Bahá'í who believed that 'Abdu'l-Bahá's Will and Testament was a forged document. She was visiting Europe to gain support for her opposition to Shoghi Effendi and his efforts to organize the believers. According to her account, she met ". . . practically all the Bahá'ís in London," and was invited to meet with members of the National Assembly at the home of Florence George. Here, she was kept waiting for two hours outside the room where the National Assembly was meeting. She could hear the sound of raised voices within.

> Finally, at nearly six o'clock, the members emerged limp and tired. No sooner were greetings exchanged than Mr. G. P. Simpson approached each member of the National Assembly and said very dramatically: "I have finished with you forever! You are not Bahais! You are not Bahais!" And then he strode from the room beside himself with rage.[25]

Ruth White later spoke with one of the members of the Assembly, a prominent Bahá'í for over twenty years:

> Lady Blomfield, who was present at this meeting, said to me that there was practically no longer a Bahai Cause in England, and she had come to the conclusion that the Bahai Cause cannot be organized.[26]

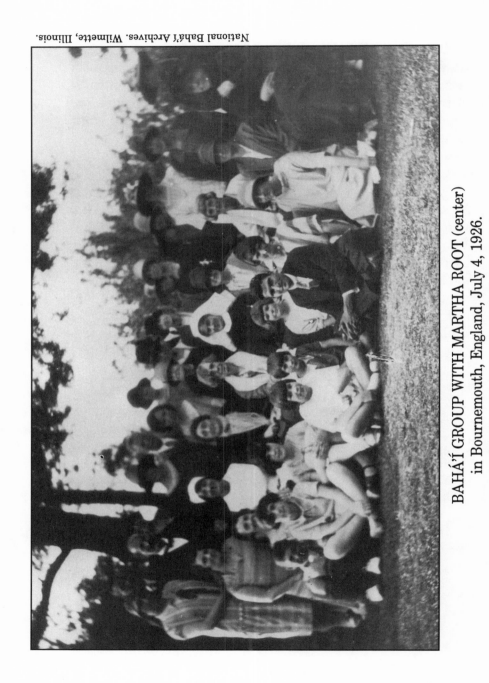

BAHÁ'Í GROUP WITH MARTHA ROOT (center)
in Bournemouth, England, July 4, 1926.

Of course, White cannot be regarded as an objective observer. She had vested interests in proving, perhaps provoking, disunity within the British Bahá'í community. However, there are indications from other sources that all was not harmonious. In the same month that White visited Britain, April 1928, Shoghi Effendi sent a brief note of encouragement to the National Assembly in which he said that he would pray for the guidance of the Beloved to ". . . help you to remove misunderstandings and difficulties amongst the friends."[27] During the next eight months only four extremely short telegrams were received from Shoghi Effendi; but on the last day of the year, he again wrote a short letter which referred to their problems:

> Not until harmony and concord are firmly established among the friends of London and Manchester will the cause advance along sound and progressive lines.[28]

Whatever the problems were, they did not result in complete inactivity, and administration never ceased altogether. In September 1929, a new Bahá'í Center was opened in London.[29] At approximately the same time, a new translation of Bahá'u'lláh's *Hidden Words* was published. It may, however, be significant that the book was published despite the Guardian's advice that its publication be delayed.[30] There is also some indication that the type of activity the British Bahá'ís were engaged in did not meet with the full approval of the Guardian, and that he may have been dissatisfied with the development of the British community:

> He is much hopeful of your new centre in Regent Street or thereabouts, and he trusts that it will mark a turning point in the history of the Cause in England — from happy tea-parties at individual homes, into a group of less personal but eager, active and thoughtful workers co-operating in a common service.[31]

It seems, however, that his hopes were to be disappointed. The ranks of Bahá'ís continued to dwindle, their numbers and activities reduced by old-age, illness, and death. While there were individuals who continued to think of themselves as Bahá'ís, the activities of the group almost ceased completely.

From the end of 1930 until early 1934, the minutes of the National Spiritual Assembly are very brief and indicate that it held only five or six short meetings a year. There are no records of any cables or letters received from the Guardian and, moreover, the minutes contain few references to him. J. R. Richards, a Christian minister, writing in London about the Bahá'ís in 1932, had no doubt that Bahaism in the West was in decline. However, he did not dismiss it entirely:

> But whilst the movement is undoubtedly losing ground its missionaries continue to be active, and their insidious propaganda must be fought down.[32]

Despite his obvious antipathy, Richards is correct in his assessment of the Bahá'í Movement in Britain. It was certainly losing ground. In a sense, he was also correct about their missionaries, as it was Bahá'ís coming from communities outside of the British Isles, where the new Administrative Order was more fully established, who were successfully to bring about the reorganization of the movement and revitalize the community.

Resurgence. In other parts of the world the Administrative Order was more fully established and the movement was moving towards greater centralization and more exclusivity. This was especially true in the United States, which would provide the model for all Bahá'í Administration in the West. Following a decline in activity there, and a possible drop in numbers in the years after the death of 'Abdu'l-Bahá, it was during the 1930s that activities and numbers once more began to increase. In the mid-1930s, the Bahá'ís of Britain began to benefit from this resurgence.

In 1934, the Guardian's communications with the British National Assembly were fully restored. From that time onwards, we can begin to detect a revival in activity among the Bahá'ís. By this time, the number of Bahá'ís in Bournemouth had dropped below the nine required to form a local Spiritual Assembly, and so there remained only the Assemblies of London and Manchester. Also by this time, the personalities who had dominated the movement since the time of 'Abdu'l-Bahá had ceased to do so. Esslemont had died in 1925, Ethel Rosenberg in 1930, and George Simpson in 1934. Mrs. Thornburgh-Cropper and several others were in such frail health that they could no longer be active. The new personalities who came to lead the community were generally people who had become Bahá'ís during Shoghi Effendi's Guardianship and who, therefore, had no difficulty in accepting the idea of the Administrative Order. Some of them, moreover, had come from other countries where the administration of the movement was already established. In 1933, Hasan Balyuzi, from Iran, was elected to the National Spiritual Assembly and was to remain a member of it until 1960. Helen Bishop was an American Bahá'í who came to Britain during the 1930s to help teach and spread the faith. Madame Gita Orlova came to London simply to help the community and established a theatrical group for Bahá'í youth in the city. All of these people helped reactivate the British community and introduce new people to it.

In 1936, David Hofman returned to his native England having become a Bahá'í in Montreal in 1933. He was immediately elected to the National Assembly. It was during the first year of his membership that a real resurgence in Bahá'í activities took place. That these two events should have coincided was a fact that was not overlooked by Shoghi Effendi. He wrote to Hofman at the very end of the year:

> Your splendid collaboration with the English believers is, as I am gradually and increasingly realising it, infusing new life and determination into individuals and assemblies which will prove of the utmost benefit to our beloved Cause. Persevere with your remarkable efforts and historic achievements.[33]

During 1936, many things of importance had, indeed, been achieved. In July, a paper on the Bahá'í Faith had been read to the newly established World Congress of Faiths, and two Bahá'ís had given short addresses there. In August, the first official Bahá'í Summer School was held.[34] In September, the first issue of the *Bahá'í Journal*, a national newsletter, was published and sent free to every registered Bahá'í. The *Journal* was to play a vital role in creating a sense of community among the British Bahá'ís and became an important tool for informing and educating them. In December, the entire National Spiritual Assembly met in Manchester for the first time in an attempt to reduce the dominant influence that London had held over the British community. This was to become an annual event, being transformed in later years into the Teaching Conference. Very early in the following year, the Bahá'í Publishing Company was established and this too would become an important part of the future community.

Having stopped the decline in numbers, the community now began to grow. For the new believers, the Bahá'í Administrative Order was an essential part of being a Bahá'í. Unlike earlier Bahá'ís, they had little difficulty in accepting the decisions and the authority of the Spiritual Assemblies. There was now a clearly accepted definition of what it meant to be a Bahá'í. In January 1937, the *Bahá'í Journal* had published Shoghi Effendi's guidance about what was necessary for a person to become registered as a Bahá'í:

Full recognition of the station of the Forerunner, the Author, and True Exemplar of the Bahá'í Cause, as set forth in 'Abdu'l-Bahá's Testament; unreserved acceptance of, and submission to, whatsoever has been revealed by their Pen; loyal and steadfast adherence to every clause of our Beloved's sacred Will; and close association with the spirit as well as the form of the present day Bahá'í administration throughout the world.[35]

Anyone who wished to become a Bahá'í had to sign a "declaration card" that stated that they understood and accepted all of the above beliefs and conditions. It was the duty of existing Bahá'ís to ensure that the new believers did fully understand and accept all of these terms and conditions before they accepted their declaration. In this way, a uniformity of belief (and a degree of exclusivity) was imposed on the community such as had never existed before. It was also made clear that a Bahá'í could not simply believe in the Bahá'í prophets, but also had to accept the administrative organization as established by Shoghi Effendi.

In 1939, the National Assembly was to take a further step towards exclusivity by applying the above restrictions to those people who had been registered as Bahá'ís before the new definition had been formulated. The *Bahá'í Journal* informed the Bahá'ís that all believers in Britain were to be issued with a ". . . registration certificate stating that the bearer is recognized by the N.S.A. as a member of the Bahá'í community of the British Isles."[36] This was ostensibly because Bahá'ís were accepted as being exempt from combat service in the armed forces on religious grounds, and the National Assembly was anxious to ensure that nobody brought the Faith into disrepute by fraudulently claiming to be a Bahá'í simply to escape combat. However, it was also an attempt to ensure that those believers who had been registered as Bahá'ís during the 1920s, or even earlier, now acknowledged the authority of the National Spiritual Assembly.

To obtain one of these registration certificates, the believers had to send two passport-sized photographs to the National Assembly along with their personal details. In April 1940, however, the Assembly announced, in their annual report, that the ". . . friends have been very slow in responding to this plan."[37] Clearly, some were reluctant to take such a step. A year later, the National Assembly reported that nearly all the believers had now registered, despite the fact that a few felt that the move ". . . conflicted with the liberal spirit of the Faith."[38] That the majority had now followed the Assembly's instruction may have been due less to its powers of persuasion than with its threat to withdraw voting rights from all those who did not register by August 13, 1940. For the first time, the National Assembly had been able to use the threat of administrative sanctions to ensure compliance with its decisions.

Such power was an effective way of imposing coherence and uniformity of belief and practice on the Bahá'í community. It is for this reason, among others, that the British Bahá'ís still carry registration documents today, despite the assurance of the National Assembly in 1941, that such a move was not permanent.[39] The issuing of registration documents completed the transition from an inclusive movement to an exclusive organization.

The British Bahá'ís of the 1930s had at last become united and organized. Their administration could now begin to serve the function that the Guardian had advocated for it more than ten years earlier. Now that its authority was generally accepted, the task of the National Spiritual Assembly was to transform the exclusive organization into a religion.

Developing the Faith. The earliest Bahá'ís in the British Isles did not consider themselves to be members of a new religion.[40] Theirs was a movement that existed within existing religions and attempted to build bridges between them. The aim of the movement was to strip away the rituals and dogmas that each religion had developed and to return each faith to the simple truths and practices of its founder. In this way, each religion would become revived and renewed. Bahá'ís believed that it would then become apparent to all that the fundamental beliefs of all religions were identical.

Because of this view, the earliest British Bahá'ís had no religious practices of their own. Those Bahá'ís who came from a practicing Christian background were encouraged to return to their churches, although they would inevitably have a different attitude towards them. It was the sharing of the ideal that made one a Bahá'í, not uniformity of worship. Religious rituals and liturgies were seen as the creations of men, not of the founders of religions. They were the outdated forms of religion which the Bahá'ís hoped to sweep away, in order to restore the original spirit of true faith.

Of course, the Bahá'ís were not the first religious group to reject liturgical practice in favor of moral behavior. Various Christian denominations had repeatedly attempted to achieve just this. Some writers pointed out the similarity between the Bahá'ís and the Society of the Friends (Quakers). Harrold Johnson, writing in 1912, saw at least two similarities between these groups:

> There are also, as in Quakerism, no priests in Bahaism and there are no ritual observances. The exceeding apprehension of the danger of mere formalism is very marked in the Bahai writings .... The important place given in Bahaism to silent prayer and to the workings of the spirit in silence are again suggestive of the Quakers.[41]

This latter point suggests what several other writers refer to, namely the importance of prayer to the early Bahá'ís. However, far less reference is made to prayer in early Bahá'í writings than is made to ethical teachings. Even when reference is made to prayer, a uniform picture of Bahá'í practice does not emerge.

There can be little doubt that prayer was part of the life of the early British Bahá'ís, but it appears to have been a private activity, with no fixed form or ritual. Even by 1923, in Esslemont's important book, *Bahá'u'lláh and the New Era*, the author states that prayer is obligatory, but the form that prayer should take is not. While he includes a translation of the short obligatory prayer, Esslemont does not refer to it as such.[42]

According to Alter and Wilson, the American Bahá'ís of this period had developed a ritual form of community worship. However, judging from the limited amount of evidence we have available, it would appear that there was no such development in Britain. During this phase, the period of the Bahá'í Movement, the meetings that were held were generally more intellectual than devotional.

The early meetings were generally gatherings in private homes held to discuss the Bahá'í teachings or to read the latest Tablet (letter) received from 'Abdu'l-Bahá. These do not represent acts of worship as we would normally accept this term, nor do they seem to have followed a set pattern or ritual. The one feature that was included in all meetings was "the delivering of prepared sermons on Bahá'í theology."[43]

At the first meetings, Miss Rosenberg and others would explain the teachings and recount their experiences of meeting 'Abdu'l-Bahá. Later, Esslemont rarely refers to a meeting without stating who gave the prepared talk:

> Tomorrow night at the meeting hall I shall speak on the Unity of Mankind.[44]

> We had a very nice meeting yesterday afternoon at the Theosophical Society's Rooms. Mrs. George spoke instead of Mr. Tudor Pole . . . . on "Religion should be a cause of love and unity."[45]

We had a fine meeting on Sunday night. Mr. Kanhere, a Hindoo Brahmin, and a friend of Mr. Eric Hammond, gave us a very interesting talk.[46]

In 1920, the Manchester Bahá'ís began to hold weekly meetings which also featured the reading of a prepared paper:

These meetings always opened with a prayer. After a few moments of silence first some letters from friends abroad were read and then a paper on some aspect of the Cause. This was followed by happy, stimulating discussion and questions and the meeting would close with a prayer.[47]

Although we can see that the more explicit forms of worship had been introduced towards the end of this early period, the meetings still seem to have remained intellectual rather than devotional. This was especially obvious to those coming from a different religious tradition. In 1919, Esslemont took Colonel and Mrs. Cuthbert, of the Salvation Army, to a meeting and later recorded their impressions:

Mrs. Cuthbert's impression is that we are not getting into touch with people as we ought—that the meeting seemed too much of a meeting of intellectual people for discussion.[48]

This seems to have been true of all Bahá'í meetings including the Nineteen-Day Feasts. Feasts were certainly held, but not on a regular basis. Those that were held do not sound like the one attended by Alter in New York. If anything, they seem to have been less devotional in content than the normal weekly meetings:

. . . we had our first "19-day Feast." We had it in a tea-room in Boscombe. 17 friends were present. We had tea in the Persian style with glass cups and saucers which Mrs. Dunsby managed to borrow for the occasion. After tea I gave a short introductory talk and read some tablets of the Master's regarding the conduct of meetings, and regarding the importance of the 19-day feasts and how they ought to be celebrated. Aflatun then gave us a most interesting talk, mostly about the life of the Beloved during the last year of the war, when Aflatun was at Haifa. Miss Pinchon read one of the tablets you sent in your last letter, and Mr. King gave us a delightful talk about the progress of the Cause in America, . . . Then we had more tea and fruit.[49]

We can conclude then that, during this early period, no fixed congregational form of service had been developed by the British Bahá'ís, but the reading of prayers and Tablets was regularly practiced by some of them.

It also seems unlikely that many of the first British Bahá'ís fasted. Although it is known that Esslemont observed the fast in 1915, when he first became a Bahá'í, because of his chronic ill-health it seems unlikely that he did so again. Although a few of the other Bahá'ís may have fasted, it is rarely—if ever—referred to and so was probably not widely observed.

The major Bahá'í festivals, on the other hand, were commonly celebrated. The gatherings seem to have been primarily social events. The two main festivals that are referred to are Naw-Rúz and Riḍván. Although the early British Bahá'ís did not observe all Bahá'í Holy Days, or adopt special religious practices connected with the ones they did observe, the recognition of such festivals marked a significant step towards the emergence of the Bahá'í Faith as a religion rather than a movement.

As we have shown earlier, the 1920s and early 1930s were years of stagnation and decline for the Bahá'í Cause in Britain. It seems unlikely that any changes in religious practices were adopted during this period. The reluctance to accept the authority of the Spiritual Assemblies, and perhaps even of Shoghi Effendi himself, made the acceptance of the change from movement to religion difficult to achieve. Even after the historic court decision in Egypt which recognized the independent nature of the Bahá'í Faith, and the legal moves undertaken by the Bahá'ís of the United States, it was possible for a prominent British Bahá'í to insist, during this period, that ". . . the 'movement' must not be called a 'religion.' "[50]

Although no changes in religious practice took place, the reduction in overall numbers may have had the effect of concentrating the existing practices within the community. In its loose inclusive stage, the Bahá'í Movement had encompassed a wide range of beliefs and opinions. Its members came from socialist, New Thought, Theosophist, and Christian Science backgrounds, as well as the more traditional Quaker and Anglican. For some of these, Bahaism was only an addition to their own more central beliefs. For others, the most committed of Bahá'í activists, Bahaism already held a central place. It was this latter group who were more likely to use Bahá'í prayers and writings in preference to other scriptures. It was also these persons who were more likely to remain Bahá'ís in years to come.

When the move towards formalization and exclusivity began, it was those whose major allegiance lay elsewhere who felt excluded. On the other hand, those who could accept the Administrative Order, and all that it involved, were also more likely to accept new religious practices. Thus the decline in Bahá'ís, brought about by the death of 'Abdu'l-Bahá and the rise of the Bahá'í Administration, paved the way for a resurgence of Bahaism in the 1930s, no longer as a loosely structured movement but as an organized religion. Numbers, in all likelihood, declined to the point where there only remained mainly those who were already observing the limited religious practice of British Bahá'ís of that time.

Thus, with the administration established and functioning effectively, the majority of Bahá'ís in Britain had accepted that they now belonged to a new religion. It is probably also true, however, that their religious practices were still of the limited form practiced during the time of 'Abdu'l-Bahá. One of the first tasks of the administration, therefore, was to standardize religious observance and to instruct its followers in the full range of Bahá'í worship.

Establishing the Faith. The first real insight we have into changes in Bahá'í worship comes with the publication of the *Bahá'í Journal.* It became the primary means whereby Bahá'ís were instructed in orthodox Bahá'í beliefs, and the primary publication from which they could learn how Bahá'ís should, and should not, behave.

From its very first issue in September 1936, the *Journal* refers to the "Faith" rather than the "Movement." Clearly the writers of the *Journal,* that is the members of the National Spiritual Assembly, saw themselves as the elected leaders of a religious community. The pages of the *Bahá'í Journal* over the next few years indicate clearly that they thought it their task to inform the rest of the community of this fact. They also attempted, in these pages, to impose a standardized form of worship on the British Bahá'ís. To a certain extent, they tell us when they were successful.

It is clear that one of the first goals that the National Assembly set out to achieve through the *Journal* was to establish the Nineteen-Day Feast as the most important Bahá'í meeting. In the very first issue of the *Journal,* a large amount of space is taken up quoting 'Abdu'l-Bahá's words on the vital importance of these meetings. Thus, the first stage of the campaign was to establish a scriptural basis for the Feast. It was not the Assembly, or the Guardian, who was attempting to elevate the Feast to some new importance. Rather, they were trying to give it the stature that Bahá'u'lláh and 'Abdu'l-Bahá had always intended it should have. Having established scriptural authority for the central importance of the Feast, the next issue of the *Journal* explains how it should now be observed:

The Feast has a threefold function and is conducted in three stages. The first part is devoted to the reading of passages from Bahá'í Sacred Writings and is the "spiritual feast". The second part is the recognised and proper occasion for consultation between the believers and between the community and local Spiritual Assembly. The third part is the material feast and provides an opportunity for a social gathering of the friends in the atmosphere engendered by the spiritual meeting.[51]

It is interesting to note that 'Abdu'l-Bahá's description of the Feast mentions only two parts: the devotional and the social. However, with the growth of the Administrative Order, there arose a need for the addition of a third part during which organizational business could be discussed. This threefold pattern of the Feast had been fixed by the Guardian, and was already widely practiced in the United States. However, to some British Bahá'ís it may have seemed a radical innovation. For their benefit, it was important to emphasize both the spiritual benefits obtained by attending the Feasts and the moral imperative to do so:

It is the source from which the spiritual life of the community is regularly renewed. By attending the Nineteen Day Feast the believer integrates himself, not only with the local community, but with the entire world organism of the Most Great Name. . . . All believers are expected to attend regularly, only sickness or absence from the city being good reason for not attending. Bahá'ís are expected to adjust their affairs so that they can attend the Feast.[52]

This latter point was frequently repeated in the *Journal.* Indeed, the National Assembly considered it to be of such importance that in November 1936, they circularized all the British Bahá'ís "urging the observance of two Bahá'í laws— regular attendance at the nineteen day Feast, and regular subscription to the Fund . . ."[53] In fact, attendance at Feasts is not obligatory according to Bahá'í law. But it is easy to see why the Assembly overstated their case in this matter. They sought to draw together this scattered group of believers and to forge them into a community. The Feast was the ideal, and to them the God-given, occasion on which to do this. By coming together to worship and to mix in a social gathering, this sense of community identity could be encouraged to develop. It was also the ideal time to deepen the believers' knowledge and understanding of the Faith.

> The National Spiritual Assembly has requested local Assemblies to arrange for a review of the current number of the *Journal* at each Nineteen-Day Feast.[54]

If attendance at the Feasts could be ensured, and the *Journal* was properly studied during the administrative part of it, then the National Assembly could be sure that their communications were getting through.

Such was the importance attached to Feasts that the *Journal* carried reports of their observance by the communities. The fact that they had become "firmly established" in Manchester by April 1937, is presented as evidence that a new and vigorous spirit was at work in that community.[55] At the same time, the lack of reports about their observance in London can be taken as an indication that the Bahá'ís of that city were less enthusiastic in their support. Mary Balyuzi recounts that her mother, Kathleen Brown, was in the vanguard of the movement to establish Nineteen-Day Feasts, but that they were introduced only gradually, and "somewhat reluctantly."[56] The fact that by May 1938, the London Spiritual Assembly could only report that its Feasts were receiving "better attendance than before"[57] would seem to confirm this.

The people who became Bahá'ís during this period would have no difficulty understanding the need to attend the Feasts. In March 1939, the *Journal* reported that the new believers in both Bradford and Torquay were holding the

Nineteen-Day Feasts regularly, even before their Assemblies had formed.[58]

After the successful establishment of Feasts as the devotional focus of the community, the *Journal* hardly mentions them again. There remained some Bahá'ís who were reluctant to attend Feasts regularly, and the National Assembly seems to have remained rather too anxious to make attendance compulsory. The Guardian pointed this out to them in June 1943:

> He feels that Bahá'ís who, though still considering themselves believers omit attending the 19-Day Feasts for long periods should not be deprived of their voting rights; they should, however, be encouraged to attend these Feasts as often as possible.[59]

The majority of British Bahá'ís did, however, attend the Feasts and, despite the addition of the administrative section, its primary purpose had become fixed as religious and devotional. By 1940, they had replaced teaching and discussion groups as the most important of all Bahá'í meetings and were in essence a form of community worship.

Prayer was always important to the Bahá'ís. Often it was not specified what form this prayer should take. But by 1936, prayer had begun to play an increasingly prominent role in the Bahá'í community. One example of this new role is the fact that the *Journal* several times calls on the Bahá'ís to pray for the success of a particular venture. For example, in April 1937, help was requested when a small group of believers had been formed in Devonshire:

> The prayers of all the friends are asked for blessings and confirmations on the efforts made in this new outpost of the Faith.[60]

Prayer is clearly seen as something positive that a Bahá'í can do to help spread the Faith. Although great emphasis is still placed upon putting the teachings into practice, no longer is religious observance seen as less important than action. Rather, it is recognized that spiritual exercises are needed to prepare oneself for material activity:

> We rise to our fullest capacity only through the power of the Spirit, and now, as never before, do we need its strength and energising influence. Let us resolve to remain continually in the clear light of prayer, individually and as a community. If we do this we know that God will use us to achieve His purpose.[61]

As this increased emphasis was being placed upon the power of prayer, there came a greater recognition of the special significance of prayers that were found in the Bahá'í scriptures. The National Assembly offered for sale, through the pages of the *Journal*, a prayer book that had been published in the United States in 1937. They also announced their intention of printing one or two prayers in each edition of the *Journal*, until the new prayer book was published.

In September 1939, the prayer book was finally in print:

> The new prayer book is now available. It is printed in two editions one with a blue cover and one with a beige. The former costs a shilling and the latter ninepence. The shilling edition contains obligatory prayers, prayers for the Fast, and the prayer for the dead; these are omitted from the ninepenny edition, with a view to making it more suitable to non-Bahá'ís.[62]

With the publication of these books, Bahá'ís were able for the first time to have a collection of prayers suitable for all occasions. These books established that there was now a distinctive Bahá'í form of prayer. Just as it was no longer possible to be both a Bahá'í and Christian, there were now prayers that should only be used by Bahá'ís. The use of these prayers reinforced their Bahá'í identity.

As we noted above, although some of the early Bahá'ís may have observed the Bahá'í fast, it is unlikely that its observance was widespread. This situation does not appear to have changed very much by the mid-1930s. Mary Balyuzi has confirmed as much in her recollections of that period:

> During the 1930s my mother observed the fast, as no doubt did some others, but I doubt if it was widely observed.[63]

The sparsity of references to the Fast in the *Journal* during the period seems to confirm this. One notice that did appear suggests that Bahá'ís knew of the Fast, but they felt it was not appropriate—nor perhaps even possible—for the British believers to observe it.

> Not all of us are able to keep the Fast, but we can all unite in making these days a special time of prayer and meditation.[64]

We have seen that the early Bahá'ís had begun to observe at least some of the Bahá'í Holy Days, principally Naw-Rúz and, to a lesser extent, Ridván. This practice appears to have continued, and the *Journal* makes regular mention of these two dates in particular. It is also clear that the other Bahá'í festivals were not widely known and certainly were not widely observed. It was not until the 1940s that the National Assembly made an attempt to change this situation.

An article printed in the *Journal* in April 1943, points out that for Jews and Christians, it is the religious festivals that stand out as milestones in the year. It says that the same situation should be true of Bahá'ís:

> Our year, with its milestones, should become indelibly engraved upon our consciousness. . . [65]

It goes on to list, and explain the significance of the nine most important Bahá'í Holy Days. This was an important step in establishing the Bahá'í Faith as a separate religion that should celebrate its own religious festivals. Although the article admits that their commemoration was not widespread, it at least began the process of promoting their observance within the community.

There are several other matters that can be mentioned as examples of further developments in the establishment of the Bahá'í religion. In September 1939, the National Spiritual Assembly advised all Bahá'ís who were eligible for military service to register as conscientious objectors. Subsequently, several Bahá'í men were granted exemption from combative service because they were members of the Bahá'í religion.

On April 15, 1940, two Bahá'ís in Bradford were married. Hasan Balyuzi officiated at the Bahá'í wedding. This was the first of several Bahá'í weddings that were to take place during the next few years. In September of the same year, Bahá'ís were urged to carry identification with them wherever they went and "to specify that in the event of death they wish to be buried according to the manner of the Bahá'í Faith."[66] These events mark an attempt to establish distinctive Bahá'í rites of passage among the British Bahá'ís.

In addition to these developments, the establishment of the Bahá'í Publishing Trust made compilations of Bahá'í Scripture easier to obtain. In addition to advertising these compilations, the *Journal* regularly urged Bahá'ís to read some scripture every day. This practice, together with daily prayer, was to become established as a distinctive Bahá'í form of worship.

All of the above changes in religious practices were urged on the community by the centralized administration of the Bahá'ís. It was only after the authority of the National Assembly had been established that religious observances could be standardized and imposed upon the British Bahá'ís. It was, in effect, the organization that created the religion and turned the Movement into the Faith.

Spreading the Faith. By 1940, the Bahá'í Movement had completed its transformation into a separate and distinct religion. Its administration, theology, and religious practices were to remain largely unchanged from that date forward. However, further changes still needed to be made before it was to become the Bahá'í Faith as it is known today. Those changes were in the area of spreading the religion.

The British Bahá'ís during the era of 'Abdu'l-Bahá do not seem to have made serious attempts to gain converts. That, of course, does not mean that they were not interested in teaching their beliefs. Much of their energy seems to have been given to this task, but the aim does not appear to have been to recruit members to the Bahá'í Movement.

Their first objective was to inform the world of the life and station of Bahá'u'lláh, and of the whereabouts of the living exemplar of his teachings, his son, 'Abdu'l-Bahá. Secondly, they sought to make known the main principles of Bahá'u'lláh's teachings, especially those concerning the unity of religions and races.

Having given their audience these two pieces of information, the Bahá'ís felt that it was then up to the hearer to decide whether to accept or reject them. The early British Bahá'ís were content that their audience might agree with and accept the principles of Bahá'í teaching. They were proclaiming Bahá'u'lláh's message, not seeking proselytes. If they spread the ideas of religious and racial unity, which they believed came from Bahá'u'lláh, then they were helping to spread the Bahá'í Spirit. If some people also recognized Bahá'u'lláh as the source of these ideas, this was an added bonus. But it was not their primary objective.

In the first edition of *Bahá'u'lláh and the New Era*, Esslemont had written that the only way "... the real success of the Movement can be gauged is, not by the number of its professed adherents, but by the way in which its principles are permeating and changing the world."[67]

The first Bahá'ís used a variety of methods to disseminate these principles. They published books and pamphlets which could be sold or given to the public. They wrote articles for publication in newspapers and journals. They held meetings in hired halls to which the public was invited. They also tried to interest their friends and their families in the teachings, often through informal gatherings in their own homes.

It was perhaps through this last method that they were most successful in leading people to accept the faith. Many of the first Bahá'í groups were formed in this way. For example, the Hall and the Craven families, who formed the nucleus of the Manchester Bahá'í community, were related to each other. The Bournemouth group was mainly comprised of the friends, former patients, and colleagues of Dr. Esslemont.

In addition to these direct teaching methods, there is some evidence that the Bahá'ís were also involved in other organizations, such as Esperanto and pacifist groups. That is not to imply that Bahá'ís infiltrated these organizations in an attempt to gain converts. They joined these groups because their own beliefs required them to work actively for world peace. In the course of their activities, they might also lead some of their coworkers to recognize Bahá'u'lláh as a prophet of God, but that was an added bonus, not their primary objective.

However, we cannot be sure how successful this teaching method was. What we can say with some certainty is that during the first twenty years of Bahá'í activity in Britain, very few people were moved to openly recognize the claims of Bahá'u'lláh. Although no precise figure is available, it was probably less than a hundred. There was perhaps a larger number, equally hard to assess, who found the Bahá'í teachings interesting and attractive, and whose thinking may have been influenced by them, but who stopped short of accepting the divine station of the Bahá'í prophet. During this early period, people in both of these groups might have been referred to as Bahá'ís.

As shown earlier, the ten to fifteen years following the death of 'Abdu'l-Bahá were ones of reduced activity for the British Bahá'ís. This was also a time during which Bahá'í identity became more carefully defined. However, teaching activities continued. The communities in London and Manchester held regular public meetings. Books by Esslemont, Florence Pinchon, and Elizabeth Herrick were published. A presentation of the Bahá'í Cause was given at the 1924 "Conference of Living Religions within the Empire" that was held in London.

Despite this activity, the tone of Bahá'í teaching during this period is one of general quiescence. Energy and direction seem to be missing from their efforts. Indeed, a letter written on behalf of Shoghi Effendi summed up their activities as "happy tea parties at individual homes."[68]

We can say, therefore, that during this period of transition of authority to the Guardian and establishment of the Administrative Order, very little was achieved in the area of growth. Few new people seem to have declared themselves Bahá'ís, in the sense of recognizing the station of Bahá'u'lláh, and many who had considered themselves Bahá'ís ceased to do so.

This situation appears to have remained unchanged until the mid-1930s. Once the administrative organization was established, and the inclusive movement had transformed into an exclusive religion, then far more organized efforts were made to draw new members into the faith. The changes in teaching methods that the organization introduced, and the effect they had on the community, can be divided into three distinct stages.

1936-1940. During this period we can trace the emergence of modern Bahá'í attitudes and methods of teaching. It was during this period that it became accepted that the greatest service one could perform for mankind was to lead people into accepting the religion of Bahá'u'lláh.

> There is undoubtedly no higher call than that of bringing the Message to a world tormented and torn on every side by the forces of destructive materialism.[69]

This message from the Guardian to the British National Assembly was quoted in the *Journal*, and became a common theme of this period. Indeed, the National Assembly went so far as to declare that "teaching is our most important obligation."[70] Much of their attention over the next few years was taken up, not only with developing methods of teaching, but also with finding ways of getting more of the Bahá'ís involved in the process of teaching.

The innovations introduced by the National Assembly to unite and educate the community were also used to promote the teaching effort. The *Journal* was used to urge the friends to new efforts and advise them of new methods. Bahá'í Summer School and the annual teaching conference were also used to develop teaching strategies and campaigns.

It was at the first teaching conference in December 1937, that an important change in activity was suggested to the National Spiritual Assembly:

> To establish three rallying points during the year for all the believers; Convention in Spring; Summer School in Summer, and a midwinter Teaching Conference.[71]

These three events were to become the highpoints of the Bahá'í year, with the National Convention in London, the Teaching Conference in Manchester, and Summer School in the Midlands whenever possible. These gatherings provided the opportunity for discussion, decision-making, and planning. But they also provided "spiritual reinforcement," through a sense of being involved, that could never otherwise have been given to isolated Bahá'ís or those from small local communities. It was the Bahá'ís who attended one or all of these events who would be most likely to become actively involved in the teaching campaigns.

A feature of the newly established administration was an increasingly centralized control of teaching. One way this control was achieved was through the Bahá'í Fund. It was the promotion of teaching campaigns that took the largest part of the Fund's resources and since the National Assembly controlled this national fund, it controlled most of the teaching. Through administration of the Fund, the National Assembly could promote teaching work in localities as far apart as Bradford and Devon, and even in areas where no Bahá'í yet resided. Increasingly, it was emphasized that teaching relied upon a steady income to the Fund, and that this was one way in which every Bahá'í could help with this work:

> The response to our appeal for funds to carry on the work until the end of April, has been most disappointing. The amount required is £30, and without this the N.S.A. will have to curtail its programme of teaching. Let every believer ask himself this question: *Do I want the Faith to progress in England?*
>
> If the answer is "yes," it means you will make sacrifices. . . . Our support of the Fund is the gauge of the measure of our Faith.[72]

This emphasis on teaching the Faith reached a peak at the National Convention of April 1938. It was at this convention, in its annual report, that the National Spiritual Assembly put forward what must have seemed to some a remarkable suggestion:

> The N.S.A. recommends for consideration the suggestion that the Faith in England should, for one year, regard itself, and attempt to function as, a teaching organism. Let all our efforts and energies be directed to this supreme aim. The work of individuals, spiritual assemblies, and the national assembly can be co-ordinated through the methods and institutions of the administration.[73]

The delegates at the convention accepted the suggestion, and the Guardian's support of it was whole-hearted. The primary purpose of the Faith was no longer to be regarded as the unification of religions, the reconciliation of races, or even as offering help to the poor and needy. For that year, the purpose of the Faith—the very reason for its existence—was to bring more people into the Bahá'í community. The Bahá'ís were to become an evangelical organization, actively and openly seeking proselytes.

Equally significant is the fact that, at the end of that year, no one suggested that the Faith should now cease to function as a "teaching organism." From that time forward, the Bahá'í Faith in Britain was to remain an organization whose main activity and purpose was to increase the number of its adherents.

This decision resulted in the first attempt at a planned and coordinated teaching campaign. The new National Assembly met in London in May 1938, and decided to concentrate its efforts in Bradford and Torquay, with the object of establishing Spiritual Assemblies in those localities as soon as possible. Of the £250 that the Assembly believed they would need during the coming year, £100 was set aside for the teaching work. At the end of the year, the Assembly was able to celebrate the success of its campaign:

> We are happy to report that owing to the persistent efforts of the resident believers, to the work of visiting teachers, to the sacrifices of all who have given to the Fund, and the unfailing assistance of the Holy Spirit, Spiritual Assemblies were elected in both places on April 21st.[74]

Undoubtedly the success was also due to the careful planning of the National Assembly that preceded and accompanied the teaching work. It was a lesson that would be noted by the Bahá'ís when later plans were drawn up.

During the period of 1936-40, teaching achieved a new priority and was centrally planned, controlled, and funded. These changes helped to achieve the establishment of the two new local Spiritual Assemblies. But this success was also due to the introduction of new teaching strategies that began to emerge at the very beginning of this period. The Annual Report for the year April 1936 to April 1937 reported these new developments:

> In the work of the Spiritual Assemblies there is apparent at this end of the year, a different and more impressive method than could be seen at the beginning. In both London and Manchester the old type of teaching in wide generalisations has been succeeded by intensive and vital discussion groups.[75]

A year later all believers were being urged by the National Spiritual Assembly to adopt this new informal approach:

> The Spiritual Assemblies are urged to arrange more meetings to which the believers can ask their friends. These should be informal, part of the time being given to teaching and part to social enjoyment. The isolated believers especially can undertake this sort of activity.[76]

This style became the normal Bahá'í teaching approach used in Britain. Public lectures and meetings were still used, but only to make contact with interested persons or "seekers." Once this contact had been made, those interested would then be invited to informal discussions, known as "firesides," usually in one of the homes of the Bahá'ís. Here their questions could be answered and the teaching focused more appropriately to their individual needs and interests. Moreover, the feeling of being part of a warm and friendly community could be given.

Another development was the establishment of a Library Committee in 1937, "to be in charge of placing Bahá'í books and literature in libraries."[77] This was a task that had been undertaken by individuals before, but it too was now to be organized on a national level.

In November 1938, a monthly newspaper called *The New World Order* was issued whose sole aim was to contact people who might subsequently be drawn into the Faith:

> The paper is chiefly a means of contact and publicity, and the first number will be sent free to five thousand people. It will contain an editorial, short articles, quotations from the Bahá'í Writings, excerpts from current speeches and other material which will help to create a body of opinion in favour of the universal principles of Bahá'u'lláh. It is intended to follow up the contacts which will be established by those people who respond to the first number.[78]

In fact the paper was never very successful and the *Journal* regularly carried appeals to the Bahá'ís to take out more subscriptions to it. During the next dozen years, its format was often changed and its frequency of publication altered. Despite all of this, it never became financially self-sustaining, and it was of only limited help in the teaching work. For these reasons its publication was suspended. It reflected, however, a new maturity in the Bahá'í approach, a more sophisticated attempt to reach a new and wider audience.

The publication of *New World Order* and the establishment, during 1937, of the Bahá'í Publishing Company mark a more businesslike attitude of the Bahá'ís in their dealings with the outside world. Here is further evidence of the increasingly centralized structure of the Faith. These businesses established by the National Assembly were to be an important aid in teaching. By 1939, the publishing company had been established as the Bahá'í Publishing Trust and was the chief subsidiary of the National Spiritual Assembly, which had become legally incorporated as an unlimited company. The Trust distributed all Bahá'í literature and also published whatever the National Assembly required. So important was its function that the Assembly regarded the Trust as ". . . its right hand in teaching."[79]

All these new developments in teaching, however, although regarded as successful, did not result in a dramatic influx of converts. The Annual Reports to the National Convention each April show a very slow increase in numbers. Nine new believers in 1937, seven in 1938, and probably about ten in 1939. During this same period, several of the older Bahá'ís died, diminishing the overall increase in numbers. The small number of converts did, nonetheless, have a large effect on the Bahá'í Administration. The increase in overall numbers of approximately ten percent at the end of 1938-39, allowed for a one hundred percent increase in the number of Local Assemblies. This was because some of those new Bahá'ís lived in areas where their presence raised the number of local believers to, or above, the nine required to form a local Assembly. And so they raised the number of Assemblies in Britain from two to four.

Thus, when we come to the end of the period 1936-40, despite only a slight increase in numbers, we can sense a feeling of both triumph and expectation within the British community. Their new teaching methods, centralized administration and planning, and relative teaching success gave the Bahá'ís the confidence to launch an ambitious teaching plan, despite the rigors and restrictions of war.

1940 to 1944. Other Bahá'í communities around the world had already organized teaching plans by this time. For example, the Bahá'ís in the United States had adopted a Seven-

Year Plan in 1937. The British community, in effect, had set themselves a one-year plan in 1938-39, when they aimed to establish Assemblies in Torquay and Bradford by the end of the year. It was the successful completion of this plan that inspired them to set themselves a more difficult task.

The Teaching Conference held in January 1939, made the following recommendation to the National Assembly:

> That a five year plan should be adopted, with the aim of having at least one believer in every county of England by the end of 1944.[80]

The Assembly seems to have ignored this suggestion, perhaps judging it to be a little too ambitious, but the following year they did accept a recommendation put at the National Convention:

> That the whole Bahá'í community should engage in a four year plan of Teaching, with the object of having nineteen local Spiritual Assemblies established by Rizwan 1944.[81]

Ultimately, this plan was also to prove too ambitious. To expect to achieve growth of nearly five hundred percent in only four years would have been optimistic at any time, but to expect such growth during wartime was unrealistic. At the completion of the four years, there were only five local Assemblies in Britain, fourteen short of the target. But this was not regarded or reported as a failure, since the plan had effectively been abandoned in 1942. Although the four-year plan was rarely mentioned after that date, the period of the plan did produce some significant and lasting changes in the Bahá'í community.

The first of these changes was administrative. At the very outset of the plan the National Spiritual Assembly appointed a separate teaching committee with well defined guidelines. Originally, all its members were based in London, so that they could consult freely. This was later changed so that the committee was comprised of Bahá'ís from all over the country. Although the plan was a failure, the idea of a National Teaching Committee was not. Such a committee has continued to exist down to the present day and has played a role in the community second in importance only to the National Spiritual Assembly itself.

Another important innovation was the employment of David Hofman as full-time editor of *New World Order* and manager of the Bahá'í Publishing Trust. These were posts which he had filled for some time in a voluntary capacity, in addition to being secretary of the National Assembly. The Assembly now paid him a salary so that he could devote himself to full-time Bahá'í work, though they seem to have adopted an unusual attitude to this appointment. On the front page of the *Journal* they announced:

> It should be emphasised that Mr. Hofman is not employed as a teacher, nor as secretary of the N.S.A., but in the capacities mentioned.[82]

However, later on the very same page they go on to mention an important side-effect of the appointment:

> Mr. Hofman will be able to spend far more time in teaching, and will be at the full service of the N.S.A.[83]

From the reports of his activities over the next few months, it is apparent that a large part of his time was spent in traveling the country, giving talks, and becoming involved in other teaching activities. In effect, despite the National Assembly's protestations to the contrary, he was employed as a full-time teacher. This was an extension of the established practice of merely paying the expenses of teachers. Although his appointment lasted only until his military call-up in 1942, it did set an important precedent.

Another minor innovation was the introduction of advertisements in the press. These first appeared during 1942, and were placed in seemingly obscure papers:

> . . . advertisements have been placed in the following: "The British Esperantist," in connection with which fourteen enquiries have been received already, "Opus," which circulates mainly amongst young people, "Stand-By," the paper of the North Regional Fire Service, and "One and All," the magazine of the National Adult School Union.[84]

The Annual Report for 1942-43 claimed that these advertisements along with others placed subsequently, had stimulated a significant response:

> So far between seventy and eighty enquiries have been received . . . . In addition to this London alone has had fifty fresh people at public meetings since Christmas, mainly on account of advertising.[85]

Again, because of its success, this was an innovation in teaching methods that survived after the demise of the four-year plan.

Perhaps the most important of the changes that were introduced during the years 1940-44, came about with the abandonment of the Four-Year Plan. The Teaching Conference held in January 1942, when failure already seemed inevitable, arrived at some important conclusions about the nature of teaching:

> The outcome of the conference was to stress the two sides of teaching: the making-known of the Cause, however slightly, to more and more of the people of the British Isles, and the gradual introduction of the more spiritually receptive individuals to a full understanding of the Revelation of Bahá'u'lláh.[86]

This could be seen as little more than putting a brave face on failure. Success in teaching was not to be judged by the number of converts alone, but also by the number of people who had learned of the Faith, even if they then rejected it. In this way, the failure of the Four-Year Plan to increase the number of Assemblies, could be transformed into the "success" of having the Faith better known to the general public.

However, it could be argued that the British Bahá'ís were facing up to the fact that only a small proportion of the public was ready to accept their new religion. If they desired large numbers of converts, then they had to accept that much larger numbers of people had first to become acquainted with the Faith. For every hundred people that heard of the Faith, perhaps only one or two would be "spiritually receptive" enough to go on to accept it. This being the case, publicity became an end in itself and could be classed by the Bahá'ís as teaching.

Later in 1942, this position was to become an official one, when the National Assembly accepted a recommendation from convention:

> To modify the Four-Year Plan to the extent of combining a publicity campaign with intensive teaching in places where there are existing groups and centres, and that special efforts be made in three places: Bournemouth, Nottingham and Blackburn, the publicity to be followed by visits from a teacher.[87]

Thus the plan of taking the Faith into new areas was officially abandoned (except for three specified towns), and for the first time publicity came to be regarded as a teaching activity in itself. Later, Bahá'ís would term this form of publicity-seeking "proclamation."

The Four-Year Plan had been a failure, but from the attempt the Bahá'ís of Britain had introduced changes that became permanent features of the community. They had established an efficiently functioning National Teaching Committee that would plan and coordinate all future teaching

CENTENARY EXHIBITION
at Bradford, Yorkshire, showing a shop window on one of the
main streets.

activities. The use of paid officials as an aid to teaching was introduced. Publicity as an aid to teaching was firmly established. Through the activities of the Publicity Committee, established in 1942, experience was gained not only in advertising but also in successfully getting reports of Bahá'í activities into the newspapers.

All of this was to be of great importance in the next few years. In 1944, the National Spiritual Assembly adopted a new teaching plan that was to see the Bahá'í Faith at last firmly established in the British Isles.

1944 to 1950. The six years from 1944 to 1950 may arguably be the most important in the history of the British Bahá'í community. At the Annual Convention held in May 1944, the delegates decided to adopt a new plan, this time to last six years. They cabled their decision to the Guardian in Haifa, asking him to set the goals, and he sent the following telex in response:

WELCOME SPONTANEOUS DECISION ADVISE FORMATION NINETEEN SPIRITUAL ASSEMBLIES SPREAD OVER ENGLAND WALES SCOTLAND NORTHERN IRELAND AND EIRE PRAYING SIGNAL VICTORY.[88]

This was almost precisely the same goal that the community had set themselves in 1940, and had abandoned as being too difficult two years later—except for the added requirement that the new Assemblies be spread throughout the British Isles.

The announcement of the plan followed successful centenary celebrations of the founding of the Faith. The British community had published a history of the Faith in England, mounted exhibitions up and down the country, and obtained a good deal of publicity. This limited success gave them the confidence to embark upon this new plan, although they were

still suffering from the same wartime restrictions and deple-
tion of numbers (due to conscription) that had led them to
abandon their previous plan.

At the beginning of the plan, there were less than one
hundred fifty adult Bahá'ís in Britain and only five local
Spiritual Assemblies. By the end of the plan, in April 1950,
there were three hundred forty adult Bahá'ís and twenty-four
local Spiritual Assemblies. All the goals of the Six-Year Plan
had been achieved.

The completion of the Six-Year Plan saw the Bahá'í Faith
at last firmly established in the British Isles. Up to this point,
the existence of the Faith in Britain had always been precari-
ous and, as has been shown, had almost ended around 1930.
From 1950 onwards, the Bahá'í presence in Britain was assured. From this base of twenty-four Assemblies, the community continued to grow. Indeed, it was soon able to send
pioneers (missionaries) abroad to found and support other
communities.

How was this success achieved? One important factor was
that the Bahá'ís were now reaping the benefit of the changes
the community had undergone and of the experience they had
gained in previous years. Teaching, or the seeking of converts, was now seen as the priority of the community, and the
Bahá'í Faith continued, in effect, to function as a teaching
organism. The Summer School program was able to function
normally after the war. From 1946 onwards, it became the
highlight of the year, with approximately half of the Bahá'í
community of the British Isles attending. This event, together
with the Teaching Conference and Annual Convention, helped
to establish a feeling of community which facilitated national
planning and action on teaching.

The National Teaching Committee continued to function
and played a vital role in the success of the plan. The now
well-established local Spiritual Assemblies organized local ac-

tivities and raised funds for the National Spiritual Assembly. The *Bahá'í Journal* continued its role of informing the believers of national decisions, as well as of exhorting the community to ever greater participation in the teaching program.

Most of these developments had been initiated in the 1930s, but their successful operation had been interrupted by the Second World War. Seen in this light, the growth of the Faith in the late 1940s was not a new development, but simply the resumption of a process that had begun before the war. However, several important changes were introduced during the Six-Year Plan.

One new feature was the energy that was injected into the community by new believers. It is a common feature of all religions that new converts can be more zealous than long-term adherents. This was true of the Bahá'ís. Those who became Bahá'ís during the plan were often more committed and active than those who had been Bahá'ís for far longer. This can be shown by an analysis that was made of those Bahá'ís who attended the Teaching Conference in January 1949:

> It is of interest to note here that of the 76 Bahá'ís who had attended during the Conference, 38 (or 50 per cent) had become Bahá'ís during the Plan, and only 18 (or 23.5 per cent) since the last Teaching Conference. Only 40 per cent of the believers attending were Bahá'ís in Britain before the Plan started.[89]

The enthusiasm and commitment brought to the community by new converts helped revitalize its teaching efforts and increase their success rate. All the new believers were aware of the plan, and they saw it as a natural part of their faith. Indeed, many may have declared because of the plan.

In the last month of the Six-Year Plan, when failure seemed inevitable, twenty-two people made their declarations of faith. Undoubtedly, many of these would have been people who had been studying the Bahá'í Faith for some time, but who were moved to make their declarations in the knowledge that their declarations would aid the plan.

Another change in the community was the success of the technique of "pioneering." It was Bahá'ís moving out from the larger established communities, particularly London and Manchester, that brought Bahá'í activity to the goal towns. Once there, the pioneers set about publicizing the Faith, organizing public meetings, and setting up study classes with any contacts they made. The hope was, of course, that these people would eventually become converts.

Some of the pioneers, having established the required nine believers in one place, would then move on to another town to begin the process again. Thus, some Bahá'ís moved two or three times during the Six-Year Plan. Any town that had numbers over the required nine was automatically a target of the National Teaching Committee, to encourage some of their number to become pioneers. What was new for the British community was the response that the committee received to their requests. Throughout the Four-Year Plan the National Spiritual Assembly had called for pioneers, but not one person had answered the call. During the Six-Year Plan many of the believers did move their residence.

In fact, it was estimated that during the first four years of the plan twelve and one-half percent (or one in eight) of the British Bahá'ís were pioneers.[90] The fact that so many were willing to move, often leaving jobs and families behind, is further evidence of the new spirit that was affecting the community.

Another development was a changed view towards the Guardian of the Faith. Shoghi Effendi at first based his authority on the instructions left in the Will and Testament of 'Abdu'l-Bahá. The establishment of the Administrative Order had reinforced his position. Even with this support, the British National Assembly had felt able to ignore an instruction of his in 1929.

However, during the Six-Year Plan we can observe a change in the way the Bahá'ís refer to the Guardian. He seems, as it were, to acquire charisma. In 1947, the Bahá'ís of the world commemorated the twenty-fifth anniversary of the Guardianship, and the *Bahá'í Journal* published an article about the Guardian by Marion Hofman. In this article, she states that for the last twenty-five years, most Bahá'ís have been blind to the "brilliance and power" of Shoghi Effendi. She goes on to describe him in words that would previously have been used only with reference to 'Abdu'l-Bahá or Bahá'u'lláh:

> . . . the depth and wonder of his nature, the sharpness and poignancy of his feelings, the weight of his inconceivable burden, his sufferings, his sacrifice, the fullness and magnitude of his dedication.[91]

From this point onwards more space in the *Journal* was devoted to printing letters and cables from the Guardian in full. Failure to achieve goals was increasingly described in terms of the community failing the Guardian. There were few believers left alive who could remember 'Abdu'l-Bahá. Gradually, Shoghi Effendi became the focus for the love and adoration of the Bahá'ís, in the same way that 'Abdu'l-Bahá had done for an earlier generation.

This new respect for Shoghi Effendi is one of the factors that animated the community during the years of the plan. It paved the way for many later Bahá'ís, who now regard him with awe and veneration, habitually referring to him as "the beloved Guardian." Some of the Bahá'ís who arose as pioneers undoubtedly did so out of that love for Shoghi Effendi.

The last change that affected the development of the Bahá'í Faith in Britain is perhaps the most significant. During the 1930s, the major achievement of the National Assembly was to unite the scattered Bahá'ís into one national community.

During the years of the Six-Year Plan the British Bahá'ís finally became part of a world faith.

This event has to be seen as part of a worldwide process. Now that National Assemblies were established in several countries, the Guardian was encouraging closer links between them and assigning them the task of taking the religion to new territories. His aim was the establishment of a world community of Bahá'ís.

This new awareness of being part of a world community allowed the British Bahá'ís to see the goals of their national plan as also being part of a much greater plan:

> Is it too much to suppose that through this task, our labours will also affect the speed and the adequacy with which the Most Great Peace, the Kingdom of God upon earth, is established.[92]

This feeling, that the establishment of local Spiritual Assemblies was not just some bureaucratic whim, but part of the unfolding plan of God for bringing peace to the world, helps to explain why so many British Bahá'ís were willing to devote their lives to achieving the goals of the Six-Year Plan. Pioneering and teaching were expressions of their religious belief and commitment.

In addition to these psychological and theological changes, the emergence of the global community of Bahá'ís was also to have important practical implications for Britain. The first of these was an increase in funds. The Guardian made regular gifts of money to the British Bahá'í Fund. This money had been donated by the larger, more established communities, principally by the Bahá'ís in Iran. Without this money, the programs of teaching and pioneering carried out in Britain would not have been possible.

One of the primary benefits of being part of the global community of Bahá'ís, therefore, was that it enabled the British community to take on far more ambitious teaching programs than would ever have been possible otherwise. While the British community remained so small, the only way it could function effectively as a teaching organism was by accepting funds from Bahá'ís elsewhere in the world.

Another practical benefit of being part of this developing worldwide community was the influence of Bahá'ís abroad. With the end of the war, Bahá'ís from overseas could again visit. Some of these Bahá'ís were students who remained for several years. Others were more or less permanent settlers. In either case, they were registered as part of the British community and helped to increase its growth. For example, the list of thirty-six adult additions to the community given in June 1950, shows that three came from Iran, two from Canada, and one each from Australia, Denmark, and Holland.[93] Many of these settlers were willing to move to the goal towns and, therefore, also qualified as pioneers.

Another major benefit from foreign Bahá'ís was in the form of "travel teaching." There were many Bahá'ís from abroad who were gifted and experienced teachers. Marion Hofman, the wife of David Hofman, came from America where she had served on the National Teaching Committee. She soon became an active teacher, traveled throughout the country, and was appointed to the British National Teaching Committee. There were also Bahá'ís who visited Britain for short periods simply to help with the teaching work. Often these visits were effective:

> It has been reported that the Canadian National Assembly sent John Robarts, its Chairman, at its own expense on a fortnight's tour of the British Isles. (He gave up most of his annual holiday to this trip.) John Robarts was instrumental in bringing about the final confirmation of about three-quarters of the 22 people who, after full study of the Faith over a period, made their declaration of Faith in the last month of the Plan.[94]

Becoming part of a world faith had a major influence on the success of the Six-Year Plan. It brought practical benefits in terms of money and foreign teachers. The immigration of overseas Bahá'ís helped to increase and invigorate the community. Perhaps most importantly, it helped British Bahá'ís to believe that their ideals of world peace and world unity could be achieved, inspiring them to greater efforts to bring them about.

Conclusion. In the early years of the Bahá'í Movement, activities had been carried out on a very informal basis. The main aim of the early Bahá'ís had been "diffusing the fragrances," by which they meant informing the world of the life and teachings of their founders. Although they were pleased if people chose to declare themselves to be Bahá'ís, this was not their primary aim. Many of them continued to practice their previous religions.

The establishment of the Bahá'í Administrative Order, while it did lead to more formalized activities, did not result in an increased number of Bahá'ís. By more narrowly defining what it meant to be a Bahá'í, it may have even resulted in an initial drop in numbers. As the Bahá'ís from the era of 'Abdu'l-Bahá grew older and died, there were few young recruits to replace them.

The 1930s saw the emergence of an effective administrative structure and the transformation of the movement into a religion. This change was accomplished largely through the addition to the community of Bahá'ís from abroad. With this change came the elevation of teaching to the foremost activity of the community. Deliberate and carefully planned attempts were made to bring new converts to the Faith. Some progress had been made when the Second World War intervened.

The period from the end of that war until 1950, saw the largest growth in the Faith. By the end of this period, Bahá'ís could be found throughout the British Isles and their numbers and organization were such that the future of the Faith on these islands was assured. Teaching was now the primary aim and purpose of Bahá'í activities. From a time when it had been considered impossible for Bahá'ís to proselytize, the community had evolved to the point where it seemed equally impossible for them not to. They were now part of a worldwide religion whose aim was to draw more and more people into it, thus uniting the world and establishing the Most Great Peace, God's Kingdom upon earth.

From this point on, the form and practice of the Bahá'í Faith in Britain was fixed. Its evolution from movement to religion was complete. The Bahá'ís of the 1950s held beliefs, lived their lives, and practiced their religion in ways that would be completely familiar to Bahá'ís of today. The Bahá'í Movement had become the Bahá'í Faith.

NOTES

1. Phillip Smith, "What Was a Bahá'í? Concerns of British Bahá'ís, 1900-1920" in *Studies in Honor of the Late Hasan M. Balyuzi: Studies in the Bábí and Bahá'í Religions,* vol. 5 (Los Angeles: Kalimat Press, 1989) pp. 219-251. I have avoided any attempt to define the word religion in this paper. The definitions that I use here are those given by the Bahá'ís themselves, at various times. As shall be seen, the early British Bahá'ís described themselves as being members of a movement, and often insisted that they did not belong to a religion. At a later date, they were equally insistent that they were members of a religion, not a movement. The purpose of this paper is to seek to establish why and how they made this change.

2. The term Bahaism is used here to cover both the period of the Bahá'í Movement (in Britain from 1900 to approximately 1930) and that of the Bahá'í Faith (from approximately 1930 onwards).

3. Written by Arthur Cuthbert, these agendas were circulated in advance of the meetings. Agendas dated 28/2/14, 25/4/14, and 30/5/14. Lotfullah Hakim papers. Bahá'í World Centre Archives. Haifa, Israel.

4. Mrs. Thornburgh-Cropper, Miss Rosenberg, Miss Gamble, Mrs. George, Miss Herrick, and Eric Hammond.

5. Mrs. Maude Holbach met 'Abdu'l-Bahá in both New York and Paris, was acquainted with Lady Blomfield in London from about 1912, and visited 'Abdu'l-Bahá in Haifa during 1914. She wrote an article about the Bahá'í Movement in the magazine *The Nineteenth Century* (February 1915).

6. John E. Esslemont to Lotfullah Hakim, December 1, 1915. Lotfullah Hakim papers. Bahá'í World Centre Archives.

7. Ibid., December 12, 1915.

8. Ibid., June 20, 1917.

9. Ibid., December 10, 1920.

10. Ibid., October 16, 1921.

11. Vernon Elvin Johnson, "An Historical Analysis of Critical Transformations in the Evolution of the Baha'i World Faith," Ph.D. dissertation (Baylor University, 1974) p. 276.

12. Ibid., p. 279.

13. See *Bahá'í News*, vol. 1 (1910) no. 1, p. 5; ibid., no. 8, p. 5; ibid., no. 19, p. 10; *Star of the West*, vol. 2 (1911) no. 3, p. 7; and Sydney Sprague, *A Year With the Bahá'ís in India and Burma* (London: The Priory Press, 1908 [Los Angeles: Kalimát Press, 1986]) p. 52 and passim, for references to Christian, Muslim, Zoroastrian, and Sikh Bahá'ís.

See Shoghi Effendi, *God Passes By*, (Wilmette, Ill.: Bahá'í Publishing Trust, 1944) p. 311; Myron Phelps, *Life and Teachings of Abbas Effendi* (New York: G. P. Putnam's Sons, 1903) p. 101 [*The Master in 'Akká* (Los Angeles: Kalimát Press, 1985) p. 132]; and Rúhíyyih Rabbani, *The Priceless Pearl* (London: Bahá'í Publishing Trust, 1969) p. 55, for references to 'Abdu'l-Bahá's Muslim observances.

14. *The Unfolding Destiny of the British Bahá'í Community: Messages from the Guardian of the Bahá'í Faith to the Bahá'ís of the British Isles* (London: Bahá'í Publishing Trust, 1981) p. 5.

15. Esslemont to Hakim, May 30, 1922.

16. Ibid., June 18, 1922. Note that this information conflicts with that given on p. 9 of *Unfolding Destiny*, which states that "Dr. Esslemont and E. T. Hall were 'chosen' to represent Bournemouth and Manchester respectively and they met with seven others representing 'The London Groups' to form the first 'All-England Bahá'í

Council' which met at the London home of Mrs. Thornburgh-Cropper 6 June, 1922."

17. *Unfolding Destiny*, p. 63.

18. Ibid., p. 71.

19. Ibid.

20. This information was supplied to me by Mrs. Balyuzi while recalling her childhood as a Bahá'í in Britain in the 1920s. She was the daughter of Kathleen Brown (later Lady Hornell), a leading Bahá'í of that period. (Letter to the author, December 19, 1984.)

21. *Unfolding Destiny*, p. 11.

22. Esslemont to Hakim, May 30, 1922.

23. *Unfolding Destiny*, p. 47.

24. Ibid., p. 54.

25. Ruth White, *The Baha'i Religion and its Enemy the Baha'i Organization* (Vermont: The Tuttle Co., 1929) p. 98.

26. Ibid., p. 99.

27. *Unfolding Destiny*, p. 74.

28. Ibid., p. 86.

29. At Walmer House, Regent Street, London.

30. See *Unfolding Destiny*, pp. 86-87.

31. Ibid., p. 87.

32. John Richard, *The Religion of the Bahá'ís* (London: S.P.C.K., 1932) p. 227.

33. *Unfolding Destiny*, p. 112.

34. "In 1933 an informal Summer School was held at Shoreham, Sussex in a bungalow lent to us, and attended by six to ten young Baha'is with my mother as chaperone and housekeeper." (From a letter to the author from Mary Balyuzi, October 13, 1984.)

35. *Bahá'í Journal*, (1937) no. 4, p. 5.

36. Ibid., (1939) no. 18, p. 10.

37. Ibid., (1940) no. 23, p. 6.

38. Ibid., (1941) no. 29, p. 3.

39. Ibid. "It is not permanent, but must be maintained as long as necessary."

40. See Smith, "What Was a Bahá'í?" *Studies*, vol. 5, pp. 240-46.

41. Harrold Johnson, "Bahaism: The Birth of a World Religion," *Contemporary Review*, vol. 101 (1912) p. 400.

42. J. E. Esslemont, *Bahá'u'lláh and the New Era*, (London: George Allen & Unwin Ltd., 1923 [Wilmette, Ill.: Bahá'í Publishing Trust, 1950]) pp. 90-91.

43. Neale S. Alter, "Studies in Bahaism," Ph.D. dissertation (Edinburgh University, 1924) p. 61.

44. Esslemont to Hakim, August 4, 1915.

45. Ibid., August 20, 1916.

46. Ibid., August 14, 1917.

47. O. Z. Whitehead, *Some Bahá'ís to Remember* (Oxford: George Ronald, 1983) p. 54.

48. Esslemont to Hakim, July 4, 1919.

49. Ibid., January 3, 1921.

50. J. R. Richards, *The Religion of the Bahá'ís*, p. 137.

51. *Bahá'í Journal*, vol. 1 (1936) no. 2, p. 4.

52. Ibid.

53. Ibid., (1937) no. 7, p. 2.

54. Ibid., (1937) no. 4, p. 3.

55. Ibid., (1937) no. 7, p. 5.

56. Mary Balyuzi to the author, December 12, 1984.

57. *Bahá'í Journal*, no. 13, (1938), p. 4.

58. Ibid., (1939) no. 17, p. 3.

59. Ibid., (1943) no. 42, p. 1.

60. Ibid., (1937) no. 6, p. 5.

61. Ibid., (1939) no. 16, p. 1.

62. Ibid., (1939) no. 19, p. 6.

63. Mary Balyuzi to the author, December 2, 1984.

64. *Bahá'í Journal*, (1939) no. 17, p. 1.

65. Ibid., (1943) no. 39, p. 4.

66. Ibid., (1940) no. 25, p. 2.

67. Esslemont, *New Era*, , p. 216.

68. *Unfolding Destiny*, p. 87.

69. *Bahá'í Journal*, (February 1938) no. 11, p. 1.

70. Ibid., (January 1938) no. 10, p. 2.

71. Ibid., (January 1938) no. 10, p. 1.

72. Ibid., (April 1938) no. 12, p. 1.

73. Ibid., (May 1938) no. 13, p. 5.

74. Ibid., (May 1939) no. 18, p. 2.

75. Ibid., (June 1937) no. 7, p. 5.

76. Ibid., (January 1938) no. 10, p. 3.

77. Ibid., (April 1937) no. 6, p. 4.

78. Ibid., (November 1938) no. 15, p. 3.

79. Ibid., (May 1939) no. 18, p. 4.

80. Ibid., (January 1939) no. 16, p. 3.

81. Ibid., (June 1940) no. 23, p. 1.
82. Ibid., (July 1940) no. 24, p. 1.
83. Ibid.
84. Ibid., (June 1942) no. 34, p. 6.
85. Ibid., (June 1943) no. 40, p. 4.
86. Ibid., (February 1942) no. 32, p. 1.
87. Ibid., (June 1942) no. 34, p. 2.
88. *Unfolding Destiny*, p. 169.
89. *Bahá'í Journal*, (March 1949) no. 71, p. 6.
90. Ibid., (February 1948), no. 65, p. 6.
91. Ibid., (March 1947) no. 60, p. 10.
92. Ibid., (November 1948) no. 69, p. 2.
93. Ibid., (June 1950) no. 79, p. 8.
94. Ibid., p. 5.

PRINCE WILLIAM STREET

St. John, New Brunswick, was the site of most of the banks and shipping offices of the city.

THE DEVELOPMENT AND DECLINE OF AN EARLY BAHÁ'Í COMMUNITY: SAINT JOHN, NEW BRUNSWICK, CANADA, 1910-1925*

by Will. C. van den Hoonaard

The Bahá'í Community of Canada is today gradually emerging from obscurity with virtually no published records of its beginnings and early development.[1] This paper attempts to make a beginning at rectifying this situation by exploring the origins, rise, and decline of an early Bahá'í group in Saint John, New Brunswick, from 1910 to 1925. The Saint John group was, during its peak years (1917-19), one of the largest Bahá'í communities in Canada, comprising almost 39% of all Bahá'ís in Canada at that time.[2] A study of this group adds to our stock of knowledge about early Canadian Bahá'ís and sheds light on the social dynamics which underlie their rise, development and, in some instances, decline.

The first Bahá'ís settled in Saint John in 1910. Considerable Bahá'í work took place through the use of itinerant teachers in the late 1910s, in Prince Edward Island, Nova Scotia, and New Brunswick. However, this work lapsed until 1937,

---

* Based on a paper presented to the 23rd Annual Meeting of the Atlantic Association of Sociologists and Anthropologists, St. Mary's University, Halifax, Nova Scotia, March 10-13, 1988.

217

when the Bahá'ís again became organized in this area. They expanded very gradually, concentrating themselves first in Moncton, Halifax, and Charlottetown. It was only in the early 1970s that Bahá'ís could be found in all of the major centers in the Atlantic Provinces. In 1991, there were 1,100 Bahá'ís to be found in nearly 90 localities.[3] Therefore, the Saint John group represents, from a Bahá'í perspective, a significant first beach-head in the area, established in 1910. But one which met with little success.

Origins of the Saint John Bahá'í Group. While a number of important figures in the early development of the Bahá'í Faith in North America originally came from Saint John, they played no role in introducing the Bahá'í Faith to the city. Miss Marion Jack (1866-1954), born in Saint John,[4] distinguished herself as a Canadian Bahá'í settler in Bulgaria from 1931 to 1954. She became a Bahá'í in Paris during the early 1900s. She is known to have visited Prince Edward Island in 1917, and that seems to have been connected with a brief stay in Saint John.[5]

Another prominent Bahá'í from Saint John was Paul K. Dealy (1848-1937).[6] He was one of the first people to have become a Bahá'í in North America while the Bahá'í teacher, Ibrahim Kheiralla, was in Chicago in 1897. Born in Saint John, Dealy left in 1865, and became a railroad engineer and inventor. He eventually moved to Fairhope, Alabama.[7] There is, however, no evidence that he played any role in establishing a Bahá'í group in Saint John.

The earliest known reference to a Bahá'í living in Saint John is to Mrs. Henry S. (Mary) Culver, in April 1913.[8] Her husband was the American consul to Saint John. The Culvers were already Bahá'ís when they moved to Saint John on September 12, 1910.[9] Henry had been a prosecuting attorney in Delaware County, where he was a mayor for four years. In

October 1897, he joined the State Department and became consul at London, Ontario, in that same month. The Culvers had become Bahá'ís as a result of their contact with the Magees, Canada's earliest Bahá'ís.[10] Henry's term as U.S. consul in London was followed by appointments in Cork, Ireland, in 1906, and in Saint John in June 1910, at the age of 56.[11]

There were many sides to Mr. Culver. He was an inveterate photographer and world traveller, having circled the globe four times, even visiting 'Abdu'l-Bahá in Haifa, Palestine. He composed poems and songs, some of which he sent to Edith Magee, Canada's first Bahá'í, for her comment.[12] He took a particular interest in the plight of destitute German and Austrian families in a Canadian war camp in Minto, New Brunswick, during the first World War.[13] Culver retired from his consular post in Saint John on July 1, 1924[14] and joined the Eliot, Maine, Bahá'í community in 1925.[15] He died in 1936, and Mary died the following year. They had seven children, but only the two daughters, (Mary) Louise and Dorothy, became Bahá'ís.

The arrival of the Culvers did not immediately lead to the growth of the Saint John Bahá'í group. It was not until well after 'Abdu'l-Bahá's visit to Canada in 1912 that the small group of Bahá'ís consisting of the Culver family began to become more active, particularly through the efforts of Louise Culver who had returned from Paris in early 1911.[16]

Louise Culver operated the Sign o' the Lantern Tea Rooms in Saint John as early as 1914,[17] along with Miss Mary Robinson Warner (also a Bahá'í)[18] and Mrs. A. Macdonnell. After 1924, Louise Culver and Mary Warner lived together and raised two boys, nicknamed "Buzzy" and "Fluffy." In the course of the following decades, after her parents' departure from Saint John, Louise eventually ceased to regard herself as a Bahá'í.[19]

Louise's sister, Dorothy (1890-1983), joined her sister in Paris in 1907, after following her parents to Ireland in 1906. She arrived in Saint John in 1912 and, except for 1916-17, lived in that city until 1920.[20]

By 1917, four more persons joined the Bahá'í group in Saint John. Very little is known about the depth of their Bahá'í commitment, but a great deal has been uncovered about their general standing in Saint John society. All of them retained their Anglican church membership until death, a fact which was noted in their obituaries. Their Bahá'í affiliations were either not known or not publicly recognized.

Mary Robinson Warner (1876-1957) ran the tearoom with Louise, and the two were inseparable. She was the daughter of General D. B. Warner, who had been United States consul to Saint John for twenty-one years. This might explain her acquaintance with the Culvers.[21] It seems, however, that others became acquainted with the small group of Bahá'ís through the coffee and tea business.

Tentatively, we suggest that Roy Wilhelm (1875-1951),[22] an importer of coffee, may have been responsible for developing the Saint John Bahá'í group after its introduction by the Culver family in 1910. Wilhelm was one of the most prominent early Bahá'ís in the United States, setting much of his coffee fortune aside to promote the interests of the Bahá'í Cause. One couple, William H. and Sophia Humphrey, were probably his contacts in Saint John.

The Humphreys appear on Bahá'í lists from 1917 to 1919. William (1852-1935) was a coffee and tea merchant who operated a retail coffee store at the foot of King Street.[23] He was a member of one of Saint John's oldest families.[24] His wife, Sophia (d. 1953) had come to Saint John from England in 1883, to visit her brother. While there, she had married William.[25] Both Humphreys were, however, well known through their affiliation with Christian churches.[26]

Arthur B. M. Hatheway, another Bahá'í in the port city, undertook in 1915, a pilgrimage to visit 'Abdu'l-Bahá in Haifa.[27] Hatheway passed away in late 1920, on which occasion his wife received a Tablet from 'Abdu'l-Bahá dated November 22, 1920.[28]

It seems reasonable to assume that the early founders of the Saint John Bahá'í community included the Culvers, the Humphreys, and Mr. Arthur Hatheway. But apparently membership in the Bahá'í group of Saint John rose quickly during the summer of 1917. There were, in all, seventeen Bahá'ís in Saint John between the summer of 1917 and 1921: though never more than twelve at any one time, and sometimes as few as seven.

Development (1917-22). The second phase in the development of a Bahá'í group in Saint John is of considerable importance in the context of the Canadian Bahá'í community as a whole. By April 1917, Saint John had an organized group which, however weak, was the second in Canada after Montreal. Two principal ingredients led to the development of this group. On one hand, the North American Bahá'ís launched a systematic campaign of traveling teachers, many of whom made their way through Saint John. On the other hand, social conditions in Saint John, especially the influence of the social gospel movement, made a number of its citizens receptive to the broad ideals of the Bahá'í teachings.

The formal existence of a Bahá'í group in Saint John, termed an "Assembly" in those days, was noted by the presence of its delegates to the ninth annual Convention of the Bahai Temple Unity at the Hotel Brunswick in Boston, between April 29 and May 2, 1917.[29] The existence of a Saint John Assembly can also be verified through an exchange of correspondence in September and October 1917, between its secretary, Miss Jean E. Nixon, and Mrs. Corinne True, the

Financial Secretary of the Bahai Temple Unity, then the national body of the Bahá'ís of Canada and the United States.[30]

The increase of membership was particularly strong in the summer of 1917. May Maxwell, a prominent Bahá'í from Montreal, had already visited Saint John as early as 1916.[31] She returned for a more extensive stay in 1917.[32] She addressed the Rotary Club on June 25, 1917, and said that she felt privileged to have met "such an intelligent, broad-minded and altruistic body of men." Maxwell stayed for a few more days to visit other groups, and then traveled on to Fredericton and Moncton. She was not a stranger to this part of New Brunswick. Her husband, William Sutherland, had a "dark and heavy" summer home in St. Andrews.[33]

The Bahá'í group in Saint John seems to have reached its peak in 1919. In that year the Bahá'ís of Saint John, along with many other American believers, were signatories to an appeal addressed to 'Abdu'l-Bahá asking him to return to North America for another tour of the continent.[34] This petition carried the names of twelve Saint John Bahá'ís, including the Nixons.[35]

The Nixons were, next to the Culvers and Humphreys, the third major family associated with the Bahá'í group in Saint John.[36] George Nixon (d. 1940) was a member of the International Order of Odd Fellows and, with his wife Agnes (1864-1940), was a member of the Anglican Church.[37] He was the owner of a well-known wallpaper store on King Street. Of the four children, a son, Murray (d. 1979),[38] and the daughter, Jean (d. 1972), became Bahá'ís.

From the Bahá'í view, the most important member of the Nixon family, at that time, was Jean, who was secretary of the Bahá'í Assembly from 1917 to 1923.[39] She was taught the Bahá'í Faith by May Maxwell and participated in a number of notable Bahá'í events. She was present at the eleventh annual national Convention in New York City where 'Abdu'l-

Bahá's *Tablets of the Divine Plan* were unveiled.[40] In April 1922, she visited Chicago, the principal Bahá'í center in North America, and attended the annual Convention there.[41] Nixon almost single-handedly kept the Bahá'í group of Saint John together by correspondence with Bahá'í communities elsewhere, and distribution of vital Bahá'í documents and general news to other Bahá'ís in the city. On August 14, 1928, however, she was admitted to the Provincial Hospital,[42] an institution for mental patients. She died there forty-four years later, in November 1972.[43] No reasons for her admission were ever given: though some have claimed that her active Bahá'í affiliation had upset members of her family. It should be clearly stated that there is no evidence to support such an assertion.

If Maxwell's visits had brought forth some results, so did the visits of other well-known Bahá'í teachers. The 1,500-strong Bahá'í community of North America picked up on the interest created by Maxwell and organized other visits to Saint John: "Mother" Ellen Beecher in 1919, and Martha Root and Jináb-i Faḍl (Mírzá Asadu'lláh Mazandarání) in October 1920. Bahá'í visitors to Saint John spent time at the "Culver Camp" up the Saint John River.[44]

Ellen Beecher's visit, in November and December 1919, proved to be an impressive occasion. On Sunday, November 30, she delivered an address in the Art Club Room[45] on the topic of "The Great Day of God." She had turned seventy-nine in the summer of the year of her visit. She was told by one of thousands attending meetings "that you are having a perfect whirlwind campaign here."[46] Beecher's report to the 1920 national Convention described her visit in glowing terms. She also speaks of her visit to several "little towns." In two of these she was not to be accepted, "unless I [Beecher] was thoroughly orthodox." Neither the YWCA nor the churches allowed her to speak in these places.[47] Even the "church of the colored people" refused her request to speak to them.[48] Her visit was ignored by the local papers.

Saint John was also visited by Faḍl-i Mazandárání,[49] known in America as Jináb-i Faḍl, in October 1920.[50] His interpreter Ahmad Sohrab, had forsaken his honeymoon to be with one of the most prominent Bahá'í teachers and scholars. They were accompanied by Mr. W. H. Randall, a Boston lawyer and Bahá'í, and both Jináb-i Faḍl and Randall spoke at the Canadian Club on Tuesday, October 12, 1920.[51] On the same day, they made a presentation at the Art Club, after which the newspaper reported that they "will be glad to meet friends interested in all vital movements for the brotherhood of man, unity in religion, universal peace and a universal language.[52] *The Standard*[53] of Saint John carried a full report of the presentation to the Canadian Club, mentioning both Bahá'u'lláh and his son, 'Abdu'l-Bahá. The two traveled with Marion Jack on the riverboat up the Saint John River to Gagetown, thirty miles from Saint John.[54] Jináb-i Faḍl also traveled to Woodstock, New Brunswick, some 120 miles from Saint John.[55]

Numerous other Bahá'ís visited Saint John, including Kate Ives in the fall of 1922.[56] She was one of the first women to accept the Bahá'í Faith in North America; her parents were Newfoundlanders. After 1923, however, the visits of such teachers became less common, and they eventually dwindled.

To what extent did the external society influence the development of the Bahá'í group in Saint John?

Social Conditions in Saint John. The late 1910s constitute a significant stage in the development of what Richard Allen calls the "social passion."[57] Canadian society was swept by an enthusiasm for reform which saw Christianity as a social religion, a phenomenon which hoped to "embed ultimate human goals in the social, economic, and political order."[58] This "passion" for social reform expressed itself in such social movements as unions, prohibition, strikes, the "open pulpit," and women's and agricultural organizations. Saint John, as a city facing the ravaging consequences of industrial development, was no exception. For example, the Workmen's Compensation Board was formed in 1918 in Saint John.[59] A climate to succor the destitute and the disenfranchised through social programs prevailed. It was in this context that three leading women in the city felt impelled to accept the reformist nature of the Bahá'í movement as well.

These women, Helen Climo, Kate Sutherland, and Mary Smith, (along with Mary Culver) belonged to the Women's Enfranchisement Association of Saint John[60] which was founded in 1894, as a women's response to social conditions brought on by modernization and industrialization. The group focused[61] on advances in education, new occupational opportunities, and the spread of democratic ideas, in addition to the improvement of women's status. The association, which had a membership of 112 during its life, dissolved after April 1919, when women gained the franchise in New Brunswick. It might be said that after its dissolution, some of its members found the social teachings of the Bahá'í Faith in line with their thoughts on the general spread of education and the position of women in society. Who were these leading women?

Miss Kate Sutherland (1854-1932) was one of the first stenographers in the city. She was born into an outstanding New Brunswick family. She used to live on Wellington Row, where a Miss Hanson lived (who later married an American, Stenner Phillips), and whose aunt, Miss Phillips, lived in New York. 'Abdu'l-Bahá gave a talk at Phillips's studio on April 12, 1912.[62] Kate Sutherland's obituary states that she "was especially interested in aiding young people who desired to take up stenography. She was keenly interested in the welfare of the community, particularly in educational endeavors."[63] Widely known as a Presbyterian, the press ignored her Bahá'í affiliation.

Mrs. Mary Colby Smith (d. 1936), a noted Saint John citizen, was a Bahá'í in 1921. Her husband, Harry, was a merchant.[64] Her son, Albert Colby Smith, became a member of the Legislative Assembly of New Brunswick. Smith's activities extended over so many areas of public life that the city's newspaper ran an editorial after her death. She presided over the YMCA Ladies' Auxiliary,[65] was elected third vice-president of the Children's Aid Society,[66] commissioner of the Saint John Free Public Library, and member of the King's Daughters, the Women's Canadian Club, the Seamen's Institute, the Red Cross, the Women's Christian Temperance Union, and the Protestant Orphanage—a total of at least seventeen societies.

Smith's acceptance of the Bahá'í Faith was probably due to personal contact with Kate Sutherland, for in 1922, the Smiths moved to Wellington Row, where Sutherland lived. Smith's Bahá'í affiliation was virtually unknown outside of Bahá'í circles. Publicly, she was a member of St. David's United Church when she lived on the east side of the harbor, and the Charlotte Street Baptist Church when on the west side.

Another prominent adherent in those later years was Mrs. Helen Travis Climo (d. 1940), also of a prominent New Brunswick family, whose husband, Harold, was a photographer.[67] She was active in the Saint John Art Club, the Women's Canadian Club, and the Natural History Society.[68] Like Sutherland she was an active Presbyterian.

Decline (1921-1925). By 1921, the social reformist movement began to wane and the Bahá'ís were experiencing difficulties organizing their affairs. By January 1921, the Bahá'ís reported to Alfred E. Lunt, a member of the national board of the Bahá'ís in the United States and Canada, that it was impossible to organize a House of Spirituality in the city.[69] Some Bahá'ís had become inactive or, as in the case of Mary and Dorothy Culver who moved to Boston, had left the city.[70] Fewer than eight believers[71] were then active.

After the passing of 'Abdu'l-Bahá in November 1921, the Bahá'í Assembly of Saint John confirmed the receipt, in March 1922, of the Will and Testament "of the Centre of the Covenant, His Holiness Abdul Baha and [t]his has been read to the firm believers and shall be safely guarded."[72] The Bahá'ís, in March 1922, also acknowledged receipt of pictures of the building of the House of Worship in Wilmette, designed by Louis Bourgeois, an architect who was Acadian through his mother's side of the family.[73]

Star of the West listed Saint John, along with Montreal, as having a Spiritual Assembly in 1922,[74] but within five months its membership had declined from eight to four. The group was represented by Jean E. Nixon and Henry S. Culver at the annual convention.[75] In that year, only four names appear on the membership list: Henry Culver, Louise Culver, George Nixon, and Jean Nixon.[76]

The last official reference in Bahá'í publications to the Saint John group was made in 1923. The Guardian of the Bahá'í Faith, Shoghi Effendi, made a reference to the Saint John Assembly in his letter of January 8, 1923.[77] In March 1923, Dorothy Culver,[78] Louise Culver's sister, forwarded papers related to the Saint John Assembly to her mother, Mary. In 1923, Saint John's delegates to the fifteenth annual Convention in Chicago were Culver and Miss Wilkinson, Roy Wilhelm's secretary in the coffee business.[79] That was the last Convention to which Saint John sent delegates. The Saint John Assembly continued until 1923, six years after its inception in 1917.

In 1923, the group was not considered large enough to finance a second visit by Jináb-i Faḍl, who had planned a teaching trip in Canada for the fall of that year.[80] There was also the matter of Bahá'í administrative reorganization. New requirements in 1923, constrained Bahá'í communities everywhere to organize their local Assemblies on stricter criteria. Local governing councils were to consist of nine adult adherents over twenty-one years of age. The Saint John Bahá'í community was too small to form its Assembly that year. Thus, the Saint John Bahá'ís were in no position to exercise administrative responsibilities. In any event, Henry Culver retired in 1924. He must have been very happy to leave Saint John, for he had hoped for a transfer from his post in New Brunswick within a year of his arrival.[81]

As late as 1925, the Saint John Bahá'í group answered a questionnaire on its activities and returned it to the National Teaching Committee.[82] The last known activity was the placement of an article, or articles, in a local newspaper regarding the renewed persecution of the Bahá'ís of Iran. The fact that there were still Bahá'ís in Saint John, although no longer organized as an Assembly, is reflected in the February 9, 1925 minutes of the Montreal Assembly.[83]

It was during the 1925 Convention that May Maxwell reported that ". . . St. John could [not] send delegates as they must concentrate all their resources upon sending representatives to the National Convention at Green Acre . . ."[84] By April 1925, Saint John was listed as a "group," indicating that there were fewer than nine believers there.[85] The name "Saint John" no longer appeared on a list of participating local Spiritual Assemblies in the forthcoming National Convention of April 1926.[86]

After this date, the group virtually ceased to exist, except for the few remaining (possibly two) individuals, one of whom was confined in the provincial mental institution in 1928. In

May 1937, it was reported that New Brunswick had only two Bahá'ís, living in Rothesay.[87] In 1940, Doris McKay, one of the earliest Bahá'í settlers in Prince Edward Island, tried to visit five Bahá'ís whose names she had—all contacts of Roy Wilhelm—to no avail.

Analysis. In retrospect, one finds several factors led to the decline of the Saint John Bahá'í group: personal factors, overwhelming traditional religious orthodoxy in the wider society, lack of deep commitment on the part of the believers, location on the geographic Bahá'í periphery, and lack of administrative experience which could have provided for continuation of the group. A number of other sociological factors played a significant role in determining the decline of the group.

First, some personal factors. By the mid-1920s, two of the key people were no longer active in the community. The departure of Henry Culver in July 1924, upon his retirement from office, had a profound impact. Culver stayed for the remainder of the summer at Crystal Beach,[88] an attractive summer-home area south of Saint John, while his wife had already left Saint John by 1923. Moreover, Nixon's confinement to a mental institution in 1928 simply left another vacuum in the already much-weakened Bahá'í group.

A second factor contributing to the further decline of the group was the climate of non-acceptance by the community at large, which led to difficulties in finding new converts. In a series of letters to the Bahá'í community of Kenosha, Jean Nixon spoke increasingly, after 1922, of the reluctant response of Saint Johners to the Bahá'í Faith. She speaks of the progress of the Bahá'í work as being "very slow," generating "criticism and a great deal of opposition." She states, "the people in this part of the country are conservative and adhere closely to the teachings of the different denominations

. . . In many cases fear keeps an individual from studying the literature that we offer." She explains that, "people here rather pride themselves in clinging to orthodoxy."[89]

One auspicious moment during these difficult days stood out, however. A new pastor of the black church, Rev. C. Stewart, had in the winter of 1923, "gladly consented" to Bahá'ís speaking to his congregation. Dr. Edna McKinney of Philadelphia spoke five times and Miss Jack gave an exhibition of her paintings. This was the first church ever to open its doors to the Bahá'í Faith on Canada's East coast.[90]

Nevertheless, the religious traditionalism and conservatism of the Atlantic region has been commented upon by such observers as Stark and Bainbridge and Bibby.[91] Our observations confirm the view of Nock and Stark and Bainbridge[92] that new religious movements (i.e., "cults") develop with the greatest difficulty in areas where sects and churches thrive. The climate of resistance, according to one Bahá'í informant, persisted well into the 1950s:

> For instance, Unitarians were very hesitant to assemble or admit their allegiance at that time. We knew one Theosophist there [Saint John] who was quite isolated and frustrated. Also a Technocrat and an Anglican Priest contacted me (through a P.O. Box number appearing in a Bahá'í ad or radio program) and arranged via the mails and then by phone (no name given) to meet me at our apartment on a given evening, where they enquired about the Faith. They were concerned that I would be both alone and discreet.[93]

It was only years later that a Spiritual Assembly was reconstituted in Saint John, in 1961.

A subsidiary element accounts for the decline of the Saint John Bahá'í group, namely the apparent lack of deep commitment to the new religious movement. The Bahá'í Faith seems to have occupied a peripheral territory in the minds of its members. More importantly, without a deep commitment the community could not establish boundaries or even common goals. In the early days of the Bahá'í Faith in North America, it was not uncommon for Bahá'ís to be simultaneously associated with established churches. Membership in the Bahá'í group was informal, requiring no registration, and the boundaries between the Bahá'í community and the larger community were not clearly demarcated. Present-day descendants of those early members of the Bahá'í group often express surprise in hearing that their ancestors were associated with the Bahá'í movement. Certainly, the obituaries of the early adherents do not indicate any affiliation with the Bahá'í Faith—on the contrary, a deep commitment to their conventional denominations is stressed. Members of the Bahá'í group were overwhelmingly of Anglican background, followed by Presbyterian and United Church affiliation.

Yet a fourth element enters into our explanation of why the early Saint John Bahá'í group declined and, for all purposes, ceased to exist. This group was not only perceived as peripheral in terms of the conservative religious tradition of the city and region, it became geographically peripheral to the extent that Bahá'í communities were developing in Vancouver, Toronto, and Montreal. We can observe this peripheral interest in the early Bahá'í history of Canada. Within the context of North America as a whole, Canada occupied a peripheral concern in the Bahá'í community. Virtually all of the recorded Bahá'í centers (or places where Bahá'ís reside) refer to United States locales. For example, the official Bahá'í organ, *Star of the West*, did not carry any news of the celebrated visit of 'Abdu'l-Bahá to Montreal in 1912, until an incidental reference to the event four and one-half years later.[94] Yet, this visit received extensive non-Bahá'í publicity. The news of this publicity in Canada did not find its way into *Star of the West*, however, until 1923, more than ten years later.[95]

Within Canada, the rising communities of Vancouver, Toronto, and Montreal attracted much of the Bahá'í attention. These cities were relatively easy to reach and, as cultural centers, had people who were not just marginally interested in new religious movements: they maintained an active involvement. If there was any opposition, it was not as sharp as that experienced by the Saint John Bahá'í group. The favorable response to the Bahá'í teachings elicited considerable interest from those Bahá'ís who were either itinerant teachers or administrators of this young religious movement.

Finally, the Bahá'ís in Saint John lacked the necessary administrative experience to marshal its resources or organize its affairs. The Bahá'í Faith was seen as a spiritual movement, in which administrative organization was of secondary importance. The Culvers, the founders of the Saint John group, became Bahá'ís in London, a community that predates any formal Bahá'í organization.[95] Thus, they had no conception of any Bahá'í administrative structure. To them, the Faith was a loose association of likeminded people interested in the teachings of Bahá'u'lláh and 'Abdu'l-Bahá.

A number of sociological factors highlight the following historical sketch of this Bahá'í group. The Bahá'í group was entirely comprised of members of the merchant class whose ideas of social reform grew out of the changing attitudes about women, education, and prison reform. Some of the early Bahá'ís were associated with the families of at least two of the American consuls in Saint John. The Bahá'í group involved women, usually unmarried, who were influenced by the social gospel and suffragette movements and who saw the Bahá'í movement as a complement to their reformist interests.

Given these parameters the informal Bahá'í group was perceived merely as a personal set of ideas, and not one gathered around a collective goal.

NOTES

1. There is a pronounced absence of historical writing on the Canadian Bahá'í community. Robert Stockman's *The Bahá'í Faith in America: Origins, 1892-1900* (Wilmette, Ill.: Bahá'í Publishing Trust, 1985) has no substantive references to early Canadian history. Memoirs have either not been written or are just now being put on paper. Doris McKay, one of the earliest Bahá'í settlers on Prince Edward Island, completed her account ("Fires in the Heart") in 1991. Rowland Estall's account ("Melodies of the Kingdom") covering the years 1926 to 1977, is yet unfinished.

There are a few other unpublished accounts: Paula C. Williams, "Candles of Guidance: The History of the Early Halifax Bahá'í Community" (Unpublished ms., 1985) 37 pp.; Linda O'Neil, "A Short History of the Bahá'í Faith in Canada, 1898-1975" (Unpublished ms., 1975) 44 pp.; Andrew Pemberton-Pigott, "The Formation of the First Bahá'í Spiritual Assembly in Edmonton, April 1943" (Honors Thesis in History, University of Alberta, Edmonton, 1988).

There have been few references to Canadian Bahá'í history in Canadian Bahá'í journals. In fact, one hardly finds any articles delving into the past. Exceptions are: "1893: The First Canadian Bahá'í," *Canadian Bahá'í News* (Sept. 1966) no. 200 (and reprinted in *Bahá'í Canada* [June 1979] p. 12); and Ritchie Rolfe, "They Built Better than They Knew: A Brief History of the Bahá'í Faith on P.E.I.," *Bahá'í Canada* (June 1987) pp. 5-6. An article on early British Columbia Bahá'í history was published outside the Bahá'í community: Roland and Ann McGee, "The Bahá'í Faith and its Development in British Columbia," in Charles P. Anderson, et. al., eds., *Circle of Voices* (Lantzville: Oolichan Books, 1983) pp. 19-26.

In addition, references to the early history of the Faith in Canada tend to focus on Montreal, Toronto, and Vancouver—even though Bahá'í communities have existed in about half a dozen localities in Canada since before 1921.

2. This figure has been calculated from a list of early Canadian believers (1893-1944) compiled by the author.

3. The 1981 Canadian census (as reported by David Nock, "Cult, Sect, and Church in Canada: A Re-examination of Stark and Bainbridge," *Rev. Can. Soc. and Anthr.*, vol. 24 [1987] no. 4, pp. 514-25) gives a figure of 546 Bahá'ís for that year.

4. *Marion Jack: Immortal Heroine*, (Toronto: National Spiritual

Assembly, 1985). Born and raised in Saint John, she left for Europe in her twenties to take up painting and art. After her enrollment in the Parisian Bahá'í community, which May Maxwell had founded in 1899, Marion Jack went on pilgrimage in 1908 and met 'Abdu'l-Bahá. She returned to North America in the Summer of 1914, spent time at the Bahá'í School of Green Acre, Eliot, Maine, and lived in Montreal and in Vancouver.

5. Jean E. Nixon, Saint John, to Alfred E. Lunt, Boston, August 26, 1918 (Alfred E. Lunt Papers. National Bahá'í Archives. Wilmette, Illinois.).

6. Stockman, *The Bahá'í Faith in America*, pp. 86-8; "In Memoriam," *Bahá'í News* (March 1937) no. 106, p. 3.

7. Letter from Robert S. Stockman to the author June 16, 1987, enclosing copies of exchanges of correspondence between Mrs. Kitty Dealy and Mr. Robert Stockman (38 pp.). Dr. Stockman gave the author a copy of Mr. Dealy's diary to be passed on to the Bahá'í National Archives in Canada.

8. Membership List, dated April 14, 1913, Lunt Papers. National Bahá'í Archives.

9. Consular Papers. National Archives of the United States. Washington, D.C. Microfilm 123.C 89/33.

10. Taped interview by Rosanne Buzell of Eliot, Maine, with Dorothy Cress (nee Culver), August 19, 1982. Eliot Bahá'í Archives, Eliot, Maine.

11. *Prominent People of the Maritime Provinces*, (Saint John, N.B.: J. & A. McMillan, 1922) p. 46.

12. Henry S. Culver, Queenstown, Ireland, to Edith Magee, March 25, 1908. Copy of letter in possession of author.

13. Consular Papers. National Archives of the United States, Washington, D.C. Microfilm 342.62/6110.

14. *The Telegraph Journal*, July 3, 1924, p.7.

15. Bahá'í Historical Record Cards. National Bahá'í Archives.

16. Lawrence Culver, "Culver-Sprague Genealogical Summary." Mimeographed, 15 pp. In possession of the author.

17. *The Telegraph Journal*, July 4, 1924, p. 3.

18. *St. John City Directory for 1916-17*, (Saint John: McAlpine Directory Co., 1916) p. 664.

19. Notes by Ken and Celia Bolton, Dartmouth, N.S., February 7, 1987. In possession of the author.

In the early 1950s, Louise was acting as chauffeur and companion to Lady Hazen who lived in an estate in the vicinity of the Catholic Hospital in central Saint John, and whose husband, Sir Douglas, was the Chief Justice of New Brunswick. Louise passed away in Saint John in December 1952.

20. Dorothy later married Adelbert F. Cress in Eliot, Maine. Julia Culver (1861-1950), who had become a Bahá'í in 1903, does not seem, however, to have been related to the family.

21. *The Evening Times-Globe*, December 30, 1957: 18.

22. "In Memoriam," *Bahá'í World*, vol. 12 (1950-54) pp. 662-64; O. Z. Whitehead, *Some Early Bahá'ís of the West*, (Oxford: George Ronald, 1976) pp. 87-99.

23. There seems to be some confusion about the identity of W. H. Humphrey in the minds of some of the later Bahá'ís. Humphrey died in 1935, but the Bahá'ís still talk about having seen a Humphrey in the 1950s. For example, they say, "he would, in the 1950s, reminisce about Roy Wilhelm, the prominent United States Bahá'í" (and coffee merchant himself). (Notes by Ken and Celia Bolton, February 7, 1987.)

24. "Information on Lot Ownership, Fernhill Cemetery, Saint John," supplied to the author

25. *The Evening Times-Globe*, June 10, 1953; and "Information on Lot Ownership, Fernhill Cemetery, Saint John," supplied to the author.

26. *The Evening Times-Globe*, January 19331, 5, p. 7.

27. *Star of the West*, July 13, 1915.

28. *Star of the West*, March 2, 1922, p. 313. A search through newspaper accounts, cemetery listings, and biographical reference works did not reveal an "Arthur" Hatheway, although the Hatheways were a very prominent New Brunswick family. There has been, however, an occasional reference to Arthur Hatheway living in Boston.

29. *Star of the West*, September 8, 1917, p. 130.

30. Jean E. Nixon to Corinne True, September 23, 1917. Lunt Papers. National Bahá'í Archives. It concerns a request for a receipt for a six dollar donation to the Bahá'í House of Worship Fund in Wilmette.

31. Cable from Mrs. May Maxwell, Saint John, to Miss Edna McKinney, Boston, December 15, 1916. Lunt Papers. National Bahá'í Archives. Wilmette, Illinois.

32. "In Memoriam," *Bahá'í World* (1938-40) p. 639; May Max-

well, Saint John, to "Beloved Sister" [presumably Corinne True], June 27, 1917. Albert Windust Papers. National Bahá'í Archives, Wilmette, Illinois.

33. Interview with Mrs. Willow Walker of St. Andrews, N.B., with Erica Ritter on "Day Shift," CBC, March 30, 1987.

34. *Star of the West*, August 1, 1919, p. 156.

35. Henry S. Culver; Mary R. Warner; Louise Culver; Sophia Humphrey; Willliam H. Humphrey; A. B. M. Hatheway; Kate M. Sutherland; Mary D. Culver; Agnes B. Nixon; George H. Nixon; Murray E. Nixon; and Jean E. Nixon. This list also appears on a membership list, dated between 1917-19. (House of Spirituality Records, National Bahá'í Archives, Wilmette, Illinois, Box 8, Folder 1).

36. *Prominent People of the Maritime Provinces*, p. 151.

37. *The Evening Times-Globe* (Saint John), November 23, 1940, p. 3.

38. "Information on Lot Owners, Fernhill Cemetery, Saint John" supplied to the author.

39. It was a chance discovery of a letter from Jean Nixon to Corinne True, dated September 23, 1917 in the National Bahá'í Archives, Wilmette, Illinois, (Lunt Papers) which led the author to the research embodied in this paper.

40. This series of letters from 'Abdu'l-Bahá outlined the areas around the world where Bahá'ís were to undertake Bahá'í teaching activity. *Star of the West*, vol.. 10 (May 17, 1919) no. 4, p. 63.

41. Postcard to L. J. Voelz, Kenosha, from Jean E. Nixon, Saint John, postmarked April 2, 1922. Kenosha Records. National Bahá'í Archives, Wilmette, Illinois.

42. Letter from Centracare Saint John Inc., Saint John, N.B., to author, July 9, 1987.

43. "Information on Lot Owners, Fernhill Cemetery, Saint John," supplied to the author; and "Obituary" in *The Evening-Times-Globe*, November 3, 1972, p. 2.

44. Dr. Ellis Cole to Alfred E. Lunt. August 27, 1917. Lunt Papers. National Bahá'í Archives. Wilmette, Illinois.

45. *Saint John Globe*, November 29, 1919, p. 12.

46. *Star of the West*, September 27, 1920, pp. 172-3.

47. The YMCA, in 1920, also excluded Jews from membership (Mortimer Lazar and Sheva Medjuck, "In the Beginning: A Brief History of the Jews in Atlantic Canada" [mimeographed] p. 5. In author's possession.)

48. Jean E. Nixon, Saint John, to Kenosha Bahá'í Assembly, April 7, 1924. Kenosha Records. National Bahá'í Archives. Wilmete, Illinois.

49. See "In Memoriam," *Bahá'í World,* vol. 14 (1963-68) pp. 334-36.

50. A good photograph of Jináb-i Faḍl can be found in *Star of the West* (April 1923) p. 2.

51. *Saint John Globe,* October 11, 1920, p. 10; October 14, 1920, p. 5.

52. *Saint John Globe,* October 12, 1920, p. 10.

53. *The Standard,* October 14, 1920, p. 12.

54. Ferne Allaby and Gaby Pelletier interviewed some relatives of Marion Jack in Saint John who remembered Marion Jack going to Gagetown "with two gentlemen dressed in Eastern clothes." (Letter from Ferne Allaby, dated July 27, 1986 to the author.)

55. Interview with Anne Chisholm, Saint John, by the author, Sept. 16, 1986.

56. Jean E. Nixon, Saint John, to Kenosha Bahá'í Assembly. March 16, 1923. Kenosha Records. National Bahá'í Archives.

57. Richard Allen, *The Social Passion: Religion and Social Reform in Canada, 1914-28* (Toronto: University of Toronto Press, 1973).

58. Ibid., p. 3.

59. See William Y. Smith, "Axis of Administration: Saint John Reformers and Bureaucratic Centralization in New Brunswick, 1911-1925," (M.A. thesis, Department of History, University of New Brunswick, 1984.)

60. Mary E. Clarke "The Saint John Women's Enfranchisement Association, 1894-1919." (M.A. thesis, Department of History, University of New Brunswick, Fredericton, 1979) pp. 155, 158-9.

61. Ibid..

62. See notes regarding interview with Anne Chisholm conducted by the author on September 16, 1986.

63. *The Evening-Times Globe,* March 17, 1932, p. 5.

64. Obituary information is found in *The Evening Times-Globe,* September 24, 1936, pp. 4, 11 and September 25, 1936, p. 9. There is a discrepancy in the date of death. *The Evening Times-Globe* indicates September 23, 1936, the Cedar Hill-Greenwood Cemetery records show September 24, 1936 (Cedar Hill-Greenwood Cemetery Co. to the author, April 13, 1987).

65. *Saint John Globe*, November 26, 1919, p. 2.

66. *The Standard*, Nov. 28, 1919.

67. Interview with Anne Chisholm conducted by the author September 16, 1986.

68. "Funerals," *Evening Telegram Globe*, February 9, 1940, p. 16. (Picture should be available from Pridham Studio).

69. It was possible to have an Assembly (i.e., a Bahá'í community) without being able to organize a House of Spirituality. Jean E. Nixon to Alfred E. Lunt, January 14, 1921. Lunt Papers. National Bahá'í Archives. Wilmette, Illinois.

70. Lawrence Culver, "Culver-Sprague Geneological Summary," (1969) 15 pp.

71. Jean E. Nixon, Saint John, to Alfred E. Lunt. Chicago, Ill., Jauary. 14, 1921. Lunt Papers. National Bahá'í Archives. Wilmette, Illinois.

72. Jean E. Nixon to Alfred E. Lunt, March 19, 1922. Lunt Papers. National Bahá'í Archives. Wilmette, Illinois. This historic document allowed the Bahá'í group to pass into the stage of administrative development, while ensuring its continuing unity.

73. Jean E. Nixon to Alfred E. Lunt, March 29, 1922. Lunt Papers. National Bahá'í Archives. Wilmette, Illinois.

74. *Star of the West* May 17, 1922, p. 94.

75. "Proceedings of the Annual Meeting of Bahai Temple Unity, Chicago, Ill. April 24-26, 1922", p. 84. National Bahá'í Archives. Wilmette, Illinois.

76. "List of Bahá'ís in U.S. and Canada," March 1922. Alfred E. Lunt Papers. National Bahá'í Archives. Wilmette, Illinois.

77. *Star of the West* (May 1923) p. 48.

78. Dorothy Culver, Boston, to Ernest V. Harrison, Montreal, March 18, 1923. Montreal Minutes. National Bahá'í Archives. Thornhill, Ontario.

79. "Fifteenth Annual Convention of the Bahai Temple Unity, Chicago, Ill. 30 April-2 May 1923," p. 61. National Bahá'í Archives. Wilmette, Illinois.

80. Dorothy Culver, Boston, to Ernest V. Harrison, Secretary of the Montreal Assembly, March 18, 1923; Minutes of the Montreal Assembly, 1922-1940. National Bahá'í Archives. Thornhill, Ontario.

81. As early as 1911, he had wanted to be posted back to Europe. Consular Papers, National Archives of the United States. Washington, D.C. Microfilm 125.7933/9.

82. *Bahá'í News* (February 1926) p. 5. This document is currently being researched.

83. Minutes of the Montreal Assembly, 1922-1940. National Bahá'í Archives. Thornhill, Ontario.

84. *Bahá'í News* (May/June 1925) p. 7.

85. *Bahá'í World*, vol. 1 (1925-6).

86. *Bahá'í News* (February 1926) p. 4.

87. National Teaching Committee, "Annual Report: First Seven Year Plan, May 1, 1937 to April 30, 1938"; Minutes of the Montreal Assembly, 1922-1940. National Bahá'í Archives. Thornhill, Ontario.

In 1934-35, Louise was apparently the sole Bahá'í in the province. (*Bahá'í World*, vol. 6 [1934-1936] p. 578.)

88. *The Telegraph Journal*, July 3, 1924, p. 7.

89. Jean E. Nixon, Saint John, to Kenosha Bahá'í Assembly, August 1, 1922; March 16, 1923; and May 2, 1923; Kenosha Records. National Bahá'í Archives. Wilmette, Illinois.

90. Jean E. Nixon, Saint John, to Kenosha Bahá'í Assembly, April 7, 1924. Kenosha Records. National Bahá'í Archives. Wilmette, Illinois.

C. Stewart organized the first soup kitchen in Saint John. K. Henry, in *Black Politics in Toronto since World War I* (Toronto: The Multicultural Society of Ontario, 1981), speaks of the Jamaican Rev. Cecil A. Stewart who lived in Nova Scotia, advocating better social conditions for blacks; his church was critical of the more conservative churches and congregations. Cecil's brother, Rev. Claude Stewart, was apparently less active. It is not known which of the two lived in Saint John.

91. Rodney Stark and William Sims Bainbridge, *The Future of Religion: Secularization, Revival, and Cult Formation.* (Berkeley: University of California Press, 1985) pp. 234-262. These authors rely also on research by Porter, Chea, and Lipset. Reginald W. Bibby, *Fragmented Gods: The Poverty and Potential of Reliaion in Canada* (Toronto: Irwin, 1987) p. 87

92. Nock, "Cult, Sect, and Church in Canada." Stark and Bainbridge, *The Future of Religion.*

93. "Notes by Ken and Celia Bolton, February 7, 1987."

94. *Star of the West*, vol. 7 (January 19, 1917) no. 17, pp. 171-2.

95. *Star of the West*, vol. 13 (February 1923) no. 13, pp. 291-3.

96. Bahá'í Historical Record Cards. National Bahá'í Archivces. Wilmette, Illinois..

THE STATE CAPITOL BUILDING

Sacramento, California. View from the northeast side. 'Abdu'l-Bahá visited here during his stay in the city in 1912. He is believed to have stood under one of the trees on this side. (California State Library, California Section.)

A HISTORY OF THE SACRAMENTO BAHÁ'Í COMMUNITY, 1912-1991

by Peggy Caton

The Sacramento Bahá'í community was the first Bahá'í group established in the Sacramento Valley of California and has played an important role in the development of other Bahá'í communities in that region. It has grown in size from only a few believers, in the 1920s, to over one hundred Bahá'ís, in the 1990s. During this time, it has evolved from a relatively homogeneous group into a more complex urban community, characterized by demographic diversity and differing perspectives.

These developments in the Sacramento Bahá'í community have not been unique in American Bahá'í history. In many ways, its history reflects the changes that have taken place in the wider Bahá'í community over the last sixty years. This essay is an attempt to study this process of continuity and change at a local level.

'Abdu'l-Bahá visited Sacramento for two days in October of 1912. Although this visit received considerable attention from local residents and newspapers, there is no record of anyone becoming a Bahá'í in Sacramento at that time. Nor is there any evidence of Bahá'í activities following his stay there.

241

Nonetheless, his visit to the city later became a symbolic link to 'Abdu'l-Bahá for the believers and an important part of the historical identity of the Bahá'í community that developed in Sacramento a few years later.

'Abdu'l-Bahá's Visit to Sacramento, October 25-26, 1912: The turn of the century was a time of religious exploration in America. In the nineteenth century, many Americans had begun embracing metaphysics, faith healing, and Eastern religions and philosophies. Among the new religious movements was Christian Science, founded by Mary Baker Eddy. Some of Eddy's students eventually began their own teaching and branched off from Christian Science. Emma Curtis Hopkins and others developed a movement which came to be known as New Thought.[1] This was a Christian-based healing movement that taught that God is All-Good and that human beings share in the Divine Essence of God.[2] New Thought adherents eschewed dogma, drew inspiration from many spiritual sources, and were usually open to new spiritual ideas. Bahá'ís during this period came into contact with persons involved in New Thought and were invited many times to give presentations on the Bahá'í Faith at their meetings and conventions.[3]

In 1887, Hopkins taught a large number of students in the San Francisco area. One of these students, Annie Rix Militz, founded the first Home of Truth in San Francisco.[4] Militz was a charismatic leader who taught, toured, and wrote books.[5] She had some correspondence with 'Abdu'l-Bahá. The Home of Truth became the main form of New Thought on the Pacific Coast.[6] Each Home of Truth was independent, though all were affiliated with and influenced by Militz herself.

Among the Homes of Truth was one operated by Christine Fraser in Sacramento from 1903 to 1921.[7] Fraser was active in the New Thought movement, spoke at the New Thought Alliance Convention in Los Angeles in 1912, and was frequently praised by Militz on her stopovers in Sacramento.[8] Although there is little information available on Fraser's origin or background, the 1910 census reveals that she was unmarried, white, a native-born American, and that she would have been forty-eight years old in 1912. Her occupation is listed as teacher at the Home of Truth.[9] The Home of Truth in Sacramento held services every Sunday and Wednesday and held healing sessions every afternoon and evening.[10]

According to Mírzá Maḥmúd Zarqání, a member of 'Abdu'l-Bahá's entourage who kept a diary of his travels in America and in Europe, it was Fraser who invited 'Abdu'l-Bahá to speak in Sacramento.[11] There is no record of how she contacted 'Abdu'l-Bahá, but she may have heard of his visit to San Francisco and gone there to see him.[12]

In 1912, Sacramento was the fourth largest city in California, after San Francisco, Los Angeles, and Oakland.[13] It was an important center of commerce and trade, as well as the capitol city of the state. The population stood at about 45,000.[14] At the center of town was the beautiful, round-domed capitol building, surrounded by a large park containing trees from all over the world. Victorian homes lined the park, and nearby there were a number of large mansions built by wealthy residents, such as Charles Crocker and Leland Stanford.

'Abdu'l-Bahá left San Francisco early on the morning of Friday, October 25, 1912. According to Mahmúd's diary, he said farewell to the Bahá'ís in an emotional address and then boarded his train with a number of believers from the Bay Area, Portland, and Seattle, who had literally begged to accompany him to Sacramento.[15] Brown notes that 'Abdu'l-Bahá was seated in a chair car: "As usual He refused the

HOTEL SACRAMENTO, c. 1912

The hotel where 'Abdu'l-Bahá stayed and lectured during his stay in Sacramento, October 25-26, 1912. (California State Library, California Section.)

comfort of a Pullman, saying, 'We are the army of God.'"[16] His entourage included: Mírzá Maḥmúd, his secretary; Dr. Ameen Ullah Fareed and Ahmad Sohrab, who acted as translators; Mírzá 'Alí Akbar; and Fugita, a Japanese Bahá'í. Also present were Mrs. Ella Cooper and her mother, Mrs. Helen Goodall, as well as other American Bahá'ís.

Maḥmúd Zarqání records that 'Abdu'l-Bahá spoke to the Bahá'ís during the train ride to Sacramento and that they arrived in the city at about noon.[17] 'Abdu'l-Bahá was met at the Central Pacific Arcade Station by Christine Fraser and Carrie Yoerk, a Sacramentan from a prominent family who was also associated with the Home of Truth. They took him, with his entourage, by car to the Home of Truth[18] and invited him to remain for lunch and stay for the night. Goodall and Cooper, along with the other Americans, went directly from the train station to the Hotel Sacramento where they were to be staying and where 'Abdu'l-Bahá was to speak that night.

Harriet Cline had arrived separately from Los Angeles and was already at the Home of Truth when 'Abdu'l-Bahá arrived there at about 11:00 a.m. She later recalled that she was the only American Bahá'í present at the luncheon. However, there were a number of New Thought people there, and they were very interested in the Bahá'í Faith. 'Abdu'l-Bahá retired to a private room to rest after lunch. At about 3:20 p.m., Cooper, Goodall, and others arrived from the Hotel Sacramento. It seems that his luncheon at the Home of Truth had come as a surprise to 'Abdu'l-Bahá, since Cooper later related that he called her into his room to scold her for arranging the meeting without consulting him, and so requiring that he separate himself from the other Bahá'ís and leave them waiting at the hotel.[19]

It seems that Cooper and Goodall were unhappy with the idea of 'Abdu'l-Bahá remaining overnight at the Home of

Truth, even though they had arranged for the luncheon. Because of their objections, he declined Fraser's invitation. He explained that it was his custom to stay in hotels and that he did not want to separate himself from the rest of his group.[20] He invited Fraser to dine with him at the hotel and to share the platform with him when he spoke that evening. He spoke again briefly to the assembled guests and then departed for the hotel.[21]

At 5:00 p.m., 'Abdu'l-Bahá was interviewed at the Hotel Sacramento by a reporter from the *Sacramento Union*. He spoke to the reporter about universal peace, the basis of divine religions, and the principles of the Bahá'í Faith.[22] After the interview, he went for a walk in Capitol Park. Seeing the trees, he is said to have commented on how like those in the Holy Land they were.[23] The Bahá'ís of Sacramento, in later years, kept an oral tradition that 'Abdu'l-Bahá gave a short talk among the trees and blessed an evergreen tree on the north side of the old capitol building below the upper tier of the northeast (or northwest) steps.[24]

The Hotel Sacramento, newly built in 1909, was the grandest of the hotels along K Street. It had a large lobby, and one newspaper reporter observed that 'Abdu'l-Bahá was mobbed there by women who literally worshipped at his feet.[25] From the Mezzanine Floor of the hotel 'Abdu'l-Bahá observed people shopping in the outer boutiques, and he seemed displeased with the spectacle. He made some informal comments concerning these activities, the difference between human beings and animals, and the need for divine civilization in such a materially advanced and preoccupied society:

> Regard how negligent these people are! All the insignificant objects are considered by them as means of happiness. How negligent they are! Like unto animals, they eat, they sleep, they walk, they sing, they dance, and, according to their belief, they think they are having a good time.

Nay, rather, the animals are preferred to them, for they enjoy the expanse of the desert. They graze on the green meadows. They drink from the cool spring. The flight of birds is higher. Their enjoyment of objects of life is great, but the blessing and enjoyment of man are through the Divine benediction, the bounties of God and the love of God.[26]

At 8:30 p.m. that same evening in the Hotel Assembly Hall, 'Abdu'l-Bahá talked about the purpose of his mission, the history of the Bahá'í Faith, and its basic teachings. He emphasized the underlying unity of reality that is the foundation of all religions. Christine Fraser gave a lengthy introduction to his talk and said a Bahá'í prayer.[27] Later, at 9:30 p.m., 'Abdu'l-Bahá gave another informal talk in the parlor on the mezzanine. He spoke about materialism and the need for spiritualization, particularly with reference to America.[28]

Early the next morning, Saturday, October 26, 'Abdu'l-Bahá spoke briefly to the chambermaids in his hotel room, anointed them with violet water and gave them fruit.[29] Mrs. Latimer brought a message to him from some Japanese believers in Portland, and he conveyed his greetings to them through her.[30] 'Abdu'l-Bahá met again with Harriet Cline before she took a train for her home in Northern California. He insisted that she take some fruit as she would be hungry on the trip. During her train ride, she missed the lunch stop and ate the fruit, as 'Abdu'l-Bahá had predicted.[31]

'Abdu'l-Bahá gave a second talk in the hotel Assembly Hall at 9:30 a.m. He spoke of the need for international peace and expressed the wish that it would first be established in California: "May the first flag of international peace be upraised in this state."[32] After the talk, he was interviewed by a reporter from the *Sacramento Bee*.

Several newspaper articles appeared about 'Abdu'l-Bahá's visit—in the *Sacramento Bee*, *Sacramento Union*, and *Sacramento Star*.[33] It seemed that his stay in the city caused quite a stir in some circles. One article states: "The novelty of seeing American women prostrate themselves before the Baha'i leader, clad in long flowing robe and turban, was a sensation for the patrons of the hotel. They stood in open-mouthed amazement at the proceeding."[34]

Mr. T. J. O'Kelly, a prominent businessman in Sacramento and a Christian Scientist, took 'Abdu'l-Bahá for a ride around the city in his car.[35] They returned at noon for lunch at the cafe in the hotel. A meal was prepared for twenty of 'Abdu'l-Bahá's guests, including the Bahá'ís from out of town, his entourage, and three guests from Sacramento (Fraser, Yoerk, and O'Kelly).[36] Mírzá Maḥmúd mentions that the hotel proprietor came in and praised the effect that 'Abdu'l-Bahá had on Sacramento: "What I have seen of the majesty of this Being is that although no one knew Him in this city, yet in the course of twenty-four hours He has created a stir in the city and attracted its people."[37]

After lunch, 'Abdu'l-Bahá spoke briefly to the friends and left for the train station. His train departed for Denver in the early afternoon.[38] Ramona Brown, Ella Cooper, and a few others were permitted to accompany him to the train station, where they waved farewell.[39] As he was leaving, 'Abdu'l-Bahá said: "A spiritual commotion has for the time being been created in this city. Let us see what God desires."[40]

Establishment of the Community, 1923-1940. Ali M. Yazdi may have been the first Bahá'í to live in Sacramento.[41] Yazdi, a Bahá'í from Iran who had immigrated to the United States, moved to Sacramento on February 18, 1923, to work for the Southern Pacific Railroad Company.[42] Within several months, however, he had moved on with his work to live in various locations in the High Sierra Mountains. He returned to the San Francisco area in 1925.[43]

The first Bahá'í group was organized in Sacramento

around September of 1924.[44] There is no record of how this group was established. However, there is some evidence that it may have come about as a result of the Bahá'í teaching efforts of Orcella Rexford.[45] Rexford was a professional lecturer who gave talks on such topics as health and healing, food, diet, and color. It was common for her to give a series of nine lectures in a particular location. For the first eight, she would charge an entrance fee. But the ninth lecture, on religion, would be free. She would deliver the Bahá'í message in the most dramatic way at the last lecture and then gather those who were interested in further investigation into a study group or club.

The first group called itself the "Bahai Assembly of Sacramento"[46] and consisted of twenty-two members. According to a newspaper article, the Assembly had for its objects: "the promotion of world peace and the universal brotherhood of man together with religious and racial tolerance among the people of all nations." There is no suggestion in the article that the Assembly considered itself to be a religious community.[47] This group was not recognized by the National Spiritual Assembly of the Bahá'ís as "an organized Assembly," and its status appears to have been somewhat ambiguous.[48] Some of the members of the Assembly did not consider themselves to be Bahá'ís until some time later.[49]

The Bahai Assembly did, however, sponsor three lectures on the Bahá'í Faith delivered by the famous Bahá'í teacher, Faḍl-i Mazandaraní (Mírzá Asadu'lláh Mazandaraní, often referred to by American Bahá'ís as Jenabe Fazel [for, Jináb-i Faḍl]), in February of 1925. Faḍl was in the city for three days and delivered three public lectures, one in a Jewish synagogue.[50] He left Sacramento to continue his teaching tour in San Francisco.

It seems that it was some time afterwards, possibly during 1925, that Henry Kuphal and his wife, Frances Kuphal,

FRANCES CLINE KUPHAL

moved to Sacramento. They had lived in Boise, Idaho, from about 1918 to 1923, and had been active Bahá'ís there. They moved to California, and Frances Kuphal was a delegate to the Second Annual Bahá'í Conference and Congress in the Western States, held in September 1924. She was also a representative to the Western States Teaching Conference in October of the same year.[51] The Kuphals eventually settled in Sacramento and remained there for the rest of their lives. They were important members of the Sacramento Bahá'í community for decades.

Before her marriage, Frances (Cline) Kuphal, a Canadian citizen, had become a Bahá'í in Glendale, California. The Clines were a well-known Bahá'í family in California in the early part of this century. However, Harriet Cline, Frances's sister-in-law, indicates that Frances had not shown any interest in the Bahá'í teachings before 1912. Her conversion to the Faith came as a result of meeting 'Abdu'l-Bahá during his short visit to the Los Angeles area in 1912. The Cline family had had an opportunity to meet with 'Abdu'l-Bahá during his visit to Southern California. At this meeting, 'Abdu'l-Bahá insisted that Frances be brought to a lecture where he was to speak. She was very impressed by the meeting and became a Bahá'í shortly after that.[52]

From Glendale, Frances moved to Idaho where she met Henry Kuphal, a German immigrant who had come to Idaho from Montana. They were married in 1918, and Frances became an American citizen after that. Apparently introduced to the Bahá'í teachings by his wife, Henry Kuphal accepted the Faith in 1919 in Idaho. The Kuphals moved to California in 1923 or 1924.[53]

Through the teaching efforts of Ali Yazdi and the Kuphals in Sacramento, James and Carmen O'Neill became Bahá'ís. Also, Carmen's son, Elmer Dearborn, and her mother, Mrs. Emma Dearborn, entered the Faith.[54] The O'Neills and Mrs.

Dearborn (as well as a Mr. I. Dearborn) had been listed as members of the Bahai Assembly of Sacramento in 1925. But this group appears to have died out, and it seems that there was little continuity between this Assembly and later Bahá'í activities. Like the early Assembly, however, the Bahá'ís in Sacramento did not openly pursue their work as an independent religion, as illustrated by Frances Kuphal's report to the *Baha'i News Letter* in the summer of 1926. She explained that one of the Bahá'ís was teaching the children at the Daily Vacation Bible School in Sacramento:

> Mrs. O'Neil's [sic] work in the school was to give the talk or sermon. She taught the children the most important thing was to live the life. It was most impressive to hear them recite from our Bahai Big Ben.[55]

She received an enthusiastic reply from the National Spiritual Assembly.[56] The Dearborn and O'Neill families soon moved to the San Francisco Bay area in 1928.

In 1930, John and Valera Allen moved to Sacramento.[57] Valera Allen had become a Bahá'í in San Francisco in 1925. A year after she married John, they came to Sacramento. When the Kuphals, now the only other Bahá'ís in the city, came to call, they simply assumed that John Allen was a Bahá'í, and he joined in all the Bahá'í activities.[58]

Before her marriage, Enola Allen (Leonard), John's sister, had attended a religious training school in San Francisco with Valera, her future sister-in-law. Enola went on to become a Methodist minister and pastor of a church near Petaluma, California. There she married, and moved to Sacramento in 1932. Through association with her brother and his wife, as well as with the Kuphals, Enola became a Bahá'í in 1934. Eventually, John and Enola's sister, Cordelia, also became a Bahá'í, as did their mother.

The Bahá'ís of Sacramento in the early 1930s were a small but active group. They were mainly educated, middle-class or upper middle-class, white women. They were all dedicated Bahá'ís, excited by the new movement. Enola Leonard later remembered the community at this time as a happy, unified, loving, and close-knit group of friends. They observed the Nineteen-Day Feasts, held regular study classes, and organized public meetings for prominent Bahá'í speakers, such as Marion Holley and Leroy Ioas.[59] They gradually increased their numbers. Marguerite Mosier became a Bahá'í and joined the community in 1932.

Though there were a number of published Bahá'í books by this time, the Bahá'ís supplemented this literature with typed and mimeographed sheets that were circulated in the community. These sheets contained Tablets (letters) of 'Abdu'l-Bahá, records of his talks, and other materials that were not published and were difficult to find. The Sacramento Bahá'í Archives now holds several scrapbooks of such sheets, compiled by Frances Kuphal and others.

The Sacramento Bahá'ís participated in Bahá'í activities in other parts of California. One of the believers, Leota Gallagher, was wealthy and owned a large Buick. The Bahá'ís in Sacramento would pile into it and travel to the Bahá'í Summer School at Geyserville, to San Francisco, even to Bakersfield for Bahá'í meetings.

In the hot summers of Sacramento, the Bahá'ís held regular study classes in Enola Leonard's backyard, under a black walnut tree. They might read from Esselmont's *Bahá'u'lláh and the New Era* or discuss various aspects of the Bahá'í teachings. The most controversial issue raised at these meetings was speculation concerning whether or not the Guardian of the Bahá'í Faith, Shoghi Effendi (who had no children), might be hiding a secret heir and would reveal this information at some time in the future. Informal gatherings of this type characterized much of Bahá'í community life in Sacramento before 1960.[60]

THE FIRST SPIRITUAL ASSEMBLY OF SACRAMENTO

elected on April 21, 1938. Standing (l. to r.): Ada Wells, Mildred Owens, Henry Kuphal, Margaret Moser. Seated (l to r.): Leota Gallagher, Myra Bradley, Frances Kuphal, Enola Leonard, Elizabeth Duffy. The Assembly sat for this photo in front of the tree under which 'Abdu'l-Bahá had stood in 1912.

Organization and Reorganization, 1938-1940: In late 1937, Myra Bradley and Stella Wainscott accepted the Faith, bringing the number of Bahá'ís in Sacramento up to ten. One other person was reported to be seriously interested. The National Teaching Committee informed the Sacramento group that they now had enough members to form a local Spiritual Assembly at Riḍván (April 21) and urged them to continue their study of Bahá'í Administration and particularly the by-laws of the Assembly.[61]

The first local Assembly was elected at a meeting of the community in April of 1938, with Prof. N. Forsythe Ward of Berkeley assisting as a representative of the National Teaching Committee. Sacramento became one of only nine local Spiritual Assemblies in California.[62] The first Assembly, eight women and one man, posed for its official photograph under the tree in Capitol Park that they believed had been visited by 'Abdu'l-Bahá.

After the election of the Assembly, the Sacramento Bahá'í community grew rapidly. Within a year, the number of Bahá'ís in the city was raised to fourteen. Two days after the Assembly was reelected in 1939, Sacramento hosted a regional teaching conference attended by eighty believers from various parts of the state. The conference was held at the Hotel Sacramento, on the same mezzanine where 'Abdu'l-Bahá was known to have delivered his informal talks in 1912.[63]

After the conference, the Bahá'ís and their guests were invited to a "Bahá'í tea" at the State Fair Grounds.[64] There Marzieh Carpenter[65] spoke to about two hundred people on the subject of "What Iran Has Contributed to World Peace." In addition, a member of the Sacramento community who was an organizer of garden clubs had arranged for a Bahá'í exhibit as a part of the Sacramento Annual Flower Show at the Fair Grounds. The Bahá'í display featured a model of the Wilmette Bahá'í Temple in a floral setting and background, and with the theme "Flowers of All Nations." The Bahá'í display was situated in the center of the hall and attracted a great deal of attention. The teaching conference and tea were considered an outstanding success. A photograph of the floral display was sent on to the Guardian by the National Spiritual Assembly and was published in *Bahá'í News.*[66]

In January of 1940, the Sacramento Bahá'í community still counted fourteen members, thirteen of them women. But the community showed the first signs of its future diversity by including the name of one black youth (marked "colored" on the membership list) who had "signified his intention to join our group when he is twenty-one years of age."[67] At that time, only adults could be considered as registered Bahá'ís.

During this year, however, the National Spiritual Assembly advised Sacramento of instructions received from the Guardian which required that all local Spiritual Assemblies confine their jurisdictions strictly to legal city limits. Only believers living within the city limits of Sacramento could officially be considered as part of the community, eligible for election to the Assembly. The new rule split the community in half. The number of believers was only brought back up to nine by the enrollment of two new Bahá'ís who lived within the city limits. The Assembly secretary noted that they were "sincere friends who had been studying for quite a long period." Their declarations of faith "saved" the Assembly.[68]

After the crisis was over, the Assembly secretary reported in 1941, that "the believers in this vicinity have met this test admirably."[69] Two of those left outside eventually returned to the community by moving inside the city limits: Enola Leonard in 1944 and Florence Keemer in 1946.[70] During this period, the activities of the Sacramento Bahá'í community consisted of a regular schedule of Feasts and Holy Day observances, study classes and firesides, punctuated by an occasional public meeting with an out-of-town Bahá'í speaker.

Community Development, 1940-1960: For many years after 1940, Frances and Henry Kuphal acted as the mainstays of the Sacramento community. They were affectionately referred to as "Auntie Frances" and "Uncle Henry." Frances Kuphal, in particular, was looked upon by the believers as a kind of mother figure. She was a considerate and loving person who acted as the community's link to an earlier generation of Bahá'ís, and to 'Abdu'l-Bahá himself.

Also in 1940, another Bahá'í woman moved into Sacramento from Spokane, Washington. Her husband would not become a Bahá'í for another twelve or thirteen years, but she immediately became an active member of the Bahá'í community. She was a capable, professional woman who worked in the office of the Western Pacific Railroad. Her husband was a carpenter at McClellan Air Force Base.[71] Another long-standing Bahá'í moved to Sacramento in 1946. She was a Canadian dress designer. In 1947, she was elected as chair of the local Spiritual Assembly.

Correspondence with the National Spiritual Assembly during the early 1940s shows intense concern over relatively mundane matters of Bahá'í administration: membership, enrollment, statistics, address changes, news of local events, Assembly elections, and annual reports. The minutes of the Assembly reveal a steady concern with the details of running its ongoing activities. The Assembly made its decisions concerning study classes and teaching activities, refreshments at meetings, publicity, the local Bahá'í library, official correspondence, and the like. In 1940, the Assembly asked the National Spiritual Assembly to clarify for them whether a Bahá'í should be permitted to contribute to her former religious group.[72] In 1944, during World War II, the Assembly agreed to sponsor a telephone call for a serviceman.[73] Issues of functions and administration dominated the Assembly's business. The Bahá'ís of Sacramento were coming to see their

BAHÁ'ÍS IN SACRAMENTO

gathered on July 9, 1953 to commemorate the Martyrdom of the Báb. Hand of the Cause Mr. Musa Banani is seated center, holding the Greatest Name. Back row (l to r.): Florence Keemer, Patricia (Keemer?), Nicki Bourget, Cordie Baker. Next row, standing (l. to r.): Mrs. Messier, Mr. Wells, Frances Kuphal, Henry Kuphal, Peggy Springer, Mildred Owens, Josephine Graham, Ada Wells, Fred Chindahl, (Nollie?) Green, and her daughter. Next row, seated (l. to r.): Louis Bourget, Amin Banani, Musa Banani, Mrs. Samireh Banani, Evanne Chindahl. Front row, seated (l. to r.): Maerea Chindahl, (Denise?) Bourget, (Delan?) Bourget, and the daughter of Patricia (Keemer?).

religion as governed by a set of prescribed procedures. Functioning in accordance with these procedures was given the highest importance.

In 1947, a new young couple became Bahá'ís. The husband was the grandson of Louis Bourgeois, the architect of the Bahá'í House of Worship in Wilmette, who had himself been a Bahá'í. However, the young man did not remember much about his grandfather. He did know that his mother had brought the remains of Bourgeois with her when they had moved to Sacramento.[74] He had only become interested in the Bahá'í Faith during World War II, while stationed in New York. There he attended some Bahá'í meetings. Both he and his wife entered the Faith after his return to Sacramento.[75]

The couple was somewhat out of place in this community of older Bahá'í women. They recalled later that the community had become something of a ladies' social club. The Bahá'ís gathered to drink tea, read from the Bahá'í scriptures, talk about gardening, and say prayers. They were uncomfortable that the community seemed to be uninterested in expanding its activities beyond its own boundaries.

The new couple was more interested in social action. They were not content with the usual round of Bahá'í meetings. At some point, during this period, the wife suggested to the community that the Bahá'ís should undertake some kind of social welfare work. The new chairman at that time gently put the idea to rest, suggesting that perhaps it would be better to devote the community's energies to completing the Bahá'í Temple (still under construction) and to strengthening their own group.[76] There was clearly a difference of perspective and approach, perhaps rooted in a difference in generations.

One incident in particular brought some of these differences into the open. In 1952,[77] the young Bahá'í couple arranged for a Bahá'í booth at the State Fair in Sacramento. It was a simple exhibit which made use of a model of the Bahá'í Temple and displayed the Bahá'í principles and quotations about progressive revelation.[78] The project was successful.[79] However, either the booth had been organized without the local Assembly's consent, or else someone disapproved of what the couple had done. Neither the husband nor the wife finally understood what the problem was, but they were both called before the Assembly.[80] Though they remained active Bahá'ís for some time, the couple eventually withdrew from the Bahá'í Faith, saying that they no longer believed in organized religion.[81]

In 1954, Frances Kuphal passed away. Although her husband continued to live in Sacramento until his death in 1965, the focal point of Bahá'í activity moved to another family. The couple from Spokane, both now Bahá'ís, became the pillars of the community. In 1958, the Spiritual Assembly of Sacramento agreed that all Bahá'í meetings would be held in their home, unless someone else asked to host a function.[82] The couple gave generously of their time and money in support of Bahá'í work. The wife especially became a strong, even a dominant, force in the Sacramento Bahá'í community.

In 1957, another relatively young person became a Bahá'í. She had learned of the Faith in Fresno, and continued her study of the Bahá'í teachings after moving to Sacramento with her husband in 1952. After her election to the Spiritual Assembly, disagreements again came to the surface. As a new and enthusiastic Bahá'í, she felt that the functioning of the Assembly did not live up to the ideal that she had read about in the Bahá'í books. She was shocked to find that a single individual held such a dominant position in the local community. Her concerns resulted in disagreements on the Assembly.[83]

Differences of opinion about administration finally came to a head in 1959, when the Assembly requested assistance from the Area Teaching Committee of the National Assembly. The Assembly requested assistance in resolving a difference of opinion concerning the correct Bahá'í procedures with regard to committees, but the roots of the problem were much deeper.[84] A Bahá'í teacher from Fresno was sent to help. She visited Sacramento in March and April of 1960, holding deepenings on administrative procedures and principles. A letter sent to this teacher by the Assembly secretary explains her view of the problems on the Assembly:

> An assembly is a body of nine "members" all with different backgrounds therefore with an ability to throw light on a different part of the picture. All can be inspired, in addition to their backlog of experience and studies in the writings, with knowledge from God, through Bahá'u'lláh. Through the Divine Hosts of Inspiration (pure souls on the other side) by the agency of the Holy Spirit directly. It seems to me absolutely vital that this point be brought out and emphasized, otherwise a caste-system is set up within the Assembly. Otherwise, the members will have a tendency to lean on a member who has been a Baha'i a long time and/or has had an opportunity to study under well-known Baha'is at summer school, etc. This discounts the condition of the soul-mind entirely and brings the members into the straight jacket of each member's estimate as to what the other one knows. Again, we're back to personalities, to the "older members" and the "younger members." We are told that only God can judge the condition of our souls. Since the "heart" (soul-mind) is the seat of our reality, of our learning, how then can we be in a position to judge another man's true learning/knowledge. Only God can do this.[85]

In 1959, the couple that had been at the center of Bahá'í activity in Sacramento became inactive. Although the issues disrupting the community are not apparent from the Assembly records, the acting secretary referred to "heartaches and turmoil" in the community in a letter to the Bahá'í Area Teaching Committee.[86]

NAW-RÚZ 1964

Poster outside Sacramento Memorial Auditorium announcing the public meeting.

The community was further disrupted by the disturbing behavior and disappearance of one of the members of the Assembly.[87] Eventually, this believer was located and voluntarily placed herself in a mental hospital for a time.

Pivotal Bahá'í Community, 1961-1968: The early 1960s was a period of tremendous activity in the Sacramento Bahá'í community. It was also a period of rapid change. A new generation of Americans was entering the Bahá'í Faith in the United States and changing the way the community viewed teaching, deepening, procedure, and morality.

In 1960, a black man and a Persian man were elected to the Sacramento Assembly, greatly increasing its diversity. At that point, the community numbered about twenty. But problems with inactivity, personality clashes, and other issues continued. In early 1961, the National Spiritual Assembly sent Florence Mayberry, a prominent Bahá'í teacher, to visit Sacramento and seek to heal the community's difficulties. Her visit seems to have had the desired effect, for she was able to report to the National Assembly that there were signs of improvement.[88]

During this time, the couple that had become inactive began to participate in Bahá'í activities again and became an important part of the community. Soon large public meetings were being organized in Sacramento which drew fifty to one hundred people, including Bahá'ís from outlying communities, from northern and central California, and from as far away as Reno, Nevada. Sacramento was able to schedule a number of prominent and popular Bahá'í speakers at these meetings, such as Eulalia Bobo, Marion West, and Dwight Allen. These speakers would attract Bahá'ís from far distances. Sacramento became a hub of Bahá'í activity. On March 21, 1964, the community held a large public meeting to commemorate the Bahá'í New Year (Naw-Rúz) at the Sacramento

Memorial Auditorium. This was the largest public hall in the city, where major concerts and sports events were held. In addition to the Bahá'í speaker, a well-known Bay Area pianist, Marilyn Raubitschek, was the guest performer.[89]

In 1965, a new couple entered the Faith in Sacramento. The husband of this couple was an enthusiastic new believer and he soon brought a friend of his into the Sacramento Bahá'í community.[90] Both were black. They began to teach the Faith vigorously, appealing to young people and others who were socially conscious. They were an effective teaching team.

The husband of the older Bahá'í couple that had become active again died in 1966. His wife remained an active Bahá'í, however. The (second) new black believer later recalled that he met her for the first time the morning after he had become a Bahá'í, and very shortly after her husband had passed away. She greeted him at her door, and said: "Isn't God wonderful! He took [my husband] and replaced him already." He said that she was smiling and radiant at the funeral.[91] Eventually, however, after a second marriage, she became inactive again and moved out of Sacramento.

The new couple held regular firesides in their home from 1967 to 1968. These meetings were very informal and relaxed. People were free to come and go during the meeting, and the firesides were open-ended. The speaker, usually the friend of the couple who had become a Bahá'í, would start the fireside by going over the Bahá'í principles found on the back of the Bahá'í Temple card[92] and then would ask for questions. The firesides attracted from twenty to fifty people, from Sacramento and the surrounding areas, and it became customary for them to last all night. Often those who were left in the morning would go out to breakfast together.[93] Those interested in the Faith were both black and white, although those who became Bahá'ís were mostly whites. The firesides accelerated growth for the Sacramento Bahá'ís, with fifteen enrollments in 1965-1966, and thirty-five in 1966-1967. Among those new Bahá'ís were young people who would shortly form the core of the active Bahá'í community of Sacramento and become the center of youth activities for the Sacramento Valley.[94]

There was resistance in the community to these new teaching methods. Some Bahá'ís felt that the new believers were being allowed to enter the Faith too quickly. A year of study before enrollment had been common in an earlier period. The new teaching was unrestrained, and those who were becoming Bahá'ís were from new social, economic, and racial backgrounds, which clashed with the white, middle-class standards that were the norm in the Bahá'í community. For example, one of the teachers convinced a prostitute whom he had met at the Greyhound Bus Station in Sacramento to declare her acceptance of the Faith. However, the Assembly declined to enroll her in the community, because of her profession.[95] The Assembly became concerned about maintaining control of the teaching activities under its jurisdiction. Eventually, they asked the teacher to stop teaching at the bus station.

Interested seekers who came to the all-night firesides were not deterred from bringing alcoholic beverages. Rumors began circulating in the community about this, and other issues. When the Assembly wrote to the couple about the drinking, they withdrew from all activity. The fireside and the teaching associated with it were discontinued. By early 1968, the Assembly had agreed that all-night firesides were no longer necessary, and perhaps had been undesirable.[96]

The fireside incident was really the final event in a series of growing conflicts between old and new members of the community concerning such issues as teaching methods, deepening, and sexual morality, caused partially by generational differences and partially by differences of race and social class. However, this brought matters into the open, causing a good deal of conflict and confusion. In April of 1968, a petition was circulated in Sacramento that asked the National Spiritual Assembly to help resolve the problem of disunity within the Bahá'í community. Later that year, the Assembly made a number of efforts to deal with the problem of inactivity, both on the Assembly and in the community. By the end of 1968, however, the majority of believers were still inactive and the community was in disarray.

Youth Movement, 1969-1975: In the late 1960s, despite the serious difficulties that the Bahá'í community of Sacramento was facing, a wave of young, new believers began entering the Bahá'í Faith in the United States. This development would soon allow the Sacramento community to once again become a locus of Bahá'í activity for the surrounding area. The history of the community from its beginnings has been characterized by a cycle of intense activity, followed by conflict and disagreement, the collapse of Bahá'í activity, and then rebirth.

The counterculture of the late 1960s and early 1970s found its fullest expression in the San Francisco Bay area, not far from Sacramento. Large numbers of young Americans revolted against the values, assumptions, and styles of middle-class culture. They were idealistic, enthusiastic, and believed in the need for dramatic and immediate change in the world. This mood in the country led many young people to accept the Bahá'í Faith. These new converts naturally saw little contradiction between the ideals of their new religion and the styles and assumptions of the counterculture they lived in.

As these youth entered the Sacramento Bahá'í community, there were almost no active believers left in the city.

Unguided and unrestrained by older Bahá'ís, they were free to reshape the community in the style and image of 1960s popular culture. Eventually, fifteen or twenty young Bahá'ís established themselves as the core of the Sacramento Bahá'í community. They were in their early twenties, with a few in their late twenties or early thirties, and mostly white. Although many were deeply involved in the counterculture, the majority were not. Some had become Bahá'ís locally, while others moved into Sacramento from the San Francisco Bay area. Their only link to the earlier Bahá'í community was one strong, black man in his forties who remained active during this period. This believer was a strong advocate of Bahá'í administration and acted as a mentor and father-figure for the new believers. He encouraged their activities and showed restraint and tolerance in his role as leader. He seldom showed disapproval. The youth knew they had pleased him when he laughed, or displeased him when he brought out the Bahá'í Writings to admonish them, or simply left a gathering.[97]

During this period, the Bahá'ís rented the first Bahá'í Center (meeting place) in the community's history. One Bahá'í recalled that since there was no home of an active Bahá'í available for meetings, the youth felt the need for a Center.[98] It became an important focal point for Bahá'í activities. The youth had decided that it should be located downtown, since that was the area of the city visited by 'Abdu'l-Bahá. His visit was a continual source of inspiration to them throughout this period. In December of 1971, a house was rented downtown in the commercial zone. It served as the Sacramento Bahá'í Center until 1974, when the Bahá'ís were released from their contract.

The new center provided a place for the Bahá'í youth to congregate. It operated in typical counterculture style. Eventually, there were Bahá'í meetings of one kind or another

MUSIC AT THE UNITY FAIR
Sponsored by the Bahá'ís in Southside Park,
Sacramento, during the early 1970s.

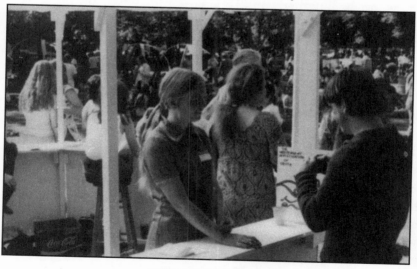

TEACHING BOOTH
at the Sacramento Unity Fair.

there almost every night—firesides, deepening classes, Assembly meetings, and committee meetings. The center was used by Bahá'í communities outside of Sacramento, as well. Gradually, many of the youth moved downtown to be near the focus of Bahá'í activity. One Bahá'í moved into the center as caretaker. He had once worked as a member of the technical crew for a touring rock-and-roll band. He had hair down to his waist, and he owned a waterbed factory in the city.[99] A local Bahá'í who visited the center during this period found a number of young people there in various costumes and hairstyles, sitting cross-legged on the floor and praying, with incense burning.[100]

The older Bahá'ís in Sacramento found this style unacceptable. They generally remained inactive, and unhappy with the state of the community, during this entire period. Some assumed that the Bahá'í youth must be involved with drugs and sexual immorality, because of their life styles. However, there is no evidence to indicate that this was the case. The new Bahá'ís generally understood the Bahá'í teachings, served on the Assembly, as well as several committees, and kept meticulous records of their Bahá'í activities. The most voluminous, complete, and well-kept archival records of community activity are found for the period of 1971-1973.

The Bahá'ís, during this period, faithfully observed communications from the National Spiritual Assembly. Their approach to most problems was to refer to the Bahá'í scriptures. They were apocalyptic in their vision of the future, feeling that the world was on the brink of dramatic and earthshaking changes. They supported this view with passages from Shoghi Effendi's books *Advent of Divine Justice* and *The Promised Day Is Come*. They were intensely involved in Bahá'í activities and became a close-knit group.

The local Spiritual Assembly at this time sponsored a number of large events. A spring Unity Fair was especially successful. The fair was a large art and music festival in Southside Park, including rock-and-roll, country, and folk bands. The event was attended by hundreds of people, mostly youth. It was well organized, and Bahá'ís from several communities participated. In 1971, the community organized an elaborate display and garden as a part of the State Fair. They arranged for several people to man the booth at all times during the nineteen days of the fair. The fair booth resulted in some people becoming Bahá'ís. Although Sacramento was the sponsor of several major events that took place within the city, it was often the case that the majority of Bahá'ís who supported these activities came from outlying communities.

The intense Bahá'í activity of this period did not last long. The youth were mobile and not permanently established in Sacramento. They began moving out of the city in 1973, many of them to Bahá'í pioneering (missionary) posts in other countries. They were encouraged to pioneer by the general Bahá'í ethos of the time, by other Bahá'í youth, and by the older Bahá'ís in the area.[101] In addition, there were urgent calls for pioneers at the end of the nine-year Bahá'í teaching plan. The middle-aged mentor of the youth eventually left the city for a pioneer post in the Caribbean. The 1960s were finally over, and the mood of the country was changing. Personal difficulties began to come to the attention of the Assembly more frequently—alcoholism, mental illness, and sexual difficulties. Hours of Assembly meetings were filled with the discussion of such problems. The Assembly struggled with the issues but could offer little help. The usual solution was to pray for troubled persons, recommend more prayer and meditation, and encourage them to become more active in the community.

Sacramento had first experienced an influx of population into its suburban areas during World War II. In 1940, the population was 105,000 in the city, and 65,000 in the rest of the county. This trend continued, and by 1960 three-fifths of the population lived in the county. Downtown Sacramento was falling into decline, and much of it became a slum. Efforts at urban renewal began around the Capitol building in the early 1960s. Some of the slum areas were cleared and replaced with modern offices and other buildings. It was not until the mid-1970s, however, that the restoration of historic Sacramento began drawing people back into the inner city.[102]

By late 1973, many of the active Bahá'í youth left in Sacramento were beginning to feel exhausted, and they could no longer sustain the same level of Bahá'í work. The Bahá'ís were unable to maintain the rent on the downtown center and lost it in 1974. The suburban Bahá'í communities were now larger and developing their own independence. Urban blight had done its work in Sacramento, and the area was no longer considered a desirable place to live. Middle-class people had moved to outlying areas.

As the youth era waned, older Bahá'ís in Sacramento gradually returned to activity. As had happened so many times before, there was little continuity—either of membership or perspective—with the earlier period.

Continuation. Following the exodus of Bahá'í youth, the Sacramento community was less active. In 1976, it was not uncommon for only five or six Bahá'ís to be present at the Nineteen-Day Feast, though there were perhaps ten times that many believers in the city.[103] Seven members of the Assembly that year were new to the community. Sacramento has continued to be characterized by more transience and less stability than its suburban neighbors. This reflects the changing nature and urban complexity of the city at large.

The size of the Bahá'í community had remained small, numbering about 20 in 1964. It increased dramatically to 55 believers by 1967. Although there was a decrease to 39 in 1969, the membership after that time, in a series of rises and falls, gradually moved up to over 100 Bahá'ís in the early 1990s.[104] Active participation in the Nineteen-Day Feasts remained the same, regardless of the community's size, until the Assembly began renting a hall for the celebration in 1989. The use of a large facility in a constant location, in combination with a change in community leadership, the influx of a number of Bahá'ís from Southeast Asia (Hmong), and the enrollment of new Hispanic believers, has increased the average Feast attendance to twenty-five or thirty adults, plus eight or ten children.[105]

During the late 1970s, some interest in mass teaching developed among the Bahá'ís of Sacramento. Tens of thousands of rural black people had become Bahá'ís in the South of the United States using this new teaching technique. Bahá'í teachers would approach people on the street, or knock on doors, to invite people to a meeting, or deliver the Bahá'í message and ask for their declaration of faith on the spot. Such radically new methods were controversial. Some Sacramento Bahá'ís did not think it was right to teach in this manner. The method was tried, but the results were generally discouraging, and such projects were discontinued.

The Sacramento community has seen no large influx of new believers since the early 1970s. However, it has witnessed a gradual increase in the number of believers. Feasts, firesides, and deepening classes have continued through the years. The Assembly has been maintained. Occasionally, large and unusual activities have been sponsored which have caught the attention and inspired the participation of surrounding Bahá'í communities.

The Sacramento Assembly sponsored a large, professional art show for three consecutive years in the early 1980s. The show drew entries from all over the country. Professional judges were used and prizes awarded. Concurrent Bahá'í teaching activities were held, as well as theatrical and musical performances. The events attracted many people and a great deal of public attention.

In June of 1987, a Bahá'í intercommunity committee organized a large commemoration of the seventy-fifth anniversary of 'Abdu'l-Bahá's visit to Sacramento. In October of the same year, the Sacramento community sponsored an even larger event for the same purpose. A crowd of Bahá'ís gathered on the capitol steps to say prayers and remember the visit. A train ride in Old Town was arranged to commemorate 'Abdu'l-Bahá's train ride into the city. The guest speaker, Joseph Ioas, the father of one of the Sacramento Bahá'ís, could still remember meeting 'Abdu'l-Bahá as a child. It was a moving testimony to the endurance of the community.

The Sacramento Bahá'í community was once the child of the larger Bahá'í communities of the San Francisco Bay area. Later, Sacramento itself became the mother-community to a number of suburban areas in the Sacramento region, sponsoring large Bahá'í activities which sustained and encouraged other Bahá'í communities in the area. Now, Sacramento has become one Bahá'í community among many, though its membership is more culturally and economically diverse than that of its suburban neighbors. However, it continues to represent the early history of the Bahá'í Faith in the region, because it was the first Bahá'í community there and because of its connection to 'Abdu'l-Bahá.

NOTES

1. Tom Beebe, *Who's Who in New Thought: Biographical Dictionary of New Thought* (Lakemont, Calif.: CSA Press, 1977) p. 104. Horatio W. Dresser, *A History of the New Thought Movement* (New York: Thomas Y. Crowell Company, 1919) pp. 231-32.

2. Charles S. Braden, *Spirits in Rebellion: The Rise and Development of New Thought* (Dallas: South Methodist University Press, 1963) p. 315. Dresser, *History*, p. 233. Rev. James Hutchinson Smylie, "New Thought," *The New Encyclopedia Britannica, Macropeadia,* vol. 13 (Chicago: Helen Hemingway Benton Publisher, 1974) pp. 14-16.

3. In 1906, in response to an invitation, the Chicago House of Spirituality decided that it was desirable for a Bahá'í to speak at the New Thought Convention. They did not want the speaker to be identified as a Bahá'í, however, to avoid any implication that the Bahá'í Faith was a New Thought group. (Minutes, Chicago House of Spirituality, March 10, 1906. National Bahá'í Archives, Wilmette, Illinois.)

In response to questions from New Thought adherents and others involved in the proliferating metaphysical healing movements of the time, 'Abdu'l-Baha addressed the subjects of healing and the nature of man while in the United States. Whereas many of these people insisted that healing was by spiritual means alone, 'Abdu'l-Bahá stated that both spiritual and physical means may have healing powers. In an interview with Mrs. Pell of the Home of Truth, he explained that man reflects the attributes of God but does not share in the Essence of God. (Ellen V. Beecher, "The Difference Between the Metaphysical Teachings of the Present Day and that of the Baha'i Revelation," *Star of the West*, vol. 2 [1911] no. 5, pp. 14-16; Ramona Allen Brown, *Memories of 'Abdu'l-Bahá: Recollections of the Early Days of the Bahá'í Faith in California* [Wilmette, Ill.: Bahá'í Publishing Trust, 1980] pp. 69-76; "Mrs. Pell Interviews 'Abdu'l-Bahá," Ella Cooper papers, National Bahá'í Archives.)

4. Braden, *Spirits*, p. 313.

5. Ibid., pp. 313-15. Dresser, *History*, p. 233.

6. Militz founded a periodical called *The Master Mind* which published from 1911 to 1924. At one point, the magazine decided to honor fifty people with a year's free subscription. These fifty were chosen from among those whom they felt were in a position to benefit humanity, such as President Theodore Roosevelt, Woodrow Wilson, and Jane Addams. 'Abdu'l-Bahá was included in this group. When he received his subscription, he sent Militz a gracious reply, commending the magazine for its efforts. The letter was published in *The Master Mind.* ("Fifty Eminent Subscribers," *The Master Mind*, vol. 3 [1913] no. 6, p. 191; 'Abdu'l-Bahá, "Letter to the Editor," ibid., vol. 3 [1913] p. 116.)

7. *Sacramento City Directory*, 1903-1921.

8. *The Master Mind*, vol 2 (1912) no. 5, p. clxxvi; ibid., vol. 4 (1913) no. 3, p. 111; ibid., vol. 1 (1911) no. 1, p. xxxix.

9. United States Census, 1910. Sacramento City, California.

10. *Sacramento Bee*, October 19, 1912, p. 11.

11. Mírzá Maḥmúd-i Zarqání, *Kitáb-i Badáyi'u'l-Áthár*, vol. 1 (Bombay: Elegant Photo-Litho Press, 1914) p. 331.

12. Ramona Brown mentions that some believers from Sacramento came to visit 'Abdu'l-Bahá in the Bay Area. Since there were no Bahá'ís in Sacramento at the time, this may be a reference to New Thought sympathizers. (Brown, *Recollections*, p. 44.)

13. United States Census, 1910. Population General Report and Analysis. *Thirteenth Census of the United States*, 1910, vol. 1 (Washington, D.C.: Government Printing Office, 1913).

14. Ibid.

15. Zarqání, *Kitáb*, p. 331. He arrived at the train at either 8:00 or 9:00 a.m. (Cf. Zarqání and Ella Cooper, "California Bahá'í History." Ella Cooper papers.)

16. Brown, *Recollections*, p. 85.

17. Zarqání, *Kitáb*, p. 331. The train schedule for that time shows train No. 24 leaving San Francisco at 7:20 a.m., arriving at the Oakland Pier at 7:47 a.m., and at Sacramento at 11:35 a.m. Train No. 4 left at 9:00 a.m. and arrived at Sacramento at 12:35 p.m. Harriet Cline mentions that 'Abdu'l-Bahá arrived around 11:00 a.m. ("A Narration of the Events Leading up to, and the Meetings with 'Abdu'l-Bahá. Ella Cooper papers, National Bahá'í Archives.)

18. At 1235 I Street.

19. Brown, *Recollections*, pp. 85-86.

20. Zarqání, *Kitáb*, p. 331.

21. There are four distinct accounts of 'Abdu'l-Bahá's visit to the Home of Truth in Sacramento. The accounts differ in some details, but they can be easily reconciled. See Cline, "Narration," pp. 8-9; Zarqání, *Kitáb*, p. 331 ff.; Brown, *Recollections*, pp. 85-86; Bijou Straun's transcripts of the talk given at the Home of Truth (Ella Cooper papers); and Cooper, "California," p. 6.

22. "Interview with 'Abdu'l-Baha by F. R. Hinkle, reporter on the Sacramento Union, Hotel Sacramento, October 25, 5:00 p.m." Ella Cooper papers.

23. Cooper, "California," p. 6; Interview No. 4. Interviews with

Bahá'ís who are or have been members of the Sacramento Bahá'í community were conducted by the author, and they remain in her possession. They will be referred to by number here to protect the privacy of those involved.

24. The first local Spiritual Assembly of the Bahá'ís of Sacramento, in 1938, had its official photograph taken standing under that same tree. A row of three evergreen trees near that place is still standing on the north side of the Capitol. I made many attempts to locate the exact tree that 'Abdu'l-Bahá may have blessed, interviewing Bahá'ís, viewing old photos, and studying archival records for Capitol Park. Though I could establish an approximate location, I have never found the tree. According to one source (Interview No. 4), this tree may have been removed to make room for the extension of the Capitol building.

Somehow for the Sacramento Bahá'ís the tree came to symbolize 'Abdu'l-Bahá's visit, a tangible link to the person and the spirit of the Master. All other landmarks associated with the visit have been torn down: the train station, the Home of Truth, and Hotel Sacramento. But, the trees in Capitol Park remain as a living legacy of his visit.

25. "Women Grovel to Persian Prophet," *Sacramento Union*, October 27, 1912, p. 1.

26. "Talk by 'Abdu'l-Bahá, Hotel Sacramento, Parlor on Mezzanine Floor, October 25, 7:30 p.m." Ella Cooper papers.

27. 'Abdu'l-Bahá, *The Promulgation of Universal Peace: Talks Delivered by 'Abdu'l-Bahá during His Visit to the United States and Canada in 1912* (Chicago: Bahai Publishing Committee, 1922-25 [Wilmette, Ill.: Bahá'í Publishing Trust, 1982]) pp. 370-76.

28. "Talk by 'Abdu'l-Bahá, Hotel Sacramento, Parlor on Mezzanine Floor, October 25, 9:15 p.m." Ella Cooper papers.

29. "Interview given by 'Abdu'l-Bahá to Ida McCormick, Maud Sickles, and Myrtle Nerhbass, Maids in Hotel Sacramento, October 26, 8:15 a.m." Ella Cooper papers.

30. "Message from 'Abdu'l-Bahá to Japanese Boys, Portland, Oregon; Hotel Sacramento, October 26, 8:25 a.m." Ella Cooper papers.

31. Cline, "Narration," pp. 9-10.

32. 'Abdu'l-Bahá, *Promulgation*, pp. 376-77. Ramona Brown, who was a teenager at the time of her visit to Sacramento, tells how she felt when she was present at the signing of the United Nations charter in San Francisco in 1945: "Then, in the most thrilling moment of

the conference, a flag was brought onto the stage: the flag of the United Nations. To my great astonishment I saw the fulfillment of prophecy. The wish of 'Abdu'l-Bahá had come true; the flag of international peace was unfurled in California." (Brown, *Recollections*, p. 88.)

33. William Lawson, "Noted Oriental Not a Prophet But a Teacher," *Sacramento Bee*, October 26, 1912, p. 1; "Noted Persian Teacher Here Pleads for World Peace," *Sacramento Bee*, October 26, 1912, p. 1; "Persian Prophet, Leader of Baha Movement, Lectures on Doctrines," *Sacramento Union*, October 26, 1912, p. 5; "Persian Priest Lectures Here," *Sacramento Star*, October 26, 1912, p. 1.

34. "Women Grovel," *Sacramento Union*.

35. Cooper, "California," p. 5.

36. "Notes by B. S. Straun, Cafe, Hotel Sacramento, October 26, noon." Ella Cooper papers.

37. Zarqání, *Kitáb*, p. 331.

38. Possibly the No. 4, at 12:50 p.m., or the No. 2, at 1:40 p.m., by the Overland Limited.

39. Brown, *Recollections*, pp. 106-107.

40. Zarqání, *Kitáb*, p. 333. Translated by the Research Department, Bahá'í World Center.

41. While living there he discovered the O'Neill family, but it is not clear how or when. They may have been living there first as Bahá'ís, or he may have brought them into the Faith. (Personal communication from Marion Yazdi [Ali M. Yazdi's wife])

42. Letter from Marion Yazdi to the author, November 25, 1987.

43. Marion Carpenter Yazdi, *Youth in the Vanguard: Memoirs and Letters Collected by the First Bahá'í Student at Berkeley and at Stanford University* (Wilmette: Ill., Bahá'í Publishing Trust, 1982) pp. 49, 115 ff.

44. *Sacramento Bee*, January 30, 1924, p. 14.

45. Enola Leonard remembered that some of the early Bahá'ís in Sacramento were taught by Orcella Rexford, though her name does not appear on a list of traveling teachers who visited the city. The size of the group and the fact that some of them did not consider themselves to be Bahá'ís at that time, also suggests Rexford's teaching methods.

46. The term *Assembly* was commonly used by Bahá'ís at this time to refer to any Bahá'í group or gathering.

47. *Sacramento Bee*, January 30, 1925, p. 14.

48. Horace Holley, Secretary, to Frances Kuphal, September 21, 1925. National Bahá'í Archives.

49. Mrs. Emma Dearborn appears to be listed as a member of the Bahai Assembly of Sacramento in 1925. (The list includes Mr. and Mrs. I. Dearborn.) She states that she did not accept the Faith until 1926, in Sacramento. (Bahá'í Historical Record cards. c.1935.)

50. *Sacramento Bee*, January 30, 1925, p. 14.

51. Letter to Shoghi Effendi, September 27, 1924. Western States Teaching Conference to National Spiritual Assembly, October 9, 1924. (Western States Region Book. San Francisco Bahá'í Archives.)

52. Harriet Cline, "Narration," p. 7. Sacramento Bahá'í Archives. (Also, Ella Cooper papers, National Bahá'í Archives.)

53. Bahai Temple Unity Contribution Journal, 1909-1920. National Bahá'í Archives. Frances Kuphal to George Latimer, March 23, 1921. George Latimer papers, National Bahá'í Archives. Bahá'í Historical Record Cards, National Bahá'í Archives.

54. Yazdi, *Youth*, pp. 71-72. Elmer Dearborn was adopted by his grandmother and used her last name.

55. Frances Kuphal to Bahá'í News Letter, n.d. [1926], National Bahá'í Archives.

56. Horace Holley, Secretary, to Frances Cline Kuphal, August 3, 1926, National Bahá'í Archives.

57. Interview No. 1 (1987).

58. Dwight Allen, "John William Allen," In Memoriam section of *The Bahá'í World*, vol. 18 (Haifa: Bahá'í World Centre, 1986) p. 725.

59. Interview No. 1.

60. Interview No. 2 (June 27, 1987). Interview No. 3 (July 1987). Interview No. 4 (June 1987).

61. National Teaching Committee to Elizabeth L. Duffy, January 5, 1938. National Bahá'í Archives.

62. "Minutes of the Meeting Covering the Formation of the First Spiritual Assembly of the Bahais of Sacramento, California on April 21, 1938," Sacramento Bahá'í Archives. *The Bahá'í World*, vol. 8 (Wilmette, Ill.: Bahá'í Publishing Trust, 1942) p. 340.

63. Spiritual Assembly of the Bahá'ís of Sacramento to Shoghi Effendi, June 12, 1939. Sacramento Bahá'í Archives. Regional Bahá'í Teaching Committee for Arizona, California and Nevada, circular letter dated April 13, 1936. Sacramento Bahá'í Archives.

64. Ibid.

65. Later Marzieh Gail.

66. National Spiritual Assembly of the Bahá'ís of the United States and Canada to Spiritual Assembly of the Bahá'ís of Sacramento, July 21, 1939. National Bahá'í Archives.

67. Membership list, dated January 11, 1940. Sacramento Bahá'í Archives.

68. Annual Report of the Spiritual Assembly of the Bahá'ís of Sacramento, California, n.d. [April 21, 1941]. Sacramento Bahá'í Archives.

69. Ibid.

70. Sacramento Assembly to National Spiritual Assembly, January 26, 1944. National Bahá'í Archives.

71. Interview No. 5 (July 1988).

72. Sacramento Assembly to National Spiritual Assembly, August 21, 1940. National Bahá'í Archives.

73. Minutes, August 24, 1944. Spiritual Assembly of the Bahá'ís of Sacramento. Sacramento Bahá'í Archives.

74. Louis Bourgeois's ashes are buried in the East Lawn Cemetery in Sacramento.

75. Interview No. 2.

76. Minutes, May 20, 1947. Spiritual Assembly of the Bahá'ís of Sacramento. Sacramento Bahá'í Archives.

77. The date is approximate.

78. The Bahá'í teaching that all religions have come from God, with the teachings appropriate for their time, in a progressive unfoldment of one divine plan.

79. The booth received two awards and won a plaque.

80. Interviews No. 2, 3, and 4.

81. Interview No. 3.

82. *News from the Bahá'í Community of Sacramento*, October 1958.

83. Interview No. 4.

84. Sacramento Assembly to Bahá'í Area Teaching Committee for the Southwest States, September 7, 1959. Sacramento Bahá'í Archives.

85. Dated April 4, 1960, pp. 3-4.

86. Sacramento Assembly to Area Teaching Committee, May 25, 1960. Sacramento Bahá'í Archives.

87. National Spiritual Assembly to Sacramento Assembly, May 12, 1960 and May 15, 1960. Sacramento Bahá'í Archives.

88. National Spiritual Assembly to Sacramento Assembly, March 10, 1961. Sacramento Bahá'í Archives.

89. Sacramento Bahá'í Archive. Personal recollections of the author.

90. Interview No. 7. Interview No. 6.

91. Interview No. 6.

92. A teaching aid published by the National Spiritual Assembly which had a color photo of the Wilmette Temple on one side and a listing of ten Bahá'í social principles on the other.

93. Interview No. 6.

94. Interview No. 10 (July 1988 and September 1991).

95. Ibid.

96. Interview No. 6. Interview No. 8. Minutes, March 5, 1968. Sacramento Assembly. Sacramento Bahá'í Archives.

97. Interview No. 8.

98. Interview No. 10 (September 1991).

99. He eventually cut his hair in response to pressure to conform to the laws outlined in the *Synopsis and Codification of the Kitáb-i-Aqdas* (Haifa: Bahá'í World Centre, 1973), which became available in 1973. (Interview 10.)

100. Interview No. 4.

101. Interview No. 10.

102. Joseph A. McGowan and Terry R. Willis, *Sacramento: Heart of the Golden State* (Woodland Hills, Calif.: Windsor Publications, Inc., 1983) pp. 85-104.

103. Interview No. 13 (July 1988).

104. There were about 110 adults and 60 children in the community in 1991. Interview No. 15 (October 1991).

105. Interview 15.

INDEX